# MICHAEL JORDAN

## Recent Titles in Greenwood Biographies

# MICHAEL JORDAN

## A Biography

David L. Porter

GREENWOOD BIOGRAPHIES

GREENWOOD PRESS
WESTPORT, CONNECTICUT • LONDON

Library of Congress Cataloging-in-Publication Data

Porter, David L., 1941-
    Michael Jordan : a biography / David L. Porter.
        p. cm. — (Greenwood biographies, ISSN 1540–4900)
    Includes bibliographical references and index.
    ISBN-13: 978-0-313-33767-3 (alk. paper)
    ISBN-10: 0-313-33767-5 (alk. paper)
  1. Jordan, Michael, 1963-   2. Basketball players—United States—
Biography.   I. Title.
    GV884.J67P67    2007
    796.323092—dc22
    [B]                2007009605

British Library Cataloguing in Publication Data is available.

Library of Congress Catalog Card Number: 2007009605
ISBN-13: 978–0–313–33767–3
ISBN-10: 0–313–33767–5
ISSN: 1540–4900

First published in 2007

Greenwood Press, 88 Post Road West, Westport, CT 06881
An imprint of Greenwood Publishing Group, Inc.
www.greenwood.com

Printed in the United States of America

The paper used in this book complies with the
Permanent Paper Standard issued by the National
Information Standards Organization (Z39.48–1984).

10   9   8   7   6   5   4   3   2   1

# CONTENTS

*Photo essay follows page 72.*

# SERIES FOREWORD

In response to high school and public library needs, Greenwood developed this distinguished series of full-length biographies specifically for student use. Prepared by field experts and professionals, these engaging biographies are tailored for high school students who need challenging yet accessible biographies. Ideal for secondary school assignments, the length, format, and subject areas are designed to meet educators' requirements and students' interests.

Greenwood offers an extensive selection of biographies spanning all curriculum-related subject areas including social studies, the sciences, literature and the arts, history and politics, as well as popular culture, covering public figures and famous personalities from all time periods and backgrounds, both historic and contemporary, who have made an impact on American and/or world culture. Greenwood biographies were chosen based on comprehensive feedback from librarians and educators. Consideration was given to both curriculum relevance and inherent interest. The result is an intriguing mix of the well known and the unexpected, the saints and sinners from long-ago history and contemporary pop culture. Readers will find a wide array of subject choices from fascinating crime figures like Al Capone to inspiring pioneers like Margaret Mead, from the greatest minds of our time like Stephen Hawking to the most amazing success stories of our day like J. K. Rowling.

While the emphasis is on fact, not glorification, the books are meant to be fun to read. Each volume provides in-depth information about the subject's life from birth through childhood, the teen years, and adulthood.

A thorough account relates family background and education, traces personal and professional influences, and explores struggles, accomplishments, and contributions. A timeline highlights the most significant life events against a historical perspective. Bibliographies supplement the reference value of each volume.

# ACKNOWLEDGMENTS

Although I did not have an opportunity to interview Jordan, his four memoirs provided numerous insights into the qualities that made him a truly exceptional athlete and successful businessman. *For the Love of the Game* (1998) and *Driven from Within* (2005) were especially helpful resources for information about his formative years.

This work especially benefited from the insights of four people who have authored previous books about Jordan. Dean Smith's *A Coach's Life* (1999) helped illuminate Jordan's years at North Carolina, and Phil Jackson's *Sacred Hoops* was an invaluable source for Jordan's years with the Chicago Bulls. David Halberstam's *Playing for Keeps* (1999) gave me a fuller understanding of how Jordan shaped the world around him, and Walter LaFeber's *Michael Jordan and the New Global Capitalism* (1999) provided perspective on Jordan's enormous influence beyond the basketball court.

I also thank the William Penn University faculty, administration, and students who listened to me share some of my ideas about Jordan at a Chautauqua lecture in March of 2006. My wife, Marilyn, patiently listened to me relate numerous stories about Jordan.

Thanks to Kristi Ward, Esther Silverman, and Apex Publishing for their valuable editorial suggestions in the later stages of writing this book.

# INTRODUCTION

## THE JORDAN MYSTIQUE

A monument stands in front of the United Center, home of the Chicago Bulls National Basketball Association team. A 2,000-pound bronze statue features Michael Jordan in full flight, ready to slam dunk the ball, to the chagrin of cowering defenders. The front panel capsulizes the phenomenal athlete: "The best there ever was. The best there ever will be."[1]

Jordan needs no introduction. He is among the best-known and wealthiest athletes in the history of organized sports. With the possible exceptions of boxer Muhammad Ali and baseball player Babe Ruth, no athlete has made a greater impact on American society. ESPN in 1999 voted Jordan the greatest twentieth-century athlete, and the Associated Press ranked him second, behind Babe Ruth. Jordan has appeared on the cover of *Sports Illustrated* more than 50 times since 1983 and was named the magazine's "Sportsman of the Year" in 1991.[2]

*Sports Illustrated* contributor Jack McCallum wrote that Jordan "stands alone on the mountaintop, unquestionably the most famous athlete on the planet and one of its most famous citizens of any kind." He called him a sportsman who "has surpassed every standard by which we gauge the fame of an athlete and, with few exceptions, has handled the adulation with a preternatural grace and ease that have cut across the lines of race, age, and gender. He transcends sports."[3]

After struggling initially, Jordan blossomed into a basketball star at Emsley A. Laney High School in Wilmington, North Carolina. He became a national celebrity as a freshman guard at the University of North Carolina, converting a 15-foot jump shot in the waning seconds of the 1982 NCAA Championship game to defeat Georgetown University. Besides making All-America as a sophomore and junior, Jordan was named *The Sporting News* Player of the Year in 1983 and 1984 and winner of the Naismith Award and Wooden Award in 1984. He co-captained the U.S. basketball team to a gold medal at the 1984 Summer Olympic Games in Los Angeles, California.

Jordan's transcendence stemmed partly from good timing. Jordan joined the Chicago Bulls after his junior year in 1984, when the NBA was enjoying an era of unprecedented popularity. Americans were fascinated with the personal duels between two modern sports folk heroes, Larry Bird of the Boston Celtics and Magic Johnson of the Los Angeles Lakers. When Bird and Johnson retired in the early 1990s, Jordan almost single handedly propelled the NBA to even more stratospheric levels of success and international visibility. Former coach Larry Brown observed, "I love Magic and Larry. But Michael,…. I'd pay money to see him play. I'd pay money to see him practice."[4]

Jordan led Chicago to six National Basketball Association titles in the 1990s. Between 1991 and 1993, the Bulls became the first team in three decades to win three consecutive NBA championships. He was selected NBA Most Valuable Player in 1988, 1991, and 1992 and became the only hoopster ever voted NBA Finals MVP three straight times. He also starred for the U.S. Dream Team, gold medal winners in the 1992 Summer Olympic Games at Barcelona, Spain.

Jordan soared to even greater heights after a nearly two-year hiatus to propel the Bulls to three more NBA titles from 1996 to 1998. Chicago shattered the NBA record for most victories in a single season with a 72–10 mark in 1995–1996, as Jordan became the first NBA player since 1970 to garner MVP awards from the All-Star Game, regular season, and NBA Finals. The Bulls still dominated the NBA the next two seasons, with Jordan snagging NBA MVP honors in 1998 and NBA Finals MVP accolades in 1997 and 1998. His intensive drive to win, extraordinary athletic ability, and uncanny basketball knowledge shone brilliantly when he battled influenza and personal fatigue to score the winning basket in Game 5 of the 1997 NBA Finals against the Utah Jazz.

Jordan retired from the Bulls in 1999, having led the NBA in scoring 10 times, including seven consecutive seasons, and won five NBA MVP awards. He is the only player to score at least 50 points in five playoff games and the only hoopster besides Wilt Chamberlain to score more than 3,000 points in a season and average more than 30 points a game during his NBA career.

In January 2000, Jordan became president of basketball operations for the Washington Wizards and minority owner of the Washington Wizards

Sports and Entertainment. He played for the Wizards from 2001 to 2003, helping rescue the franchise from a $20 million deficit to a $30 million profit in two years. Jordan did not lead the Wizards to the NBA playoffs, but he became just the fourth NBA player to score 30,000 career points and passed Chamberlain as the third leading scorer in NBA history. In June 2006, he became the second largest shareholder of the Charlotte Bobcats, fulfilling his dream of sharing in the ownership of an NBA club in North Carolina.

Jordan's transcendence stemmed from his phenomenal athleticism and personal magnetism. Coach Bob Knight in 1995 proclaimed, "Michael Jordan is the best that will ever play this game."[5] Even those who never saw Jordan play a college or professional basketball recognize him. He combined exceptional athletic ability with a relatively clean public image. *Gentleman's Quarterly* correspondent David Breskin termed him "the most admired, idolized, and moneyed team-sport hero in the entire American-hero business. For some folks he has come to *represent* America."[6] Sociologist Harry Edwards declared, "if I were charged with introducing an alien life form to the epitome of human potential, creativity, perseverance, and spirit, I would introduce that alien life form to Michael Jordan."[7]

Jordan personifies the imaginative, individual skills that Americans emulated in a society that adores graceful, successful individualism, but he also embodies the all-out competitive spirit and discipline that Americans believe drove the nation to the peak of world power.

Jordan's extraordinary basketball skills translated into enormous money and power in the late twentieth century. He has endorsed numerous commercial products, including Nike's Air Jordan footwear, Wilson basketballs, Wheaties cereal, Coca Cola soft drinks, Chevrolet automobiles, and McDonald's hamburgers. Nike designed a whole new line of athletic shoes after the legend with uncanny ability to hang four feet above the floor while shooting. The Air Jordan line revived Nike's sneaker sales.

These commercial enterprises netted the likable star millions annually in revenues. Biographer David Halberstam labeled Jordan the first super-athlete of the satellite age, the initial professional to benefit on a grand scale from a global audience for his talents and his products. "Jordan has created a kind of fame that exceeds sports. He is both athlete and entertainer. He plays in the age of the satellite to an audience vastly larger than was possible in the past and is thus the first great athlete of the wired world."[8] Jordan became a multimillionaire and a role model not only for African Americans but others as well. Along the way, he also became one of the most successful advertising figures in the world.

This book traces Jordan's career chronologically. The first chapter treats his formative years with his family in Wilmington and at the University of

North Carolina. The next four chapters feature his role with the Chicago Bulls. Chapter 2 treats the building years from 1984 to 1988, and Chapter 3 discusses the ascending years from 1988 to 1991, culminating in Chicago's first NBA crown. Chapter 4 examines the triumphant years of the Bulls' second and third NBA titles from 1991 to 1993 and the transition years from 1993 to 1995, when he played baseball with the Birmingham Barons and returned to the Bulls. Chapter 5 highlights the pinnacle years of Chicago's last three championships from 1995 to 1998, and Chapter 6 reviews the disappointing years with the Washington Wizards.

The book features his on-court accomplishments, but it also examines his disagreements with Chicago's coaches over offensive strategy, his clashes with Bulls' management over team policies, and his reluctance to rely on teammates. It also details his role as a phenomenally successful advertising figure and the way in which his competitiveness led to gambling problems.

## NOTES

1. Mark Kram and Rebecca Parks, "Michael Jordan," in Shirelle Phelps, ed., *Contemporary Black Biography*, Vol. 21 (Detroit, MI: Gale Research, Inc., 1999), p. 15.

2. ESPN, "Michael Jordan," Sportscentury Top 50 Athletes, December 26, 1999; "Michael Jordan," *Sports Illustrated* 75 (December 23, 1991), pp. 64–81.

3. Jack McCallum, "The Everywhere Man," *Sports Illustrated* 75 (December 23, 1991), pp. 64–69.

4. "Michael Jordan," *Current History Yearbook* (New York: H. W. Wilson Company, 1997), p. 252.

5. Mike Lupica, "Let's Fly Again," *Esquire* 123 (May 1995), p. 54.

6. David Breskin, "Michael Jordan," *Gentleman's Quarterly* (March 1989), pp. 319–397.

7. Walter LaFeber, *Michael Jordan and the New Global Capitalism* (New York: W. W. Norton & Company, 1999), p. 28.

8. David Halberstam, "A Hero for the Wired World," *Sports Illustrated* 75 (December 23, 1991), pp. 76–81.

# TIMELINE OF EVENTS IN THE
# LIFE OF MICHAEL JORDAN

1963    Jordan is born on February 17 in Brooklyn, New York.

1975    Jordan pitches two no-hitters in the Wilmington, North Carolina Little League. He hurls a two-hitter in the Little League Eastern regionals, but his team loses, 1–0, and just misses making the Little League World Series.

1978–1979    Jordan fails to make the varsity basketball team at Emsley A. Laney High School in Wilmington, North Carolina.

1980–1981    Jordan grows to six feet four inches by his senior year and averages 29.2 points, 11.6 rebounds, and 10.1 assists. He attends Howard Garfinkel's summer Five All-Star Basketball Camp in Pittsburgh, Pennsylvania for major college prospects.

1981–1982    Jordan enrolls at the University of North Carolina on a basketball scholarship and becomes one of the few true freshmen to start for Dean Smith. He averages 13.5 points and four rebounds, earning Atlantic Coast Conference (ACC) Rookie of the Year accolades. His 15-foot corner jump shot in the closing seconds gives the Tar Heels a one-point victory over Georgetown University in the National Collegiate Athletic Association championship game and gives Smith his first national title.

1982–1983    As a sophomore, Jordan leads the ACC in scoring
             with a 20-point average. His 78 steals rank second
             to Dudley Bradley in the Tar Heels single-season
             record book. A unanimous All-America, he is
             selected *The Sporting News* College Player of the
             Year. He stars in the Pan American games in
             Caracas, Venezuela, where the United States wins a
             gold medal.

1983–1984    Jordan leads North Carolina to the ACC
             Conference regular-season title, averaging 19.6
             points and 5.3 rebounds. He repeats as *The
             Sporting News* College Player of the Year and an
             All-American, winning the Naismith Award
             and Wooden Award, and contributes to the U.S.
             Olympic team gold medal win at the 1984
             Los Angeles, California games.

1984–1985    Jordan leaves North Carolina after his junior year
             to enter the National Basketball Association draft.
             The Chicago Bulls select him in the first round
             as the third overall pick and sign him to a seven-
             figure, five-year contract. Jordan becomes an instant
             success, reviving interest in the floundering Chicago
             franchise. He leads the NBA in points (2,313),
             averaging 28.2 points, 5.9 assists, and 2.4 steals and
             pacing the Bulls with a 6.5 rebound average. The
             NBA Rookie of the Year and an All-Star game
             starter, Jordan scores a season-high 49 points and 40
             or more points seven times. He mesmerizes crowds
             with his blinding speed, physical artistry, and ability
             to soar upwards, momentarily hang in mid air, and
             make balletic slam dunks. The Bulls increase home
             attendance by 75 percent and lead the NBA in road
             attendance. Jordan signs a lucrative contract with
             Nike athletic shoe manufacturer, which releases its
             very popular Air Jordan basketball shoes.

1985–1986    Chicago wins its first three games, but Jordan breaks
             a bone in his foot in the third game and misses all
             but 18 games. Without him, the Bulls lose 43 of
             their next 64 games. On his return, Chicago finishes
             the season 30–52 and makes the playoffs. The
             Boston Celtics sweep the Bulls in the first round,

but Jordan averages 43.7 points and scores an NBA-playoff record 63 points in a double overtime loss in Game 2 on April 20.

1986–1987    Jordan wins his first NBA scoring title with a 37.1 point average, becoming only the second NBA player (Wilt Chamberlain was the first) to tally 3,000 points in a season and the first player in NBA history to register 200 steals and 100 blocked shots in a season. He wins the slam-dunk competition on All-Star weekend in February in Seattle and scores 61 points in a 117–114 loss to the Atlanta Hawks on April 16 at Chicago Stadium. Jordan registers at least 50 points eight times during the regular season, makes the All-NBA first team, and finishes runner-up to Magic Johnson in the NBA Most Valuable Player voting, but Boston again sweeps Chicago in the first playoff round.

1987–1988    Jordan repeats as NBA scoring champion with a 35.0 point average and leads the NBA with 3.16 steals per contest, helping the Bulls post a 50–32 mark and advance beyond the first playoff round for the first time in seven seasons. He wins his second consecutive slam-dunk contest with a dunk from the free-throw line and tallies 40 points as the All-Star game MVP. His 259 steals and 131 blocks are exceptional for an NBA guard. The NBA MVP and defensive player of the year, Jordan makes the All-NBA first team and the All-Defensive team. In the playoffs, he averages 45.2 points to help Chicago eliminate the Cleveland Cavaliers in five games before losing to the eventual Eastern Conference champion Detroit Pistons in five games in the second round.

1988–1989    On January 25, Jordan scores his 10,000th career point against the Philadelphia 76ers, reaching that total in just 303 games, fewer than any other NBA player except Wilt Chamberlain. He records perhaps his best all-around performance, leading the NBA with 32.5 points per contest, averaging a personal-best 8.0 assists, and hauling down a career-high 8.0 rebounds per outing. A perennial All-Star

and All-NBA first teamer, Jordan makes the first
team All-Defensive squad and finishes second in
the NBA MVP balloting. He joins the NBA's great
clutch performers with his last second shot against
Cleveland in decisive Game 5 of the first playoff
round. After defeating the New York Knicks in
the Eastern Conference semifinals, the Bulls lose
to Detroit in the Eastern Conference Finals. The
physical Pistons invoke the Jordan Rules, double-
and triple-teaming Jordan every time he touches the
ball, preventing him from going to the baseline, and
hammering him when he drives to the basket.

1989–1990   Jordan marries Juanita Vanoy in September at Las
Vegas, Nevada. Chicago finishes 55–27 under new
coach Phil Jackson. Jordan again paces the NBA in
scoring with a 33.6 point average, finishing third
in the NBA MVP balloting and repeating on the
All-NBA first team and the All-Defensive team.
Besides tallying a career-high 69 points at Cleveland
on March 28, he leads the NBA in steals, with 2.77
per game, and averages 6.9 rebounds and 6.3 assists.
Jordan averages 33.1 points in the playoffs, but Detroit eliminates the Bulls in the seven-game Eastern
Conference Finals.

1990–1991   Jordan silences his critics who claim that his brilliant
individual performance had not elevated the play of
his teammates or brought the Bulls an NBA title. He
wins his second NBA MVP Award after leading the
NBA again in scoring with a 31.5 point average and
averaging 6.0 rebounds and 5.5 assists. After winning
a franchise record 61 games and finishing in first
place for the first time in 16 years, Chicago sweeps
Detroit in the Eastern Conference Finals and defeats
the Los Angeles Lakers in the five-game NBA Finals
for its first NBA title. During the playoffs, Jordan
averages 31.1 points, 6.4 rebounds, and 8.4 assists
and changes hands in midair while completing a
layup against Los Angeles. He wins his first NBA
Finals MVP Award and weeps while holding the
NBA Finals trophy.

1991–1992   The Bulls continue their dominance, with 67
victories, as Jordan snags another NBA MVP

Award. He paces the NBA with a 30.0 point scoring average and averages 6.4 rebounds and 6.1 assists, repeating on the All-NBA first team and the All-Defensive first team, and averages 34.5 points in 22 postseason contests. After overcoming the physical New York Knicks in the second round, the Bulls eliminate the Cleveland Cavaliers in the Eastern Conference Finals. Jordan again earns NBA Finals MVP honors with his dominating performance, as Chicago defends its title in six games over the Portland Trail Blazers. His six 3-pointers and 35 points in the first half highlight Game 1. The "Dream Team," a collection of NBA superstars, including Jordan, breeze to a gold medal at the 1992 Olympic games in Barcelona, Spain. The star-studded roster cruises through the medal round, keeping America at the top of the basketball world. The Olympics promote the NBA and Jordan's potent image to a growing international market of basketball fans.

1992–1993 Jordan helps the Bulls become the first team to win three consecutive NBA titles since Boston's victories during the mid-1960s. He again paces the NBA in scoring with a 32.6-point average, but Charles Barkley of the Phoenix Suns takes the NBA MVP Award. The Bulls lose the first two games of the Eastern Conference Finals at New York but rally behind Jordan to win four straight. Chicago bests Phoenix in the six-game NBA Finals, as Jordan's 41 point scoring average sets an NBA Finals record. He becomes the first NBA player to earn three straight NBA Finals MVP awards, capping off perhaps the most spectacular seven-year run by any athlete.

1993–1994 Jordan announces his initial retirement from basketball, citing a lost desire to play the game. Other factors include his physical exhaustion, ever-rowing celebrity, and the murder of his father, James, that July . Jordan also suffers gambling losses on the golf course and is spotted at an Atlantic City, New Jersey casino. His photo-filled book, *Rare Air: Michael on Michael*, celebrates his remarkable athletic skills. Jordan spends 1994 pursuing a childhood dream he shared with his father—playing professional baseball. He trains with the Chicago White Sox and plays outfield for the Birmingham Barons of the Class AA Southern League, drawing large crowds. In 127 games, Jordan hits only .202 and strikes out 114 times in 436 at bats. He belts 17 doubles, drives in 51 runs, and steals 30 bases.

1994–1995    Jordan plays baseball for the Scottsdale Scorpions in the Arizona Fall League and scores 52 points on September 9 in the final basketball game at the old Chicago Stadium, a charity contest arranged by Scottie Pippen. The entrance to the United Center, new arena of the Chicago Bulls, is adorned with a 12-foot bronze statue of an airborne Jordan. His disappointing baseball performance and the prolonged professional baseball players' strike prompt him to return to the NBA. On March 18, Jordan issues a two-word press-release, "I'm back." The next day, he rejoins the Bulls and dons jersey Number 45, as his familiar Number 23 had been retired in his honor during his first retirement. Besides scoring 55 points against New York at Madison Square Garden on March 29, Jordan leads Chicago to a 9–1 record in April and the NBA playoffs. He averages 26.8 points in 17 regular-season games and 31.5 points in the playoffs, but the Bulls lose to the Orlando Magic in the six-game Eastern Conference semifinals. His sequel, *I'm Back! More Rare Air*, provides more reflections on his remarkable athletic career.

1995–1996    The playoff defeat motivates Jordan to train aggressively over the summer. The Bulls, strengthened by the acquisition of rebounder Dennis Rodman, dominate the NBA with an all-time best 72–10 mark. Jordan wins both the regular season and All-Star Game MVP awards and captures an eighth scoring title, averaging 30.4 points, hauling down 6.6 rebounds, dishing off 4.3 assists, and making 2.2 steals per outing. He averages 30.7 points in postseason, as Chicago sweeps Orlando in the Eastern Conference Finals and defeats the Seattle SuperSonics in the six-game NBA Finals

to win the title. Jordan earns the NBA Finals
MVP Award for the fourth time, surpassing Magic ·
Johnson, and becomes the first player since Willis
Reed in 1970 to capture all three MVP awards
during the same season.

1996–1997   Jordan leads the Bulls to a 69–13 record and fifth
championship in seven years, although Karl Malone
edges him for the NBA MVP Award. He wins
another NBA scoring title with a 29.6-point average and tallies his 25,000th career point at the San
Antonio Spurs on November 23. Jordan averages
31.1 points in the playoffs and 32.3 points in the
NBA Finals, helping the Bulls conquer the Utah
Jazz in six games. He wins Game 1 with a buzzer-
beating jump shot. Despite being feverish and
dehydrated from a stomach virus, Jordan scores 38
points and makes the game-deciding three-pointer
with less than one minute left to lift the Bulls to a
dramatic 90–88 victory in Game 5. He earns a record
fifth NBA Finals MVP Award and signs an unprecedented $3 million, one-year contract that August.

1997–1998   Chicago compiles a 62–20 record for a second
three-peat. Jordan leads the NBA for a record tenth
time in scoring with a 28.7 point average, securing
his fifth regular-season MVP Award. His other accolades include making the All-NBA first team for
the tenth time, the NBA All-Defensive team for the
ninth time, and All-Star Game MVP for the third
time. The Bulls win the Eastern Conference playoffs
for the third straight year and vanquish Utah in the
six-game NBA Finals. In decisive Game 6, Jordan
enjoys perhaps the greatest clutch performance in
NBA Finals history. He steals the ball from Malone
and sinks a dramatic shot with less than 10 seconds
left, giving the Bulls an 87–86 victory and their
sixth NBA championship. Jordan scores 45 points in
that historic game and averages more than 30 points
in the NBA Finals, earning his sixth NBA Finals
MVP Award, twice that of any other NBA player.
A third memoir, *For the Love of the Game: My Story*,
provides more reflections on his career.

1999        Jordan retires from the Bulls for the second time
            on January 13 during an owner-induced lockout of
            NBA players, "99.9 percent" certain he will never
            play another NBA game. Phil Jackson leaves as
            coach and Pippen is traded to the Houston Rockets.

2000        On January 19, Jordan becomes part owner
            and president of basketball operations for the
            Washington Wizards NBA team. He wins four
            Excellence in Sports Performance for the Year
            (ESPY) awards: Athlete of the Century, Male
            Athlete of the 1990s, Pro Basketball Player of the
            1990s, and Play of the Decade for switching the ball
            from his right hand to his left for a dunk against
            Los Angeles in the 1991 NBA Finals. Jordan trades
            or releases several highly paid, unpopular players,
            including Juwan Howard and Rod Strickland, but
            unwisely drafts high school prospect Kwame Brown
            with his first 2001 draft pick.

2001        Jordan spends the spring and summer training for a
            second comeback, holding several invitation-only
            games for NBA players in Chicago, and hires Doug
            Collins as Washington head coach. On September
            25, he leaves the Wizards front office and returns as
            a player.

2001–2002   Despite an injury-plagued season, Jordan still paces
            Washington in scoring (22.9 point average), assists
            (5.2 average), and steals (1.42 average). He nearly
            leads the youthful Wizards to the playoffs and in-
            spires sellouts for all 41 home games at the MCI
            Center. Jordan sparks Washington to a franchise-
            record nine-game winning steak in December and
            scores his 30,000th career point on January 4 against
            Chicago at the MCI Center. Kareem Abdul-Jabbar,
            Chamberlain, and Malone were the only NBA play-
            ers to score 30,000 career points previously. A knee
            injury shortens his season to 60 games.

2002–2003   Jordan averages 20 points as the only Wizard to
            play all 82 games, but Washington again misses
            the playoffs. He appears in his 13th All-Star game,
            surpassing Abdul-Jabbar as leading scorer in All-
            Star history. Jordan scores 43 points on February

21 against the New Jersey Nets, becoming the first 40-year-old to tally 40 points in an NBA game. The Wizards again sell out all 41 home games. Jordan retires with 32,292 career points, third on the NBA's all-time scoring list behind Abdul-Jabbar and Malone. He assumes that he will return to his director of basketball operations position, but Washington owner Abe Pollin fires him on May 7.

2003–2006    Jordan spends time with his family in Chicago, golfs in celebrity charity tournaments, and promotes his Jordan Brand clothing line. In 2005, his inspiring story, *Driven from Within*, stresses the importance of authenticity, integrity, passion, commitment, and other qualities in his personal life. The book also describes how challenging events have pushed him to new heights. On June 15, 2006, Jordan becomes the second-largest owner of the Charlotte Bobcats NBA team. Owner Bob Johnson gives him final authority on player personnel decisions as managing member of basketball operations. The Jordans file for divorce in December 2006, citing irreconcilable difference, ending their 17-year marriage. They retain joint custody of their three children.

# Chapter 1

# THE FORMATIVE YEARS, 1963–1984

## MIDDLE CLASS ORIGINS:
## EARLY YEARS (1963–1977)

Jordan attributes his success to his home, family, and hometown. He came from a close-knit upper-middle class family. His parents, James Jordan and Deloris Peoples, grew up in limited economic circumstances on eastern North Carolina farms. They met after a basketball game in Wallace in 1956. James, a sharecropper's son, served in the U.S. Air Force, and Deloris briefly attended Tuskegee Institute. They were married shortly after Deloris quit Tuskegee. Both parents were average height and nonathletic.

Michael Jordan was born February 17, 1963 in Brooklyn, New York. His parents lived there temporarily while his father attended a General Electric training school. The fourth of five children, he has two older brothers, Larry and James, the most athletic sibling; an older sister, Deloris; and a younger sister, Roslyn. When Jordan was still young, his father retired from the Air Force and moved to Wallace. James worked as a forklift operator at the General Electric Company factory outside Wallace, and Deloris was a drive-through window teller at a branch of United Carolina Bank in Wallace.

In 1970, the Jordans got better jobs in larger Wilmington, near where James had grown up. James, who built a large house in a wooded area near an ocean beach, was promoted at General Electric to dispatcher, foreman, and equipment supervisor of three departments. Deloris advanced to head teller at United Carolina Bank and then head of customer relations at the downtown office. The Jordans fared well financially with incomes from their jobs and James's Air Force pension.

The five Jordan children attended integrated schools and missed the worst of the civil rights violence. The Jordans encouraged Michael to develop friendships with both African-Americans and whites. Deloris wanted Michael to judge others on their merits rather than their skin color. Jordan seldom experienced racial discrimination, but he was suspended from school for crushing a Popsicle into the head of a white girl who called him a "nigger."[1] When a neighbor refused to let him use a swimming pool, he quietly left. "Don't worry about race unless somebody slaps you in the face,"[2] he said.

Jordan's parents influenced him in different ways. Both parents imbued him with their strong work ethic, the will to strive for excellence in their chosen fields, and a sense of priorities. Jordan developed his outgoing personality, sense of humor and order, love of athletics, mischievousness, and tongue-wagging from James. "My father is a people person," Jordan explained. "He can talk to someone for five hours and have any conversation you could imagine." Deloris gave him motivation, discipline, a perfectionist attitude, competitiveness, and a drive to win. "My mother has always been more of the business side of the family," he observed. "She had a kind of [get up and get it] attitude."[3]

James described Michael as carefree, kind, and easy to please. The laziest sibling, Michael avoided doing household chores. As a teenager, he was the only sibling who did not maintain a steady job and would have been viewed as the least likely to succeed. "I was the black sheep of the family," Jordan confessed. "I didn't want to work."[4] He often bribed his siblings to avoid household chores that his strict, hard-working parents demanded of their children. Deloris forced him to take a job at a hotel doing maintenance work, but he quit after a week. She was upset and warned him that he would not have any spending money. Jordan just wanted to play basketball and other sports. He admitted, "my focus was to be the best player in whatever sport I played. That was all I ever thought about." Unlike James or his older brothers, Ronnie and Larry, Michael lacked mechanical skills. James wanted Michael to help him in the garage, but Michael was not interested. "He didn't think I'd amount to anything," Jordan recalled.[5]

Jordan was not focused academically until high school. Although he had perfect school attendance through eighth grade, he had discipline problems in ninth grade. "Ninth grade was the toughest year of my life,"[6] Jordan recollected. The principal suspended him for leaving the school grounds without permission on the first day of school to buy a soda, for swearing at a teacher, and for fighting a boy who erased the white lines he was drawing to form base paths on the school infield for a baseball game that day. He tried to stay out of further trouble.

Jordan considered baseball his favorite sport and made his first athletic accomplishments in that sport. He wanted to become a professional baseball player He was one of few African Americans on his Wilmington Little League team and pitched two no-hitters. At age 12, Jordan hurled a two-hitter in the Little League Eastern Regionals, but Wilmington lost the championship game, 1–0, and just missed making the Little League World Series. He fared even better in the Babe Ruth League, earning Most Valuable Player honors when his team captured the state baseball championship. Jordan considered the award his favorite childhood memory and biggest accomplishment as a youth. He also excelled at pool, cards, Monopoly, and other games and played the trumpet in seventh and eighth grades.

In Wilmington, the African American youngsters usually played basketball rather than baseball. Basketball seemed a distant dream for Jordan because of his skinny frame. Not a born basketball player, Jordan worked hard to improve his jumping and other hoop skills. He worshipped his competitive, athletic older brother, Larry. As a middle school student, Jordan often played one-on-one basketball with Larry on the small court that his father built in the back yard. Although only five foot seven inches, Larry dominated Michael for several years because he was taller and much stronger. Jordan repeatedly lost the one-on-ones, but loved competition and overcoming obstacles. Their spirited rivalry sometimes even led to fights. Frustrated by his lack of height, Jordan often hung from a chin-up bar to stretch his body. He eventually outgrew Larry, but both could jump. Despite his later athletic accomplishments, Jordan remained an adoring younger brother and looked to Larry as a source of inspiration. James often complimented Larry more often, leading Michael to work even harder.

## LEARNING THROUGH FAILURE: 9TH AND 10TH GRADES (1977–1979)

By the ninth grade, Jordan began exhibiting more athletic ability and even more competitiveness. Six-foot six-inch Harvest Leroy Smith, Jordan's closest friend, considered him small, but very quick and the best ninth-grade player. Jordan's quickness compensated for his lack of size. Jordan needed to win whether it was a game or just playing HORSE. If he lost, he played again until he won.

Emsley A. Laney High School was desegregated when Jordan entered. Approximately 40 percent of Laney students were African American. Laney lacked the racial tensions that sometimes occurred at southern schools. After ninth grade, Jordan and Smith attended varsity basketball coach Clifton "Pop" Herring's basketball camp. Herring invited them to try out for the varsity squad as sophomores in 1978, and he liked Jordan's quickness and Smith's size, but the other varsity players were older and stronger. When Herring posted the varsity team names in the gymnasium, Smith made the final cut, but 5-foot 9-inch Jordan did not. Although admitting that the varsity squad was very good, Jordan still insisted he could contribute.

Assistant coach Fred Lynch decided that Jordan should spend his sophomore year on the junior varsity squad. Jordan would see more playing action there. The Laney coaching staff should have known how the decision to accept Smith would impact Jordan and should have told him that his time would come.

Jordan considered that day the worst of his young life. Herring listed the varsity team in alphabetical order. Jordan repeatedly reread the list, thinking that he might have missed seeing his name or that the list was out of alphabetical order. He walked home alone that day. "I went to my room and I closed the door and I cried," Jordan recalled. "For a while I couldn't stop. Even though there was no one else home at the time, I kept the door shut. It was important to me that no one hear me or see me."[7] Harvest Smith knew the pain that Jordan was experiencing because he considered Jordan a much better basketball player. Although his friends were playing, Jordan did not even want to cheer for the varsity team. "I guess I wanted them to lose to prove that they had made a mistake by leaving me off the team,"[8] he remembered.

Jordan starred for the junior varsity basketball team that year, exhibiting dominant quickness. He averaged 28 points as a point guard, popularizing the jayvee games. The entire varsity squad watched Jordan play. Despite his stellar play, however, Jordan was not promoted to the varsity for the state tournament. He rode the team bus to the state tournament only because he asked to be statistician and the team manager was sick. Jordan desperately wanted to be part of the varsity. He did not have a ticket and had to carry the star player's uniform just to get into the gymnasium.

As a sophomore, Jordan briefly played safety on the football team, competed in track and field, and played baseball. He began thinking that perhaps baseball was best suited for his talent. The failure to make the varsity basketball squad enhanced his determination and competitiveness. It embarrassed and irritated him, especially because the team roster was posted for a long time. He did not want that to happen again.

Herring, however, knew that Jordan would make the varsity basketball team as a junior and encouraged him to stop playing football. Herring, who lived a block from the Jordans, picked up Jordan every morning at 6:30 A.M. that fall and drove him to the high school gymnasium for an extra hour of practice before classes started. During those sessions, Jordan worked diligently to improve his skills, fundamentals, and work ethic. "Whenever I was working out and got tired and figured I ought to stop," he said, "I'd close my eyes and see that list in the locker room without my name on it, and that usually got me going again."[9] His game improved, and he became more confident. Herring realized Jordan's potential and urged him to stay focused both athletically and academically. Jordan suddenly grew four inches to six foot three inches. The height change transformed him from a promising all-around athlete to a potential basketball star.

## THE BLOSSOMING OF A TALENT: 11TH AND 12TH GRADES (1979–1981)

Jordan made the varsity basketball squad his junior year, joining his brother, Larry, who wore uniform Number 45. He requested uniform Number 23 because he aspired to be at least half the player his brother was. "Mike was real skinny," teammate Kevin Edwards recounted, "and we called him 'Peanut' because of the way his head was shaped."[10] Jordan, though, possessed much larger hands than Edwards and towered over other family members. He added strength to his quickness and began dunking the ball.

Laney, led by Jordan, finished 13–10 and verged on being an excellent basketball team. Jordan enjoyed an impressive junior season at power forward, averaging 20.8 points. He played with intensity and practiced the hardest, working out every morning before school. Jordan implored his teammates to play harder and urged his coaches to inspire them more. Herring wanted Jordan to shoot more, but he declined. Jordan was not even included among the 300 leading high school prospects before his senior year.

Jordan liked athletics more than academics. He disliked doing homework, but Deloris made sure he did it anyway rather than waste time watching television. She adamantly insisted that he make good grades and that academics take priority over basketball. Jordan described himself as a C+ or B- student before entering high school. He often sneaked out of his biology class to practice his jump shot in the gym. After doing that so many times one year, Jordan was suspended from school. James warned Michael to cease this behavior because he had special athletic ability.

By high school graduation, Jordan had raised his academic average to a 3.2 or 3.3 grade point average and could have earned a college academic scholarship. He increasingly realized the importance of getting a good education and performed well in math, science, and his other precollege courses. Jordan also took a home economics course. "I wanted to learn how to cook and clean and sew," he explained. "I figured no girl would ever want to marry me, and I didn't know if I'd have enough money to eat out."[11] Jordan wanted to be admired and respected by his classmates, but encountered difficulty getting dates and often drew taunts for playing basketball with his tongue wagging.

In February 1979, Mike Brown, athletic director of the New Hanover (Wilmington) County schools, phoned Roy Williams, a University of North Carolina assistant basketball coach, about Jordan. "There's this junior down here at Laney that's starting to really come on," Brown noted. Bill Guthridge, North Carolina's top assistant basketball coach, saw Jordan play once that season and told revered head basketball coach Dean Smith that he took quite a few jump shots, exhibited exceptional quickness and great hands, and tried hard. "He's unmilked,"[12] Guthridge observed. Although possessing natural athletic skills, Jordan still needed to learn a lot. Guthridge concluded that Jordan probably could compete in the Atlantic Coast Conference. North Carolina scouted him and monitored his development.

During the summer of 1980, Williams arranged for Jordan to attend Smith's prestigious basketball camp. Neither Smith, Williams, nor assistant coach Eddie Fogler had seen him play. Approximately 400 high schoolers, including heralded prospects Buzz Peterson and Lynnwood Robinson, attended. Jordan dominated the camp. After Jordan's group finished a scrimmage on the first day, Williams asked him if he wanted to continue scrimmaging. Jordan agreed and played another game. He was supposed to leave after that scrimmage, but sneaked back for a third session. Williams liked Jordan's athletic skills, quickness, jumping ability, defensive intensity, and nose for the ball and boasted to Fogler, "That's the best six-foot-four-inch high school player I've ever seen."[13] They told Smith about his stellar performance. Smith, who saw Jordan play the next morning for the first time, especially noticed his quickness and competitiveness and also liked his defensive potential and jumping ability.

Williams considered Jordan to be North Carolina's top recruit. Jordan began to show explosive athletic moves, driving to the basket, reversing himself, and scoring effortlessly. He enjoyed playing basketball, exuding a natural self-confidence, and realized that he possessed virtually unlimited potential if he applied himself. Smith lunched with him twice. The coaching staff urged his family to strongly consider North Carolina.

Williams suggested that the Jordans send Michael to Howard Garfinkel's prestigious Five-Star Camp near Pittsburgh, Pennsylvania that summer. Prospects competed there against the nation's best high school players. The other North Carolina coaches were concerned that other universities would notice Jordan's talent. Smith advised, "It would be better for us if we didn't send him up there for everybody else to see."[14] Williams and Fogler countered that North Carolina could learn how good Jordan really was against premier talent.

Jordan was excited, but apprehensive about the camp. Unlike many other attendees, he had received very few inquiries from colleges. Jordan told himself, "You must emerge as somebody—somebody to be admired, to achieve big things. But don't lose your identity."[15] He played well against the nation's best young players. Garfinkel, an astute appraiser of talent, saw Jordan showcase his physical ability and he raved that that week was the moment a star was born. Jordan stole a ball, sped down the court, and gently laid the ball in the basket. According to Garfinkel, he was quicker than the other players, possessed great jumping ability, and played with exceptional poise and control. Garfinkel persuaded Jordan's parents to let him stay another week at the camp. Jordan relished the opportunity to improve his game.

Jordan, however, did not make any prospective high school basketball All-America lists. Garfinkel told Dave Krider, who selected the players for *Street and Smith*, that he considered Michael among the nation's 10 best prospects. Although Krider had never heard of Jordan, Garfinkel insisted that he be included on the All-American team. He predicted "the kid's going to be a great star, and they'll make fun of you if you don't have him."[16] Krider phoned back several hours later that it was too late to include Jordan's name. Jordan won five trophies the first week and was named the camp's Most Valuable Player, besting 17 high school All-Americas.

Peterson also performed well there. Jordan edged him in the one-on-one championship. He suggested that they attend North Carolina as roommates, dreaming they could win a national championship there. They exchanged telephone numbers and agreed to stay in contact.

Jordan considered attending UCLA, North Carolina State University, North Carolina, the University of South Carolina, or the University of Maryland. He preferred UCLA, but the Bruins never recruited him. As a youth, Jordan rooted for North Carolina State because of its star, David Thompson, and disliked the University of North Carolina. Smith's camp and personal interest influenced him to reconsider North Carolina. South Carolina and Maryland also recruited Jordan.

The Jordans accompanied Michael on his visits to Chapel Hill. Their involvement convinced Smith that Jordan was serious about attending North Carolina. In the fall of 1980, Smith, Guthridge, and Fogler visited the Jordans in the living room of their spacious Wilmington home. Jordan sat on the floor palming and stroking a basketball. The Jordans asked many questions, mostly about academics. Deloris appreciated Smith's emphasizing the importance of education and disciplined work habits rather than the glories of Tar Heel basketball. Jordan's sister, Roslyn, who graduated from high school in three years, also planned to attend North Carolina.

Williams and Fogler befriended the Jordans during Michael's senior year. Williams told James that he liked to chop wood for exercise and wanted to make a wood stove for his house. Unbeknownst to Williams, James made wood stoves for a hobby and loved to give them to friends. James built a wood stove for Williams and delivered it to his house. Williams insisted on paying for it, but James refused to accept any money.

After being persuaded by Deloris, Jordan signed a letter of intent to attend North Carolina in November 1980. The Jordans liked the North Carolina basketball tradition, Smith, and especially Williams. Jordan enjoyed meeting prominent North Carolina athletes Kelvin Bryant, Lawrence Taylor, Al Wood, James Worthy, and Sam Perkins sitting on "The Wall," the brick fence encircling the campus library.

Jordan's reputation blossomed his senior year. Smith saw him perform well against formidable Southern Wayne High School. Jordan recorded a triple-double, averaging double figures at in least three different statistical categories. He averaged 29.2 points, 11.6 rebounds, and 10.1 assists as a senior. Wilmington finished 19–4, but a fluky regional tournament setback kept them from the state tournament. Jordan helped persuade Peterson, the state's Mr. Basketball and top athlete, to attend North Carolina. They played in the Capital Classic in Washington, D.C., McDonald's All-American Game in Wichita, Kansas, and National Sports Festival in Syracuse, New York.

Jordan made the McDonald's All-American team and started at guard in the McDonald's classic, converting 13 of 17 shots and scoring 30 points. Adrian Branch, a Maryland recruit who scored 24 points, won the MVP Award because his baskets came at more crucial times, but Jordan appeared the most dominant player. Deloris protested the decision and approached judges John Wooden and Sonny Hill, but Guthridge intervened. CBS announcer Billy Packer consoled Deloris, "It's only an all-star game. . . . I think your son has a great career ahead of him."[17]

## THE SHOT HEARD ROUND THE NATION (1981–1982)

Jordan arrived on the University of North Carolina campus in August 1981 with a basketball scholarship; he majored in geography. He roomed with Buzz Peterson, a reserve from a prominent business family whom he had befriended when both were prep All-Americas. "What impressed me most about Michael was his love for his parents and family," Peterson recalled. He described Jordan as "a fun guy to be around," but "deadly serious"[18] on the basketball court.

North Carolina had supplanted UCLA as the nation's premier collegiate basketball program. The Tar Heels had reached the NCAA Final Four six times during coach Dean Smith's tenure and were eliminated in the 1981 NCAA semifinals. North Carolina was ranked Number 1 in preseason polls and returned four starters, including senior Jimmy Black, junior James Worthy, and sophomores Sam Perkins and Matt Doherty. Smith's very disciplined program featured the team over the individual. Smith believed that the maximum results were achieved when players sacrificed individuality for the team.

Smith realized that Jordan was a little apprehensive and brought him along slowly. Some Emsley A. Laney High School friends predicted that Jordan would not succeed in basketball there and urged him to attend the University of North Carolina-Wilmington. "They thought I'd sit on the bench for four years, come home and work at the local gas station," Jordan recalled. Jordan initially doubted if he could compete with the talented North Carolina players and did not dominate his freshman year. "I thought I would go in and be a flop," Jordan admitted. "Everyone was expecting so much." Smith encouraged him to have fun playing basketball and work diligently, and assured him "you will get the opportunity to play." [19] Jordan followed his advice and gradually gained self-confidence.

Jordan quickly learned that he could fulfill expectations during campus pickup games with Worthy, Mitch Kupchak, and Al Wood before the Tar Heels' first practice. Wood was guarding Jordan, with the score tied and the next basket to determine the winner. Jordan went to the baseline, drove past Wood and seven-foot Geff Crompton, and dunked the ball. The game winner gave him motivation to push further. Jordan began telling upperclassmen in pickup games that he would dunk the ball and usually backed up his promises. He amazed teammates with his offensive acceleration, exceptional moves to the basket, and dazzling defensive plays. Upperclassmen considered him cocky, but he assured Smith that he could help North Carolina immediately.

Worthy, Perkins, Black, and Doherty were pictured on the front cover of *Sports Illustrated*'s annual preseason college basketball issue. Larry Keith, college basketball editor, told Smith that the picture would look peculiar with just four players and urged him to include Jordan. "He made himself and the others available," Keith said, "but he was adamant about not letting a freshman get that attention."[20]

Jordan desperately wanted to make the starting five. During Smith's 20-year tenure, Phil Ford, Mike O'Koren, and Worthy were the only freshmen starters. Freshmen practiced against the varsity but usually made cameo appearances in games because Smith feared they would make critical mistakes. Jordan battled junior Jimmy Braddock and Peterson to replace guard Al Wood. Smith regarded Braddock as a better outside shooter and ball handler; considered Peterson very athletic, more experienced, better coached, and a finer pure shooter; and regarded Jordan a better jumper, quicker, a superior defender, and more motivated. He did not know that Jordan possessed a compulsion to be the best and a rare ability to motivate himself.

Jordan readily learned the guard position and new defensive techniques. He had played forward in high school, but Smith wanted him to play big guard. Smith did not name players as starters unless they demonstrated superior skill and defensive execution. Jordan mastered the guard drills so quickly that Smith knew he would see extensive action. To contend for a starting position, however, Jordan needed to be a more complete player defensively. Smith and Williams pushed Jordan to work harder in practices. Jordan assured Williams, "I'm working as hard as everyone else." Williams replied, "But Michael, you told me you wanted to be the best. And if you want to be the best, then you have to work harder than anyone else." Jordan responded, "Coach, I understand. You'll see. Watch."[21] He consequently began to take his game to another level.

Smith spent considerable time explaining defensive techniques and how to counter backdoor plays. Jordan had been taught to turn and defend facing the ball, but Smith wanted him to look over his shoulder and see both player and ball. Smith walked through each step of this technique with him. Jordan amazed Smith by executing the technique perfectly at the next practice.

Two preseason Blue-White scrimmages helped Smith determine the starting lineup. Jordan convinced Smith "he knew our principles defensively better than most freshmen."[22] Two days before the season opener, Smith selected Jordan over Braddock at big guard. His athletic ability, quickness, offensive creativity, enthusiasm, work ethic, and innate athletic intelligence impressed Smith. Smith informed Jordan that he was starting just before the first game against the University of Kansas at Charlotte Coliseum. Jordan was jubilant about joining Worthy, Perkins, Doherty, and Black in the starting lineup.

North Carolina proved ideal for Jordan, who played with experienced, talented teammates in a demanding, disciplined program. Smith's tightly organized practices challenged Jordan and proved excellent learning experiences for him. Jordan worked hard to improve, learned quickly, and showed exceptional concentration; but his defense, passing skills, and outside shot needed improvement. According to Smith, Jordan's exceptionally large hands made it more difficult for him to shoot.

Smith and about half the players called him Michael; the North Carolina media guide and remaining teammates referred to him as Mike. Sports information director Rick Brewer asked him how he preferred to be listed in the media guide. Jordan replied that he had no preference. Brewer claimed that Michael sounded better. Jordan nodded his approval and has been called that ever since. He wore uniform Number 23 and long, loose-fitting baggy shorts.

Opponents often used a zone defense against North Carolina in 1981–1982, denying Worthy and Perkins the ball on the inside, while giving Jordan, Doherty, and Black open shots. Smith advised his guards not to take quick outside shots, but rather wait patiently for high percentage shots. North Carolina implemented Smith's strategy well, averaging 67 points and restricting opponents to just 55 points. The Tar Heels shot 53.7 percent, with Perkins and Worthy both averaging more than 57 percent, Jordan more than 53 percent, and Doherty and Black more than 51 percent. Opponents often resorted to ball control, but the Tar Heels used their four corners delay game with leads.

On December 26, North Carolina defeated second-ranked University of Kentucky, 82–69, at the New Jersey Meadowlands. The Wildcats applied a packed-in zone, forcing the Tar Heels to rely on jump shots. Jordan shot inconsistently in the first half, but finished with 19 points in 35 minutes. North Carolina was ranked first nationally by midseason, and Jordan was the leading scorer.

North Carolina and the second-ranked University of Virginia, led by seven foot, four inch center Ralph Sampson, split two regular-season games and shared first place in the ACC. Wake Forest University inflicted the Tar Heels' only other loss when influenza sidelined Perkins. North

Carolina faced Virginia in the ACC tournament championship game to determine which school would stay in the NCAA East Regional at nearby Charlotte and Raleigh. No national champion had ever reached the NCAA Final Four from outside its natural region. Jordan spent five days in the infirmary with a bad throat infection but recovered by the ACC tournament.

In that ACC title game, Jordan converted four consecutive jump shots to give North Carolina a 44–43 lead with 7 minutes and 34 seconds left. Smith instructed the Tar Heels to spread their offense with his patented four corners and not shoot again unless Sampson and the Virginia zone moved away from the basket. The Cavaliers let nearly five minutes elapse before starting to foul North Carolina. With 28 seconds left, Virginia accumulated enough fouls to send Doherty to the line. Doherty converted one foul shot, giving the Tar Heels a 45–43 lead. After North Carolina regained possession, Doherty sank two more free throws with three seconds remaining. Sampson's meaningless dunk at the buzzer produced the 47–45 final score.

James Madison University nearly upset the Tar Heels in the second round of the NCAA East regionals at Charlotte. Worthy scored North Carolina's last five points, giving the Tar Heels a narrow 52–50 victory. North Carolina spread the court late in the second halves to preserve victories over the University of Alabama and Villanova University at Raleigh and make the NCAA Final Four.

In the NCAA semifinals at the Superdome in New Orleans, Louisiana, the Tar Heels shot 76 percent in the second half to defeat the high-scoring University of Houston, 68–63. Houston featured All-America guard Rob Williams, Hakeem Olajuwon, and Clyde Drexler. Perkins tallied 25 points and 10 rebounds, but Williams tallied only two points.

North Carolina faced Georgetown University in the NCAA cham-pionship game before 61,612 fans and a huge national television audi-ence. Georgetown, coached by John Thompson, played pressure defense with 7-foot 1-inch All-America freshman Patrick Ewing and three quick guards. North Carolina countered with speed, power, finesse, and excel-lent passing. Smith had not won an NCAA title in six previous Final Four appearances.

Georgetown displayed tenacious defense, with Ewing being called for goaltending on five of the first nine North Carolina shots. The Hoyas led, 32–31, at halftime. Ewing and Eric "Sleepy" Floyd combined for 18 points; Worthy tallied 18 points. Jordan delivered the best performance of his freshman season, leading both teams with nine rebounds, scor-ing 12 points in the first 24 minutes, setting up two monster dunks by

Worthy, and playing great defense. He prevented a sure Ewing basket by intercepting a pass and finding Worthy for another flying slam dunk to give the Tar Heels a 57–56 lead. North Carolina used its four corners offense. Black drew Ewing's fourth foul and converted both free throws, widening the lead to 59–56 with 5 minutes and 30 seconds left. After Georgetown's Fred Brown made two free throws, North Carolina ran two minutes off the clock. Jordan spotted a slight opening and drove down the middle lane to the basket. Ewing tried to block his path. Jordan, already airborne, switched the ball to his left hand and laid it up just over Ewing's outstretched arm. The ball touched high off the glass and gently through the net, giving the Tar Heels a 61–58 lead. Georgetown regained the lead, 62–61, on baskets by Ewing and Floyd.

Smith called a timeout with 32 seconds left. He preferred to get the ball inside to Worthy or Perkins, but he figured Georgetown's pressure defense would deny them the ball. Smith anticipated that Jordan would be open and instructed the other players to pass the ball to him for the final shot. "Take the first great shot, and pound the boards," he instructed Jordan. Smith uncharacteristically trusted a talented freshman to take the decisive shot. He tapped him on the knee and said, "If it comes to you, Michael, knock it in."[23]

When play resumed, Jordan breathed deeply and just waited. Black took the inbound pass but found neither Worthy nor Perkins open. He faked a pass to Perkins and passed to Jordan, who sank an open 16-foot corner jump shot with 17 seconds left to put North Carolina ahead, 63–62. The arena roared at what North Carolinians termed "The Shot." Jordan shut his eyes after releasing the ball and admitted, "I honestly did not know that the shot had gone in until Georgetown took the ball out of bounds."[24] At crunch time, Jordan always wanted the ball. "He didn't have a hesitation or a doubt that he was going to shoot the ball,"[25] Doherty recollected. A picture of Jordan launching the shot became the cover of the Chapel Hill phone book.

The Hoyas pushed the ball down court quickly, but Jordan blocked the lane when Fred Brown tried to pass to Floyd. Brown instead threw an errant pass to Worthy, who missed two foul shots with two seconds remaining. Georgetown's desperation 50-foot shot missed at the buzzer, preserving North Carolina's 63–62 victory. Smith, who won his first NCAA title, told Thompson, "It was the best team we played all year, and it was our best game."[26] The Tar Heels shot 53.2 percent in the classic game; the Hoyas converted 52.9 percent. Worthy led North Carolina with 28 points and won the NCAA Final Four Award, and Ewing paced Georgetown with 23 points.

The decisive basket marked the making of the legendary Jordan. Fogler observed, "That kid doesn't realize it yet, but he's part of history now. People will remember that shot 25 years from now."[27] The 19-year-old Jordan won acclaim for his graceful success under immense pressure, performing in a way that few freshmen could. Classmate Davis Love noted, "He wanted the ball in that situation. How many freshmen would have that confidence to take it, then make it?"[28] Smith, impressed with Jordan's intelligence and court savvy, was amazed by how often he played heroic roles at crunch time. Although later winning six NBA titles, Jordan considered the 1981 NCAA Championship his favorite moment. "It's hard to outrank Carolina," he explained, "because that started everything. The confidence, the knowledge, and everything I gained from that, is without question the beginning of Michael Jordan."[29] James warned him, "Your life will never be the same after that shot."[30]

Michael's dramatic shot relieved Smith, who had taken six previous North Carolina teams to the NCAA Final Four without winning a national title. Smith gleamed, "I would never have to answer another question about not winning a national championship. That so-called monkey was off my back." At a press conference, Smith acknowledged, "we were the best team in college basketball in 1982." He added, "We were solid defensively, difficult to stop on offense, and a good rebounding team. Also we were mentally tough."[31] Besides playing smart and unselfishly, his youthful squad remained healthy.

Several Tar Heels won personal accolades, and the NCAA title benefited the basketball program. Worthy was named national Player of the Year and made first team All-America with Perkins. Jordan garnered NCAA Freshman of the Year honors, averaging 13.5 points and four rebounds in 34 games and performing brilliantly in the clutch. North Carolina signed another highly rated recruiting class, featuring center Brad Daugherty and guards Steve Hale and Curtis Hunter.

## A MOVE TO THE HEAD OF THE CLASS
## (1982–1983)

Under Smith, Jordan learned tight all-around team play and mastered rebounding and defense. After the title season, Smith told Jordan that he needed to improve his defense. As a freshman, Jordan did not win one defensive game award. If he worked hard on his defense over the summer, he could become a more complete player. Smith explained that good defense ultimately won games and remained consistent even when the offense struggled. Jordan worked so diligently on his defense that summer that he became more interested in defense than offense. Smith also asked Jordan to improve his left-handed dribble and his outside shot because the ACC was adopting the shot clock and three-point shot. Jordan toiled assiduously on each facet of his game. His extraordinary athletic gifts, determination, and work ethic astonished Smith. "I have never seen that kind of improvement in anyone, ever," Smith observed. "We weren't prepared for the exponential leap he made in his game."[32] Besides being more mature physically, Jordan was a more consistent shooter and savvier player.

By August, Jordan exhibited new confidence and a quiet swagger. He already possessed the qualities to become a great player, but his confidence matched his physical talent. Jordan looked impressive during preseason pickup games against established NBA players Mike O'Koren, Al Wood, Dudley Bradley, Phil Ford, Mitch Kupchak, and Walter Davis, Tar Heel returnees Perkins and Doherty, and incoming freshmen. He once soared over Davis to dunk the ball with tongue wagging and eyes wide open. During these games, Jordan became the most dominant player. Besides scoring at will, he elevated the weaker phases of his game and performed moves that could not be taught.

Jordan seemed bigger, faster, and stronger at fall practice. He had grown from six feet, four inches to six feet, six inches and ran the 40-yard sprint in 4.39 seconds, .16 of a second faster than during his freshman year. His height and speed complemented his talent, passion, and willingness to accept coaching advice, making him a dominant player. He almost always won the one-on-one drills against Hale, Peterson, and Braddock, frequently dunking the ball. After observing one practice, Philadelphia 76ers coach Billy Cunningham proclaimed "He's going to be the greatest player who ever came out of here."[33]

Jordan needed to win whether in practice, basketball games, or other activities. At some practices, Smith played Jordan with four nonstarters to let him experience the desperation of getting blown out in scrimmages. Jordan developed a disdain for losing and the foundation of a killer instinct. Smith often stacked five-on-five games against him, but his team usually prevailed anyway. Every competition meant life or death for him, occasionally landing him in trouble. Jordan, Peterson, and their dates were playing Monopoly one night. Jordan threw the Monopoly board and stormed out of the room when Peterson built hotels on Boardwalk and Park Place. "I stayed with my sister that night," he recalled. "I just couldn't face Buzz."[34]

As a sophomore, Jordan played small forward. Although Worthy and Black graduated, North Carolina ranked first nationally in 1982–1983 preseason polls. Jordan, Perkins, Doherty, Braddock, and Warren Martin returned from the national championship team; 16-year-old center Daugherty and guards Hunter and Hale gave the Tar Heels considerable depth. Injuries, however, intervened. Jordan broke his hand and played with a hard cast during the first four games, and injuries also slowed Perkins and Daugherty. North Carolina dropped its first two games at the University of Missouri and St. John's University and struggled to win three of its next four contests. Jordan showcased his exceptional defensive ability, natural basketball instincts, and blazing speed, usually being assigned to guard two players. He often freelanced, stealing the ball at very opportunity. His 22-foot jump shot against Tulane University forced overtime in North Carolina's initial victory. In late December, the Tar Heels won the Rainbow Classic in Honolulu, Hawaii. Jordan's road to glory continued on January 12 at Chapel Hill, where he blocked Chuck Driesell's shot to preserve a 72–71 victory over the University of Maryland. In the rematch at College Park later that month, Jordan took an outlet pass from Perkins, accelerated toward the basket, and launched an experimental Air Jordan dunk. He moved laterally while elevating toward the basket. "Before you know it," he recalled, "I'm cranking the ball back, rocking it left to right, cuffing it before I put it down. Every breakaway after that seemed like a chance to try something new."[35]

North Carolina defeated Virginia twice. The Tar Heels snapped the top-ranked Cavaliers' 34-game winning streak in January in Charlottesville, where Perkins tallied a career-high 36 points in the 101–95 upset. Near the end, Jordan stunned the crowd by soaring across the lane to block Ralph Sampson's shot. North Carolina extended its victory streak to 18 games against Virginia at Chapel Hill on February 10, when Jordan sparked a comeback. Virginia exploited Sampson's enormous size, amassing a 16-point lead with nine minutes left, and still led, 63–53, with 4 minutes and 12 seconds left. Braddock's three pointer, coupled with two free throws each by Doherty and Perkins, sliced the margin to 63–60 with 2 minutes and 54 seconds remaining. Jordan scored with 1 minute and 7 seconds left and stole the ball from Rick Carlisle. After driving toward the basket, he ascended with his arm cocked and slam-dunked the ball to put North Carolina ahead, 64–63. The crowd reached a frenzied pitch. After Carlisle missed a last second shot, Jordan snatched the rebound to preserve the victory.

The Tar Heels finished eighth nationally with a 28–8 record, sharing first place in the ACC with Virginia. Injuries sidelined Peterson and Hunter for the rest of the season, and Daugherty played with a stress foot fracture. North Carolina lost to eventual NCAA champion North

Carolina State University in the ACC Tournament semifinals at Atlanta. The University of Georgia upset the Tar Heels, 82–77, in the NCAA East regional finals at Syracuse, New York, abruptly ending North Carolina's quest to repeat as national champions. Georgia continually penetrated North Carolina's trapping defense.

Jordan, benefiting from the ACC's three-point shot experiment, averaged 20.0 points and 5.5 rebounds in 36 games and won 12 defensive game awards. He earned numerous honors, including All-Atlantic Coast Conference, All-America team, and *The Sporting News* College Player of the Year, and he ranked second to Sampson in the Associated Press Player of the Year balloting. Jordan led the ACC in scoring and recorded 78 steals, trailing only Dudley Bradley in the North Carolina record books. *The Sporting News* described his court versatility, "He soars through the air, he rebounds, he scores (more than 1,100 points in two years, a school record), he guards two men at once, he vacuums up loose balls, he blocks shots, he makes steals. Most important, he makes late plays that win games."[36]

The next afternoon, Jordan told Roy Williams that he had been playing basketball for two consecutive years without a respite and wanted a breather. Williams encouraged him to take time off and was surprised to find him practicing that night in the gym. Jordan responded that he needed to improve his game.

Jordan toured that summer with various All-Star teams and starred in the Pan-American Games in Caracas, Venezuela, where the U.S. basketball team won a gold medal. The South American trip intensified his interest in cultural geography. Peter Alfano observed, "He can excite a crowd like a Sunday morning preacher and lift a team to new heights, and yet people are impressed by his unassuming nature and friendly manner. There are times when he seems too good to be real."[37] Jordan also enjoyed playing golf with roommate Peterson and future pro golfer Davis Love.

## NATIONAL AND OLYMPIC HONORS (1983–1984)

During Jordan's junior year, most 1983–1984 preseason polls ranked North Carolina best nationally. *Sports Illustrated* predicted that the Tar Heels would win the national championship and pictured Jordan with Perkins on the front cover of its college basketball issue. Jordan and Perkins led North Carolina, complemented by Brad Daugherty and Kenny Smith. Besides being stronger and more articulate, Jordan began exhibiting his killer instinct on the court, and Perkins scored from both inside and challenged the Tar Heels' career rebounding records. Daugherty, slimmer and stronger, was the best pure center to play under Smith. Point guard Smith, New York City hoop star, was considered the final link to another NCAA title and became just the fifth Tar Heel to start as a freshman.

North Carolina started the 1983–1984 season with 21 consecutive victories, including Smith's 500th career win. The Tar Heels dominated most opponents, routing Syracuse University at the Carrier Dome and capturing both the Stanford Invitational and the Holiday Classic in New York, but Jordan was disappointed at not making either All-Tournament team. He tried to fulfill his own high expectations and win player of the year awards. Smith told him, "So what if you don't? Don't worry about other people's expectations."[38] The conversation helped relieve pressure for Jordan. The only close contests were a three-point win at Virginia and a five-point victory at Duke University.

During the winning streak, Smith reminded Jordan about the importance of teamwork. Jordan stole the ball against Maryland, sped down the court, and converted a spectacular slam dunk to defeat the Terrapins. As the ecstatic Tar Heels charged into the dressing room, Smith reminded Jordan that Maryland had left Kenny Smith unguarded Jordan displayed his mental fiber when he saw Maryland's Ben Coleman slap Doherty in the face while running down the court. When Coleman was positioned near the basket late in the game, Jordan dunked the ball right over him and sternly warned him not to hit North Carolina players again.

Freshman point guard Kenny Smith broke his left wrist against Louisiana State University and missed nearly a month of play. A 65–64 loss at the University of Arkansas ended the Tar Heels' 18-game winning streak. North Carolina won its last seven games to finish the regular season 26–1. In the first two games of that winning streak, Jordan tallied 57 points, 14 rebounds, and 9 steals. The Tar Heels ended the regular season by defeating Duke, 96–83, in double overtime in the home finale for Jordan, Perkins, and Doherty. North Carolina fared 14–0 in the ACC, its first undefeated conference record in a decade, and ranked first in the final regular season poll.

Jordan experienced a disappointing postseason. Duke upset North Carolina, 77–75, in the ACC Tournament semifinals at Greensboro. Smith's broken wrist prevented him from dribbling with his left hand and limited his outside shooting, and Daugherty played with injured ligaments in his shooting hand. After defeating Temple University in the NCAA tournament second round, North Carolina was eliminated by Indiana University, 72–68, in the NCAA Eastern Regional semifinals at Atlanta, Georgia. Indiana, coached by Bob Knight, controlled the tempo and denied open shots to Jordan and Perkins. Guard Dan Dakich shadowed Jordan, challenging his jump shots and denying him dunking and rebounding opportunities. Jordan accumulated two quick fouls and sat out most of the first half. He recorded just 13 points and one rebound in 26 minutes before fouling out.

North Carolina finished 28–3 and again missed the NCAA Finals. The Tar Heels averaged 80 points, played excellent defense, and rebounded well, but they watched Georgetown defeat Houston for the NCAA title. Coach Smith dejectedly reflected, "it was the third time that I thought we had the best team in the country."[39] Smith equated that squad with his stellar 1977 and 1982 aggregates.

Jordan averaged 19.6 points, 5.3 rebounds, and approximately 4 assists and 3 steals in 31 games, shooting 55.1 percent as a junior. He fed the ball to Perkins and Daugherty, who shot 59 percent and 61 percent, respectively. Jordan won both the Naismith Award and Wooden Award, repeating as *The Sporting News* College Player of Year and an All-America. Jordan surged to the forefront as a result of his ability to excel at crunch time. "Jordan," *The Sporting News* opined, "is a showman under control. Sometimes Jordan spontaneously performs an electrifying high-wire act."[40] At other times, he waltzed in for a layup, pulled up for a soft jump shot, or improvised with a critical steal or blocked shot.

During Jordan's three years at North Carolina, the team compiled an 88–13 record and made three NCAA tournaments. He scored 1,788 points for a 17.7 point average and averaged 5.0 rebounds and 1.8 assists in 101 games. He also tallied 165 points in 10 NCAA Tournament games.

Coach Smith believed that Jordan had little left to prove at the collegiate level and advised him to enter the National Basketball Association draft. Jordan was ready to adjust to the faster, more challenging NBA. If he remained at North Carolina, Smith anticipated that defenses would use difficult zones against him and triple team him. He also feared that any major injury might hinder Jordan's professional career. "What's best for my players always comes first,"[41] Smith counseled.

Smith expected Jordan to be drafted high in the first round and called Chicago Bulls Rod Thorn, who held the third pick. Thorn told Smith the Bulls planned to select Jordan if he was still available, but the Houston Rockets and Portland Trail Blazers held the first and second choices. Smith discussed the draft situation with the Jordans at his office two weeks after the season in his office. Houston or Chicago would select Jordan second or third and offer him at least $2.5 million for five or more seasons. James advised Jordan to turn professional, but Deloris wanted him to remain at North Carolina and graduate with his class, which included his sister, Roslyn. Jordan was undecided about turning professional because he loved the North Carolina basketball program, coaches, and friendships and wanted to win one more national championship. "An awful lot of people," he realized, "didn't feel it was the right thing for me to do."[42] Fogler, Williams, Guthridge, and many alumni wanted Jordan to remain for his senior year.

The Jordans agreed that night that Michael should turn professional and informed Smith the next morning. Deloris realized that entering the NBA draft would delay Jordan's graduation by only one or two years. Smith assured the Jordans that they had decided wisely. (Indeed, Jordan did graduate with a bachelor's degree in geography in 1985 and he claims he would have become a meteorologist if he had not pursued professional basketball.) At the press conference, Jordan announced his decision to enter the NBA draft and delay his senior year at North Carolina. Smith also guided Jordan through the agent process. Jordan chose Donald Dell and David Falk of Pro Serv to represent him in contract negotiations. Smith asked Dell to call Thorn to discuss contract terms if the Chicago Bulls drafted Jordan.

Jordan remained passionate about North Carolina and coach Smith, who he considered "[m]y second father."[43] "I wasn't going to the NBA until he advised me to do it,"[44] he confided. Smith knew that Jordan would play guard in the NBA and made him play the point in pickup games that spring. He had taught Jordan great discipline to accompany his natural ability and how to behave both on and off the court. Jordan later wrote, "He was the perfect guy for me. He kept me humble, but he challenged me. He gave me confidence."[45]

Smith attributed Jordan's North Carolina success to his athleticism and diligent work ethic. "Michael," he reflected, "was extremely gifted athletically and is perhaps the most competitive person I know." His incredible determination to improve in all facets of the game provided an excellent role model for others. Smith concluded, "Nobody I know works harder at his craft than Michael Jordan."[46] Jordan had listened carefully to Smith's instruction, applied what he was learning, and worked hard daily.

## NOTES

1. Walter LaFeber, *Michael Jordan and the New Global Capitalism* (New York: W. W. Norton & Company, 1999), p. 29.

2. Curry Kirkpatrick, "The Unlikeliest Homebody," *Sports Illustrated* 75 (December 23, 1991), pp. 70–75.

3. Michael Jordan, ed. by Mark Vancil, *Rare Air: Jordan on Jordan* (San Francisco, CA: Collins Publishers, 1993), p. 87.

4. Ibid., P. 73.

5. Michael Jordan, ed. by Mark Vancil, *Driven from Within* (New York: Atria Books, 2005), pp. 17–18.

6. Ibid., p. 55.

7. LaFeber, *New Global Capitalism*, p. 30.

8. Sam Smith, *The Jordan Rules: The Inside Story of a Turbulent Season with Michael Jordan and the Chicago Bulls* (New York: Simon & Schuster, 1992), p. 65.

9. United States Olympic Committee, "Michael Jordan," http://www.usoc.org/26_604.htm

10. Ken Rappoport, *Tales from the Tar Heel Locker Room* (Champaign, IL: Sports Publishing L.L.C., 2002), p. 128.

11. Ibid., p. 125.

12. Dean Smith with John Kilgo and Sally Jenkins, *A Coach's Life* (New York: Random House, 1999), p. 182.

13. Art Chansky, *The Dean's List: A Celebration of Tar Heel Basketball and Dean Smith* (New York: Warner Books, 1997), p. 105.

14. Smith, *Coach's Life*, p. 184.

15. "Michael Jordan," *Current Biography Yearbook 1987* (New York: H. W. Wilson Company, 1987), p. 291.

16. David Halberstam, *Playing for Keeps: Michael Jordan and the World He Made* (New York: Random House, 1999), p. 66.

17. Halberstam, *Playing*, p. 71.

18. *The Sporting News*, March 26, 1984, p. 3.

19. Rappoport, *Tales*, pp. 120–122.

20. Chansky, *Dean's List*, p. 105.

21. Halberstam, *Playing*, pp. 88–89.

22. Smith, *Coach's Life*, p. 188.

23. Ibid., p. 195.

24. Chansky, *Dean's List*, p. 111.

25. Rappoport, *Tales*, p. 134.

26. Smith, *Coach's Life*, p. 197.

27. LaFeber, *New Global Capitalism*, p. 31.

28. Rappoport, *Tales*, p. 121.

29. Roland Lazenby, *Blood on the Horns: The Long Strange Ride of Michael Jordan's Chicago Bulls* (Lenexa, KS: Addax Publishing Group, 1998), p. 200.

30. Michael Jordan, ed. by Mark Vancil, *For the Love of the Game: My Story* (New York: Crown Publishers, 1998), p. 7.

31. Smith, *Coach's Life*, pp. 197–198.

32. Ibid., p. 203.

33. Ibid., p. 203.

34. Rappoport, *Tales*, p. 121.

35. Mitchell Krugel, *One Last Shot: The Story of Michael Jordan's Comeback* (New York: St. Martin's Press, 2003), p. 23.

36. *The Sporting News*, March 26, 1984.

37. *New York Times*, December 26, 1983, p. C1.

38. Smith, *Coach's Life*, p. 206.

39. Chansky, *Dean's List*, p. 119.

40. *The Sporting News*, March 26, 1984, p. 3.

41. Chansky, *Dean's List*, p. 119.
42. Ibid., p. 119.
43. Jordan, *Driven from Within*, p. 9.
44. Chansky, *Dean'.s List*, p. 119.
45. Jordan, *Driven from Within*, p. 29.
46. Smith, *Coach's Life*, p. 216.

# Chapter 2

# THE BUILDING YEARS, 1984–1988

## WELCOME TO THE NBA (1984–1985)

The Chicago Bulls, who owned the second worst NBA record in 1983–1984, desperately needed a superstar to move them out of the doldrums. The Bulls had not made the NBA playoffs since 1980–1981 and had won more games than it lost only twice in nine seasons. They selected third after the Houston Rockets and Portland Trail Blazers in the NBA draft on June 20 at the Conrad Hilton Hotel in New York City. Houston chose Hakeem Olajuwon, a 7-foot Nigerian center and University of Houston star, and Portland picked Sam Bowie, a 7-foot 1-inch University of Kentucky center. Olajuwon developed into an NBA star, winning two NBA titles.

Chicago Bulls general manager Rod Thorn drafted Jordan. He preferred a center, but Olajuwon was not available. "Jordan isn't going to turn this franchise around," Thorn predicted. "I wouldn't ask him to." Chicago fans, who had assembled two floors below, enthusiastically shouted "Jordan, Jordan" loud enough for Thorn to hear. Bulls assistant coach Mike Thibault observed, "He's one of those players who comes along once a decade,"[1] and *Chicago Tribune* columnist Bernie Lincicome ventured that Jordan "maybe the greatest natural basketball talent, inch for inch, in this young decade."[2]

Jordan performed that August on the star-studded U.S. basketball team, which included Patrick Ewing of Georgetown University and Steve Alford of Indiana University, at the 1984 Los Angeles Olympic Games. The American squad, coached by Bob Knight of Indiana, moved faster, leaped higher, and drove stronger, routing opponents by 32 points per game and overwhelming Spain, 96–65, for the gold medal. "We can put any five we have out there and get the job done,"[3] Jordan insisted.

Jordan, the flashiest Olympian, penetrated zone defenses for at least one dunk per game. He dunked three shots against Uruguay and sank a 28-foot jump shot at the first half buzzer against Spain. He finished that preliminary game with 24 points, the best for any American Olympian. After the gold medal game, Fernando Martin of Spain described Jordan, "Jump, jump, jump. Very quick. Very fast. Very very good."[4]

Knight remarked that Jordan possessed immense talent, exhibited natural leadership, played tenacious defense, and was very competitive and coachable. An ultimate perfectionist, however, Knight considered Jordan a subpar shooting guard and occasionally admonished him during games. When Jordan carelessly dribbled the ball out of bounds against West Germany, Knight bellowed, "Michael, get in the game!"[5] During the gold medal game against Spain, Knight yelled, "when are you going to start setting some screens—all you do is rebound and score!" Jordan smiled, "Coach, didn't I read some place where you said I was the quickest player you ever coached?" Knight responded affirmatively. "Coach, I set those screens faster than you could see them,"[6] Jordan answered. He became one of the most reliable perimeter players and contributed mightily to the gold medal. He likened Knight to Dean Smith except that the former used four-letter words while the latter used the four-corner offense. George Raveling, assistant Olympic coach, lauded Jordan as "probably the best athlete playing college basketball."[7] After receiving his gold medal, Jordan touchingly placed it around Deloris's neck.

The Olympics enhanced Jordan's leverage in contract negotiations with the Bulls. Agents Donald Dell and David Falk of the ProServ Agency represented him. He signed a seven-year, $6.3 million contract, larger than any NBA rookie except for Olajuwon and Ralph Sampson. At a Chicago press conference, he revealed, "I'm anxious to meet the team and start fitting in with them."[8]

Dell also lined up prospective advertisers, giving assurance that Jordan had "a charisma that transcends his sport" and that he belonged "in a category with Arnold Palmer or Arthur Ashe."[9] Michael, articulate, well mannered, and hardworking, was a mass-market icon who appealed to all demographic groups, transcending age and race barriers. Falk obtained a commercial endorsement with struggling Nike athletic shoes. He believed that the popular Jordan could increase Nike shoe sales and profit handsomely from those sales. Jordan signed a seven-year contract with Nike, which designed the signature Air Jordan shoe. Nike guaranteed him $18 million and a royalty on every Air Jordan shoe sold. The Air Jordans sold very well in the United States, Europe, and Asia. The hype and demand for the Air Jordans even sparked "shoe-jackings," where young boys were robbed of their sneakers at gunpoint. The innovation of designer Tinker Hatfield spurred the basketball shoe industry to new heights. The Air 180 Shoe, introduced in 1991, likewise featured Jordan and was advertised worldwide. Jordan admitted, "I never knew it could be nation-based—or, if you want, world-based."[10] He also endorsed McDonald's fast-food chain, Wilson Sporting Goods basketballs, Coca-Cola, Chevrolet automobiles, Johnson Products, Excelsior International, and Guy LaRoche watches.

Jordan, who possessed an effervescent smile, owned a townhouse in Northbrook, a Chicago suburb. Before being married, he handled his personal shopping and housecleaning. Jordan spent free time watching videotapes of games, following stock car racing, bowling, playing pool, and listening to music. He often sought the counsel of coach Smith on basketball and other matters and enjoyed little social life, considering "the game (his) wife."[11] He traveled to home games in his silver Corvette, often chatting with maintenance and food-concession workers and signing autographs.

Jordan began practicing with the Bulls in September 1984, dominating the camp with his work ethic. He played primarily for the love of the game rather than financial remuneration, always arriving first at practice and leaving last. Jordan never relaxed in practice because he was the highest paid Bull and wanted teammates to understand he was worth it. He felt pressure "to prove I deserved to play on that level."[12] He worked diligently to improve his jump shot and was virtually unstoppable in one-on-one drills. After watching Jordan make a resounding dunk, coach Kevin Loughery told general manager Thorn, "I think we've hit the jackpot."[13]

Jordan exhibited exceptional athletic ability and boundless energy, using superior speed, jumping ability, strength, and huge hands to create his shot. Loughery dismissed practice early once because Jordan was exhausting his teammates. He also devised a strategy in practice to hone Jordan's skills as a clutch player. At practice, Loughery pitted the five best players against the next five best in a simulated game. Jordan's team usually built an 8–1 or 9–2 lead, with 11 baskets needed to win. Loughery then switched Jordan to the losing team. Jordan, who usually got that team back in the scrimmage game, built his confidence the most during those workouts.

Jordan initially found the transition to the NBA somewhat difficult. The North Carolina basketball program had been first rate, well designed, and brilliantly organized with outstanding coaches. The Tar Heels recruited many excellent, committed players who always worked hard in practices and games in premier facilities and with clearly defined goals. The Bulls program paled by comparison. Loughery was a good coach, but his assistants did not match North Carolina's. The Bulls practiced at subpar Angel Guardian, a converted orphanage, and played regular games in aged Chicago Stadium before small crowds. They had limited scouting and videotaping resources. Jordan called his teammates "The Looney Tunes," very talented, but lacking goals, the passion to win, and mental toughness. The roster was riddled with substance abusers and partygoers. Quintin Dailey and Orlando Woolridge later entered drug rehabilitation; and Steve Johnson, Jawann Oldham, Sidney Green, and Ennis Whatley faded into mediocrity. Jordan seldom socialized with teammates except for Rod Higgins, refusing to drink alcohol or take drugs and deploring their late night lifestyle.

Jordan performed well in exhibition games, leading the Bulls in scoring with a 22.7-point average and helping Chicago finish 5–2. Thorn declared "there are certain guys who seem to bring out the best in their teammates. I think Michael Jordan has the potential to be like that. He is a terrific offensive player—a great, great player."[14] Jordan considered Loughery, who had coached Julius Erving in the American Basketball Association, an ideal first coach. "He understood my skills and provided me with the freedom to develop," Jordan observed. Jordan initially liked Erving more than either Magic Johnson or Larry Bird. He wanted to convince his teammates, coaches, and owners that he possessed the right skills and motivation and hoped to dominate and excel. "I tried to win every drill, every scrimmage."[15]

The Bulls built a promotional campaign around Jordan, billing him as Chicago's newest athletic star. Newspapers advertised "Here Comes Mr. Jordan" in "his first starring role since the Olympics." Movie critic Gene Siskel rated him four stars. Jordan, however, wanted to ensure that the "Whole New Breed" Bulls was something he contributed to rather than inspired. He vowed, "to help make this basketball team into a winner. And I want to have fun."[16] His personality inspired teammates to perform better and gave Bulls fans extra adrenaline.

At the outset, Jordan preferred to lead through example rather than words. He was reluctant to speak to veteran teammates, most of whom were paid lower salaries. "My leadership came from action, all action," he noted. He never became good friends with Dailey or Woolridge because "I was stealing some of their thunder."[17]

Jordan ignited a swift transformation of the floundering Bulls. He excited spectators with his youthful enthusiasm and charm and provided endless enjoyment and entertainment, dunking the ball and defying gravity with amazing shots. WGN, the Chicago superstation that carried 15 Bulls home games, attracted 30,000 more households the year Jordan joined the team. The Bulls drew more than 1 million fans. Their average Chicago Stadium attendance rose 87 percent, from 6,365 to 11,887, as ticket sales climbed from $2 million to $3 million. The Bulls drew crowds best on the road, selling out in eight of Jordan's first 13 road appearances. More than 19,000 witnessed his Madison Square Garden debut in New York. He also drew sellout crowds at Los Angeles, Portland, Golden Gate, Milwaukee, Detroit, and Indianapolis.

Jordan enjoyed a spectacular rookie season, operating the Bulls offense, penetrating the basket, scoring at least 40 points seven times, and nabbing NBA Rookie of the Month honors twice. Acrobatic on the fast break and breathtaking in the air, he portrayed both mental toughness and willpower. Chicago won during his debut, 109–93, over the Washington Bullets at Chicago Stadium on October 26, as he netted 16 points. "The first NBA game I ever saw was one I played in,"[18] he recollected. Jeff Ruland knocked him down after a drive. Jordan sank two free throws and drove right at him in the next series. The next night at Milwaukee, he astonished Bucks Coach Don Nelson by taking off from near the foul line on a long dunk attempt. Nelson was amazed to see him convert the basket like only Julius Erving had done.

In his next NBA game on October 29, Jordan set a Bulls record by exploding for 22 fourth-quarter points in a 116–110 home victory over Milwaukee. Bob Love had scored 21 points in a quarter in 1972. The Bulls overcame a nine-point deficit in the fourth quarter when Loughery decided to revolve the offense around Jordan. Sidney Moncrief, two-time NBA Defensive Player of the Year, could not stop Jordan. Nelson assigned more players to guard Jordan, but he still tallied a game-high 37 points. "He was sensational," exclaimed Nelson. "Down the stretch, we couldn't do anything with him."[19] The game marked a significant milestone for Jordan and the Bulls. "That is when . . . I felt like I earned my stripes," he reflected, "and the city of Chicago started to believe we could change the fortunes of the Bulls."[20] On November 13, Jordan broke the Bulls' single-game scoring record with 45 points to edge the visiting San Antonio Spurs, 120–117. "Nobody knew Michael would play this well as quickly as he has," Thorn acknowledged. "He's been a tremendous player from day one."[21]

Chicago slumped in late November, but Jordan helped the Bulls return to the win column in December. On December 7, his 20-foot desperation jump shot at the buzzer nosed the New York Knicks, 95–93, at home.

Jordan's 32 points and 12 rebounds on December 22 handed the visiting Boston Celtics their worst defeat, 108–85, in two years. Celtic legend Larry Bird had never seen one player transform a team like Jordan had. "Even at this stage of his career," Bird raved, "he's doing more than I ever did."[22] Five nights later at home, Jordan equaled his club single-game scoring record with 45 points, including a season-best 20 baskets and 6 slam dunks, and added 11 assists, 7 rebounds, and 3 steals in a 112–108 triumph over the Cleveland Cavaliers. During a cradle jam, he shook the ball twice before dunking it. Jordan improvised the cradle jam, double pumping the ball underhanded and spreading his legs to maintain altitude while dunking the ball.

Jordan led the Bulls to eight victories in 15 January games. On January 5, he tallied 42 points in a loss to New York at Madison Square Garden. At Chicago Stadium nine nights later, Jordan performed the first triple-double in Bulls history with 35 points, 15 assists, and 14 rebounds in a 122–113 triumph over the Denver Nuggets. Despite a sprained ankle, he scored 45 points with 10 rebounds and 8 assists on January 26 in a 117–104 home victory over the Atlanta Hawks. Jordan's yeoman-like performance helped earn him his first NBA Player of the Week Award.

Jerry Reinsdorf, a wealthy Chicago real-estate developer, bought the Bulls for only $16 million. The franchise had lost money throughout its two decades of existence. An executive committee, including Lester Crown, Phillip Klutznick, Jonathan Kovler, and William Wirtz, had operated the team.

The Bulls limped through February with just two wins. Jordan tallied 41 points in a February home loss to Boston and was voted the first rookie to start in the All-Star Game since Isiah Thomas in 1982, outpolling legends Bird and Julius Erving. He trailed only Dominique Wilkins in the slam-dunk contest at the Indianapolis Hoosier Dome. Some NBA All-Stars resented his overnight commercial success with the Air Jordans. When Jordan wore clanking gold chains and a sweat suit boldly bearing the Nike logo in the slam-dunk competition, several veterans considered his action disrespectful. "I thought I was doing Nike a favor," Jordan explained. "They had invested so much in me."[23] In the February 10 classic, Jordan was nervous and scored just seven points because Eastern Conference teammates gave him little opportunity to handle the ball. Two nights later, he broke his Bulls single-game scoring record again with a season high 49 points, including 19 baskets, in a 139–126 overtime home victory against the Detroit Pistons. Teammates were amazed that Jordan strengthened during the grueling NBA 82-game season. Sidney Green conceded, "Michael

Jordan is the truth, the whole truth, and nothing but the truth, so help us God."[24]

Jordan started March by thrilling home fans with his second triple-double, recording 21 points, 10 rebounds, and 10 assists in a 109–104 victory over New York. He recorded 92 points, 27 rebounds, and 25 assists in one three-game stretch, scoring at least 30 points in four consecutive contests. Jordan tallied 35 points in a loss at Cleveland on March 28, giving him a team record 2,043 points for the season. Six nights later, the Bulls clinched their first playoff berth in seven years.

Chicago finished third in the Central Division behind Milwaukee, with a 38–44 mark, recording 11 more victories than in 1983–1984. Jordan became just the sixth rookie to lead the NBA in points with 2,313. He ranked third in scoring with a 28.2 point average and fourth in steals with 2.39 per game, easily capturing NBA Rookie of the Year honors and winning the Seagram Award for best NBA player. His point average marked the highest for a rookie since Kareem Abdul-Jabbar in 1969–1970 and sixth best all-time. He broke six Chicago records and led the Bulls in scoring, free throw percentage (.845), rebounds (534 or 6.5 per game), assists (837 or 5.9 per game), steals (196 or 2.4 per game), and minutes played (3,144). Jordan became only the third NBA player to lead his team in scoring, rebounding, and assists. Jerry West, former Los Angeles Lakers star, boasted, "He's the only player I've seen who reminds me of me."[25]

Jordan captivated the NBA his rookie season. According to Jim Naughton, "With his blinding speed and his ability to soar upwards and then momentarily hang in midair, thwarting more earthbound defenders, Jordan mesmerized crowds with his Njinsky-esque physical artistry and, especially, his balletic slam-dunks."[26] Experts marveled at his scoring, rebounding, and defense. He often stopped his opponents' best guard or forward, but could not elevate his teammates to a championship level and often alienated them with his intensity, showboating, and commercial successes.

Milwaukee eliminated Chicago, three games to one, in the opening round of the Eastern Conference playoffs. Jordan tallied 35 points, including a jump shot with 17 seconds left, to give the Bulls their lone victory, 109–107, on April 24 at Chicago Stadium.

Chicago's firing of coach Kevin Loughery disappointed Jordan. Reinsdorf wanted the Bulls to play team-oriented basketball, but Loughery centered the offense on Jordan and shaped him into the game's most dominant player. Jordan related exceptionally well to Loughery. "He was a player's coach," Jordan recollected. "He liked my game and wanted me to be the leader."[27] Loughery, who preferred one-on-one style basketball, enabled Jordan to demonstrate his skills and develop self-confidence. Jordan quickly realized that confidence was the most important quality to have in the NBA. Loughery's decision to let him test his individual skills convinced him that he could become a great player. Stan Albeck replaced Loughery.

Reinsdorf appointed Jerry Krause, former sportswriter and Chicago White Sox scout, to replace general manager Thorn. Krause, nicknamed "Crumbs" by Jordan because of his disheveled appearance, wanted the Bulls to retain only Michael, Dave Corzine, and Higgins and hired veteran Tex Winter as assistant coach. He acquired Charles Oakley, an exceptional rebounder that the Bulls sorely needed, from Cleveland in the June draft. Krause also obtained guard John Paxson, an ideal supplement to Jordan, from San Antonio.

## SOPHOMORE INJURY JINX (1985–1986)

During Jordan's second season, Chicago won all eight exhibition games, as coach Albeck let him run the offense. Jordan scored at least 30 points in three contests, but realized he should pass the ball more. "I may have to score less and pass more this season,"[28] he admitted.

Jordan led the Bulls to three consecutive wins to start the 1985–1986 season, averaging 31 points, 6.5 rebounds, and 4.5 assists. He contributed 29 points, including three crucial baskets down the stretch, in the opening home game 116–115 overtime victory against Cleveland on October 25. After pacing Chicago to a 121–118 victory the next night over Detroit, he broke a bone in his left foot on October 29 in a 111–105 triumph over the Golden State Warriors. With 45 seconds left in the second quarter, Jordan landed awkwardly after leaping high for a rebound and severely jammed his left ankle. "It felt like something popped out of place when I came down flat on my foot,"[29] he revealed. Although the initial x-ray films were negative, Jordan experienced difficulty stopping and starting. He hobbled on crutches and nursed his left foot, which was wrapped in a protective brace.

A computed tomography (CT) scan on November 5 showed that Jordan had fractured the navicular tarsal bone in his left foot. In a state of disbelief, Jordan revealed, "I went home and cried. It was like a part of my life had been taken away, and there was nothing I could do."[30] Chicago anticipated that Jordan would be sidelined for two months, but he missed most of the NBA season. The slow recovery frustrated Jordan, who desperately wanted to return to action by the All-Star break, and forced him to learn more self-discipline and patience. He watched the Bulls from his living room sofa and threw soda cans at the television when teammates lacked the resilience to fight.

As his foot healed and the pain lessened, Jordan became convinced that he was ready to play. He visited Dr. John Hefferon, Bulls orthopedist, hoping his cast would be removed soon. Hefferon, leery of making that decision, consulted other orthopedists in Eugene, Oregon and Cleveland, Ohio. The next CT scan four weeks later indicated that Jordan could put stress on his left foot. The doctor gave him a removable split instead of another cast.

Jordan asked the Bulls for permission in mid-January to return to the University of North Carolina, Chapel Hill, to take a geography class, improve his conditioning, and shoot baskets several hours daily. He owned a condominium there and conversed with his many friends, including the North Carolina coaching staff. Unbeknownst to Bulls officials, Jordan began testing his left foot in pickup games. The experience convinced him how much he really loved basketball. In mid-March, he informed Chicago that his injury had healed and that he could resume playing.

Reinsdorf, Krause, and the Bulls' doctors wanted Jordan to forgo the remainder of the season because he already had missed more than 50 games. "I was scared to death," Krause recalled. "I didn't want to go down in history as the guy who put Michael Jordan back in too soon."[31] Jordan, Reinsdorf, Krause, and the Bulls' doctors conversed at least twice. Dr. Stan James told them that Jordan's risk of breaking the bone again stood at 10 percent. Jordan, an extremely passionate competitor who was separated from his main source of enjoyment, desperately wanted to return. He knew his body better than Bulls executives did and estimated that the odds were 85 to 90 percent that he would not reinjure his foot.

The disagreement soured relations between Jordan and Krause. Krause initially rebuffed Jordan's pleas to play. Jordan claimed that Krause did not want him to return that season so that the Bulls would miss the playoffs and qualify for the NBA lottery, where the seven teams with the worst records received an opportunity to draft the best collegians available that year. "You're trying to lose games," he confronted Krause, "so you can get a better draft pick."[32] Krause viewed basketball as a business and wanted to control the Bulls organization, but Jordan wanted to determine his fate. He wanted to participate in the game he had been involved with for a long time, but management insisted on safeguarding its multimillion dollar investment. "That's when I really felt used,"[33] he revealed.

Jordan insisted that Chicago could still make the playoffs if he returned. The Bulls ranked ninth in the Eastern Conference with a 22–45 record, one spot below making the playoffs. Reinsdorf permitted Jordan to practice two hours daily, but Krause and Albeck limited him to just seven minutes a half.

Tim Hallam sat at the scorer's table with a stopwatch to make sure Jordan did not exceed his limit. After missing 64 games, Jordan returned on March 15 to the Bulls. With 5:59 left in the second quarter against Milwaukee, he entered the game to a standing ovation in Chicago Stadium and immediately dunked the ball over 7-foot 3-inch center Randy Breuer. He tallied 12 points in just 12 minutes in the overtime loss. Chicago dropped its first five games after Jordan returned. Jordan scored 13 points in seven minutes in the fourth quarter on March 17 in a setback at Atlanta, setting a Bulls record for most steals in a quarter, with five. He complained that his limited playing time disrupted team chemistry. When Albeck left him in one game for an extra three minutes, Krause warned him he would be fired if that occurred again.

Reinsdorf upgraded Jordan's playing time to 10 minutes a half and then increased it two minutes per game. Jordan's 19 points in 19 minutes sparked a 111–98 home win over New York on March 25, and his 24 points in 23 minutes four nights later lifted the visiting Bulls to a 106–96 triumph over the Knicks. Chicago won four of its final six games, as Jordan averaged 29.6 points, and overtook Cleveland for the last playoff spot. Albeck upset Jordan by removing him with just 30 seconds left on April 3 when the Bulls trailed the Indiana Pacers by just one point because he had reached his 28-minute limit. Jordan averaged more than 1 point a minute in a reserve role. He scored 10 points in the first quarter in his first start, helping Chicago vanquish visiting Milwaukee, 107–101. Reinsdorf waived Jordan's playing time restriction four days later, when the host Bulls clinched the final playoff spot at home by defeating Washington, 105–103.

Chicago finished fourth in the Central Division at 30–52, 27 games behind Milwaukee, as Jordan averaged a career-low 22.8 points in 18 games. The Bulls entered the first round of the Eastern Conference playoffs as heavy underdogs against Boston. The Celtics boasted the NBA's best record at 67–15 with Bird, Kevin McHale, Robert Parish, Dennis Johnson, and Danny Ainge.

Undaunted by the formidable challenge, Jordan captivated the nation with some of the greatest playoff performances in NBA history. Boston bested Chicago, 123–104, in Game 1 on April 17, but Jordan dazzled the Boston Garden crowd with 49 points. He single handedly kept the Bulls ahead nearly the entire first half.

Jordan tallied 30 first-half points in the Game 2 on April 20 before a national television audience. The prototype of the new super player, he dribbled, drove, jumped, shot, and passed without any perceptive weakness. Jordan froze Johnson and blew by Bird as he banked a shot from the right side, soared by McHale for an over-the-shoulder, no-look reverse slam dunk, and jumped over Ainge for a jam. The Boston Garden crowd shifted from disbelief to apprehension to admiration, as Jordan added 22 second-half points and converted two free throws to send the game into overtime. At the end of the first overtime, he missed a jump shot that would have won the game. The Celtics prevailed, 135–131, in double overtime. An exhausted Jordan played 53 minutes, the final 39 minutes without a rest. He broke the NBA single-game playoff scoring record with 63 points, surpassing Elgin Baylor's 62 points on April 14, 1962. Jordan converted 22 of 41 shots from the field and 19 of 21 free throws. Of his 22 baskets, 13 were jump shots, 7 came on drives, 1 was a dunk, and 1 resulted from goaltending.

Jordan performed at an unprecedented playoff level against the best NBA team. He drew 10 fouls from Bill Walton, Johnson, Ainge, Parish, and McHale, among the best NBA defensive players. "No one can guard him," Johnson claimed. Bird, who paced Boston with 36 points, was amazed that any player could put on such a dazzling performance against the Boston Celtics and proclaimed, "I think he's God disguised as Michael Jordan."[34] Ainge concurred, "he was so good you were tempted to stop playing and just watch. It was not just what he did, but the way he did it."[35] Ray Sons of the *Chicago Tribune* penned, "He painted his own masterpiece on the ceiling of basketball's Sistine Chapel, and he didn't need a scaffold to lift him there."[36] Jordan even admitted, "I don't think I had ever played a game as good as that one."[37] The double-overtime marathon loss, however, erased any sense of personal accomplishment for Jordan. "I'd give all the points back if we could have won the game. I wanted to win so badly."[38]

Boston doubled-teamed Jordan in the Game 3 finale two nights later at Chicago Stadium. Because he experienced much more difficulty getting the ball, Chicago dropped the game, 122–104, and lost the series, 3–0. Although Jordan averaged 43.7 points, the Celtics exhibited their superior talent, mental toughness, sense of purpose, and depth.

Krause fired Albeck as head coach, hiring youthful, intense, intelligent Doug Collins. Collins wanted Jordan to take the summer easy to prevent reinjuring the foot. Jordan reminded Collins, "too many people who didn't know anything about me or my body were telling me what to do. . . . I never want to go through that again."[39] He refrained from basketball workouts all summer for the first time in several years, but played for the North Carolina alumni against the University of Nevada Las Vegas alumni. Collins let Jordan run the Bulls' offense.

## JORDAN'S FIRST SCORING TITLE (1986–1987)

Jordan wanted the Bulls to draft guard Johnny Dawkins of Duke University. To Jordan's dismay, however, Krause selected 7-foot forward

Brad Sellers of Ohio State University and Stacey King of the University of Oklahoma. He traded forward Orlando Woolridge to the New Jersey Nets for draft rights to King and acquired point guard Steve Colter from the Portland Trail Blazers. Jordan argued that Sellers lacked the physical strength to sustain NBA punishment and criticized Colter, too.

Jordan thought about basketball all summer and entered the 1986–1987 season more mentally prepared to play than ever before. Doctors reported that his foot had healed completely and that he possessed very little body fat. He tallied 36 points before a sellout crowd of 22,500 at the debut of the Dean Dome in Chapel Hill and averaged 33 points in eight exhibition contests.

Jordan played intensely and relentlessly during team practices. His presence and daily work ethic made his teammates work harder. During one scrimmage, he accused Collins of intentionally misstating the score so that his team would lose. Jordan stormed out of practice and delayed reporting for the Bulls' flight the next day until a few seconds before take-off. When Collins removed him from scrimmages, Jordan often checked back into the game a minute later to work on his defense or post moves. "Every day he had this need to show you he was the best,"[40] Collins recalled. He practiced at an intensity level not attainable by teammates.

Chicago opened the 1986–1987 season on November 1 with a 108–103 victory at New York. Jordan dominated the first half with 16 points and several steals and assists. At halftime, Collins told him, "You don't have to do it all." Jordan scored 20 of the Bulls' 31 fourth-quarter points, including the final 11 points. With two minutes left, he assured Collins, "I'm not going to let you lose your first game."[41] Jordan tallied 50 points in a regular season game for the first time, setting a Madison Square Garden record for most points by an opponent.

Chicago won five of its first six games, as Jordan garnered NBA Player of the Month honors. He averaged 39.4 points, 5.6 rebounds, and 2.8 steals during the first week. He netted the final eight points, including a game-ending slam dunk after being knocked to the floor, in a 104–99 triumph over host Cleveland on November 2, and scored 16 of his 34 points in the fourth quarter to give the Bulls a 111–104 home win over San Antonio two nights later. His 39-point performance in a 101–86 victory over the visiting Phoenix Suns featured a decisive cradle jam. "Jordan is so great," Phoenix coach John MacLeod proclaimed, "it takes five guys just to hold him to 20 points." Chicago edged Atlanta, 112–110, four nights later at home, where Jordan challenged three defenders for the winning layup. "It was your routine, twisting, 360-degree, double-pump, reverse lay-up,"[42] coach Collins explained.

He outscored Bird, 48–37, in a decisive loss to Boston on November 14 at Chicago Stadium.

A week later, Jordan led a spectacular Bulls home comeback with 40 points in a 101–99 triumph over New York. He set an NBA record by scoring Chicago's final 18 points in the last 6 minutes and 29 seconds and stole the ball three times in the last three minutes. He made a running bank shot with 13 seconds left against three defenders and sank a 22-foot jump shot to clinch the win. Collins conceded, "its kind of nice to have a nuclear weapon on your team."[43]

Jordan soared to even greater heights, tallying at least 40 points in nine consecutive contests. Wilt Chamberlain remains the only NBA player with longer consecutive game streaks, notching 14 in 1961 and 10 in 1962. Jordan began his string with 41 points on November 28 in a setback to the Los Angeles Lakers, matching The Forum single-game scoring record set by Jerry West in 1969. He netted 40 points, including two baskets and free throws in the last 46 seconds, to defeat the host Seattle SuperSonics, 115–109, in overtime on December 2 and exceeded 40 points in consecutive road losses to the Utah Jazz, Phoenix, and San Antonio. The streak continued on December 9 with 40 points in a 106–100 home win over Denver, 41 points in a loss the next night at Atlanta, and 41 points in a 106–93 victory at Milwaukee on December 12.

Chicago ironically finished just 3–6 during Jordan's scoring barrage. He averaged 41.1 points during that span, but was reluctant to pass the ball to teammates except for Oakley. His nine-game streak abruptly ended the next night in a home loss to Milwaukee when he tumbled after driving to the basket with five seconds left in the first half. After lying motionless for nearly six minutes, Jordan appeared sparingly in the second half. Despite the injury, he connected for at least 40 points in wins over New Jersey, Indiana, and Cleveland.

The Bulls made their first regular-season national television appearance with Jordan on Christmas against New York at Madison Square Garden. CBS billed the contest as "a Michael Jordan showcase." Jordan scored 30 points, but was triple-teamed and shot poorly in the 86–85 loss. Despite suffering influenza and a 101-degree fever two nights later, he still tallied 44 points in a 105–93 home victory over Indiana. "When I'm sick, I always play better," Jordan claimed. "My concentration level is much higher."[44]

Although Jordan dominated the NBA in scoring, Chicago just split its first 42 games through January. Collins asked him to move from big guard to small forward to enable guards Paxson and Sedale Threatt to play simultaneously. Jordan tallied 47 points, including 17 last-quarter points, in a 124–118 home win on January 3 over Detroit. Five nights later, he thrilled Chicago Stadium spectators with 53 points, lifting the Bulls to a 121–117 triumph over Portland. His next test came on January 17 at home against the Philadelphia 76ers. Michael responded with 47 points, including 16 in the fourth quarter, 10 rebounds, and 6 assists in the 109–85 rout. He followed with 20 third-quarter points in a 117–96 trouncing of Cleveland six nights later and 49 points in a setback at Philadelphia on January 30. Coach Matt Guokas, of the 76ers, who wondered if Jordan could tally all the Bulls points in a game, added, "I'd certainly like to see him try. He is certainly capable of doing it."[45]

Jordan received more than 1.4 million votes for the All-Star game, shattering Magic Johnson's all-time record. Paxson explained, "He's such an easy person to like. Wherever he goes, people want to touch him, say 'hi' to him. He is one of God's special children."[46] In the NBA Slam-Dunk semifinals on February 7 at the Seattle Skydome, Jordan replicated the dunk that Erving had made at the inaugural 1976 competition. As the capacity crowd roared, he moved down the court, accelerated to full speed, gained momentum as he passed midcourt, and catapulted off the free-throw line to complete a thunderous double-pump slam. "I added a little with the pump," he explained, "but the roots started with Dr. J."[47]

Jordan bested Jerome Kersey of Portland in the slam-dunk finals, 146–140, to claim the $12,500 prize. He flaunted hang time with a slashing slam, ducking the rim as he floated by. Next came a swooping cradle jam in which he double-pumped the ball underhanded and spread his legs to maintain his altitude. Then, Jordan assaulted the hoop from the left side with a sideswiping rock-a-baby. He dribbled the full length of the court, took off at the foul line, leveled off in midair, and rose again for the dunk. Jordan credited his move to instinct and intuition. "I never know until I get there what's going to happen,"[48] he said. His dominance did not extend to next day's All-Star Game, as he tallied a disappointing 11 points for the Eastern Conference as a point guard in the 154–149 loss to the Western Conference.

Jordan often dazzled Chicago Stadium crowds in February. He registered 45 points, including 16 final-period points, in a 106–98 victory over Seattle on February 13. Nine days later, his 43 points and season-high eight steals lifted Chicago past Cleveland, 102–98. Jordan struck for 43 points, 6 assists, and 5 blocked shots in a 113–103 win over Atlanta. He dominated the first three quarters with 39 points, recording 15 points in one five-minute span. On February 26, Jordan broke the Bulls' regular-season scoring record with 58 points to overwhelm New Jersey, 128–113. Chet Walker held the previous single-game mark with 56 points in 1972.

Jordan made 16 of 25 field goals and 26 of 27 fouls shots, third best in NBA history. He notched 17 points in both the first and second quarters, including Chicago's last 11 points in the first stanza and 15 of their last 17 points in the second. With just 2 minutes and 44 seconds left, he made a soaring reverse layup and free throw to break Walker's record.

In March, Jordan snagged NBA Player of the Month honors for a second time with several memorable road masterpieces. He soared to new heights on March 4 with an NBA season-high 61 points, including 22 baskets and 17 free throws, to edge Detroit, 125–120, in overtime at the Pontiac Silverdome. Jordan notched 26 fourth-quarter points, a one-period record against Detroit, making the Bulls' first 13 points and 24 of their first 26 points. His hanging fall-away jump shot in the waning seconds of regulation sent the contest into overtime. In a setback at Philadelphia a week later, he tied The Spectrum single-game scoring record with 49 points. His 40 points and acrobatic moves keyed a 114–97 romp over the Los Angeles Clippers on March 19 at the Forum. "All the people came out to see me play, and to see if all the ink about Michael Jordan was true,"[49] he observed. He also netted 44 points in a heartbreaking defeat at Houston on March 16, 40 points in a 112–97 win at the Sacramento Kings on March 21, and 46 points in a loss at Portland the next night.

Jordan's masterpieces continued at Chicago Stadium. He tallied 56 points, including 22 of 32 field goals, and eight steals to nose Philadelphia, 93–91, on March 24. His 36 points en route to a 101–75 romp over Washington one week later clinched a third consecutive playoff appearance. Jordan became the only NBA player except for Chamberlain to record three consecutive 50-point games, garnering 53 points in a 116–95 rout over Indiana on April 12. He converted 14 of his first 16 first-half shots and on seven consecutive possessions for 13 fourth-quarter points. His 50-point performance the next night sparked a seven-point triumph over Milwaukee.

Jordan matched his NBA season-high 61 points, including 22 baskets and 17 free throws, in falling to Atlanta on April 16. He recorded his 3,001st point of the 1986–1987 season on a layup, joining Chamberlain as the only other NBA hoopster to reach that plateau. Jordan tallied 23 straight points, including the last 17 of the first half, a feat Chamberlain never accomplished. "But these records and marks meant nothing," he reflected. "I'd rather have had the win because it would have clinched the seventh playoff spot in the Eastern conference."[50] Atlanta coach Mike Fratello exhausted ways of defending Jordan.

Despite Jordan's stellar performance, Chicago finished a lackluster 40–42. The Bulls placed a disappointing fifth in the Central Division, 17 games behind Atlanta. Jordan led the NBA in scoring for the first time with 3,041 points, third highest in NBA history, and a career-best 37.1 points average, fifth highest in NBA history. The NBA had not witnessed such prolific scoring since Chamberlain averaged 50.4 points and Elgin Baylor averaged 38.3 points in 1962. Jordan reached at least 60 points twice, 50 points in eight games, 40 points 28 more times, and 30 points 26 other times. The Bulls finished 22–15 when Jordan registered at least 40 points. He netted 40 points against every NBA team, producing the top three and seven of the top 10 NBA scoring performances, and outscored his next three teammates combined. Oakley averaged 13.1 rebounds, second best in the NBA.

Jordan made the All-NBA team for the first time, but Magic Johnson, who led the Los Angeles Lakers to the NBA title, won the NBA Most Valuable Player Award. He scored 35.4 percent of Chicago's points and paced the Bulls in steals and blocked shots, becoming the first NBA guard to record more than 200 steals and 100 blocked shots in the same season and blocking more shots than 13 NBA starting centers. Besides ranking second on Chicago in assists and third in rebounds, he led the NBA in minutes played, with 3,281, and averaged more than 38 minutes a game.

Boston again swept the Bulls in the first round of the NBA Eastern Conference playoffs. At Boston Garden, Jordan scored 35 points in a Game 1 108–104 defeat on April 23 and 42 points in the Game 2 105–96 setback three days later. The Celtics eliminated Chicago, 105–94, on April 28 at Chicago Stadium. Although Michael experienced his greatest offensive season, the Bulls still did not survive the first playoff round.

## JORDAN'S FIRST MVP AWARD (1987–1988)

Krause, meanwhile, began building the foundation of a championship team. He traded Jawann Oldham to New York for a first-round draft choice, which he sent to Seattle for the draft rights to Scottie Pippen of Central Arkansas University. The Bulls that June also selected Horace Grant of Clemson University. Pippen could play small forward, off guard, or point guard; shoot from any range; pass; rebound; and play exceptional defense. He possessed strength, unusually long arms, great hands, natural grace, fluidity, and quickness, combining Jordanesque speed and hands with a unique talent for stealing the ball defensively. Grant, a tall, limber, strong, and agile power forward, gave Chicago a natural rebounder. Jordan had wanted the Bulls to draft center Joe Wolf and guard Kenny Smith from North Carolina.

Phil Jackson, member of two New York championship teams and Continental Basketball Association coach, joined Winter and Johnny Bach as an assistant coach. His relations with Jordan did not start smoothly. Jackson told Jordan that the great basketball players were those who improved their teammates. Collins also wanted the Bulls to play more team offense. Jordan, however, preferred to shoot rather than pass to less talented personnel and was reluctant to share the ball with Pippen and Grant until they had earned his respect. He considered it his personal responsibility to improve the Bulls.

By November 1987, Chicago began elevating to another level. Oakley blossomed as a power forward, Paxson emerged as a talented partner to Jordan, and Grant and Pippen gave the Bulls more depth. Pippen, unlike other Bulls who usually kept their distance from Jordan, tried to learn all he could from Jordan in practice. In turn, Jordan worked with Pippen on his moves, jump shot, and defense and taught him mental toughness.

For the first time in seven seasons, Chicago won a majority of its regular-season games in 1987–1988. Jordan won NBA Player of the Month honors in November, helping the Bulls capture 10 of their first 13 games. Detroit inflicted an overtime loss on November 21, despite Jordan's 49 points. Chicago snatched two road wins to start December. The Bulls' 98–97 victory over Golden State on December 1 marked the only time that Jordan did not lead the team in scoring. Paxson paced Chicago with 19 points that night. The next night, Jordan responded with 47 points in a 105–101 triumph over Utah. Chicago struggled the rest of December, but Jordan scored 44 points in a 112–103 victory over Houston on December 12 and a second-best 52 points in a 111–100 conquest of Cleveland at home on December 17.

The Bulls waltzed through January with an 11–4 mark, as Jordan again snagged NBA Player of the Month accolades with several Chicago Stadium masterpieces. He netted 45 points in a 113–91 rout over Utah on January 9 and outscored Larry Bird, 42 to 38, three nights later in a setback to Boston. Dominique Wilkins of host Atlanta outscored him, 41 to 38, one week later. Jordan's 42 points lifted Chicago to a 118–108 triumph over Phoenix on January 22. One week later, he recorded a career-high and NBA season-high 10 steals against victorious New Jersey.

Chicago boasted a 27–18 mark at the All-Star break. After edging Wilkins for his second consecutive slam-dunk title with a dunk from the free-throw line, Jordan won the NBA All-Star Game MVP Award at Chicago Stadium on February 7. He tallied 40 points, second best in All-Star history behind Chamberlain's 42 in 1962, to lift the Eastern Conference to a 138–133 triumph over the Western Conference. He delighted the 18,403 spectators by converting 17 of 23 shots from the field and all six free throws, and by notching 16 points in the final 5 minutes and 51 seconds.

The Bulls fared poorly in February but rebounded with a 10–4 mark in March. Jordan netted 49 points in a 111–90 rout over visiting Sacramento on February 19. Chicago wasted two of his stellar efforts later that month. His 46 points did not avert a loss on February 21 at Cleveland. Five nights later, he recorded 52 points and NBA-season high 21 baskets in a loss to visiting Portland. Jordan snatched consecutive NBA Player of the Week honors in late March and early April, scoring 50 points in a 113–103 victory over Boston at Chicago Stadium on March 18 and 49 points in a 118–102 romp over host Philadelphia five nights later.

Chicago fared 9–3 in April, featuring a season-best six game winning streak from April 6 through April 19. Jordan reached an NBA season-high 59 points, including 21 baskets in just 27 attempts, on April 3 to edge the Bulls past host Detroit, 112–110, in a nationally televised masterpiece. Five nights later, his eight steals helped the Bulls conquer visiting New York, 131–122. He scored 44 points in a 105–97 home triumph over Milwaukee on April 17 and 47 points to edge New York, 121–118, at Madison Square Garden two nights later. His season ended brilliantly with 46 points in a 115–108 victory over Boston at Chicago Stadium.

Chicago enjoyed its first 50-victory campaign since 1973–1974, with the seventh best NBA record. The Bulls finished 50–32, an 18-game improvement over two years, and shared second place in the Central Division with Atlanta, four games behind Detroit. Thanks mainly to Jordan, Chicago averaged 18,080 in home attendance, nearly triple its 1984 total and trailing only Detroit. The Bulls sold out a record 40 times. Chicago became the second biggest road attraction after Boston, averaging 16,461 fans.

Jordan finally realized that he belonged in the same class as Johnson and Bird, elevating his teammates to a 50-win season. He repeated as NBA scoring champion with 2,868 points, averaging 35.0 points. He shot 53.5 percent from the field compared with 48.2 percent the previous year and converted 84 percent of his foul shots. Although still the offensive anchor, he passed the ball more often. Jordan scored 173 fewer points, but compiled 108 more assists and 19 more rebounds. He averaged 5.9 assists and 5.5 rebounds and became the first NBA player to record 200 steals and 100 blocked shots in two consecutive seasons.

Jordan repeated as an All-NBA first team selection and won his first NBA MVP Award, besting Bird and Johnson. He became the first Bull and only the fourth guard since 1956 so honored. "Winning the award has always been one of my biggest goals in basketball," Jordan acknowledged. "It is a similar feeling to winning College Player of the Year. But this means a little more because of the caliber of the athletes. You're talking about 276 of the best athletes in the world." Jordan claimed that he had played better in 1986–1987, but the Bulls had won fewer games. "I had more explosive games last year, but better all-around games this year. And, I played better defense this year."[51] *The Sporting News* likewise named him NBA Player of the Year.

Acrobatic Jordan was selected NBA Defensive Player of the Year, leading the NBA with 259 steals (3.16 steals average) and blocking 131 shots, exceptional for a guard. He recorded 23 more steals and six more blocked shots than in 1986–1987. No other NBA player had won the scoring title, MVP Award, and defensive award in the same season. Jordan and Oakley helped Chicago hold opponents to a league low 101.6 points a game. Oakley led the NBA with 1,066 rebounds, averaging 13 rebounds. Defense gave Jordan his biggest thrills. "I'd rather be on the all-defensive team than all-NBA," he insisted. Jordan especially cherished winning the Defensive Player of the Year Award. "Now I wasn't just seen as a scorer," he explained. Jordan elevated his game past that of Johnson and Bird by using his superior athletic ability to outplay them defensively. "I realized defense could be my way of separating myself from them,"[52] he noted. Opponents discovered that he could win games at both ends of the floor.

Chicago survived the initial round of the Eastern Conference playoffs for the first time in seven years, nosing Cleveland, three games to two. The Bulls defeated the Cavaliers 104 to 93 on April 28 and 106 to 101 on May 1 at Chicago Stadium, with Jordan tallying 50 points and a playoff high 55 points, respectively. No NBA player ever had recorded consecutive 50-point games in the playoffs. Cleveland evened the series at home, but Jordan's 44 points enabled the host Bulls to take decisive Game 5, 107 to 101. Jordan set a five-game playoff record with 226 points, averaging 45.2 points.

Detroit, however, eliminated Chicago, four games to one, in the Eastern Conference semifinals. Coach Chuck Daly instituted "the Jordan Rules" for stopping Jordan defensively, double- and triple-teaming him. Joe Dumars, Dennis Rodman, Bill Laimbeer, and Isiah Thomas disrupted the Bulls' game plan by pushing and shoving Jordan physically whenever he tried to move, touch the ball, and take a shot. Jordan experienced difficulty penetrating that defense and was taunted about his selfish play. "Their game was to intimidate, to divide, and to conquer an otherwise united team," he noted, "by forcing players to react emotionally."[53]

The Pistons bested the Bulls, 93–82, in Game 1 on May 25 at Detroit, but Jordan's 36 points helped Chicago even the series, 105–95, the next night. At Chicago Stadium, Detroit routed the Bulls, 101–79, in Game 3 on May 14 and 96–77 in Game 4 the next afternoon. The Pistons clinched the series, 102–95, at home on May 18, limiting Jordan to a career-low eight points. Chicago needed to learn how to keep their composure and play through situations without losing sight of their objective.

David Falk, meanwhile, negotiated a new contract for Jordan with owner Reinsdorf. Jordan still played under a seven-year, $6.3 million contract, with a $750,000 base salary for 1987–1988. The talks progressed very slowly. Falk stressed how Jordan benefited the Bulls financially, citing vast increases in season-ticket and single-ticket sales, concession and parking revenue, and a lucrative radio and television contract. He claimed that Jordan brought approximately $40 million to the Bulls annually, and he sought $4 million a year for the superstar. Reinsdorf demurred because Johnson's 10-year, $25 million contract was the maximum NBA player salary. He considered Jordan the biggest gate attraction in sports history, but he refused to pay him $4 million a year. Reinsdorf offered him $3 million a year. He and Falk finally settled on an eight-year, $26 million contract, an average of $3.25 million annually, best in the NBA and a quadrupling of Jordan's old salary. The new contract put Jordan's salary approximately 30 percent higher than Johnson's. The Bulls issued a press release that Jordan had signed an eight-year contract.

## NOTES

1. Mitchell Krugel, *Michael Jordan* (New York: St. Martin's Press, 1988), p. 37.

2. *Chicago Tribune*, June 21, 1984.

3. Amateur Athletic Union. *Olympic Summer Games '84* (Upper Montclair, NJ: proSport, 1984), np.

4. David Halberstam, *Playing for Keeps: Michael Jordan and the World He Made* (New York: Random House, 1999), p. 150.

5. *Olympic Games '84*, np.

6. Halberstam, *Playing*, p. 150.

7. "Michael Jordan," *Current Biography Yearbook 1987* (New York: H. W. Wilson Company, 1987), p. 291.

8. Krugel, *Michael Jordan*, p. 37.

9. *Current Biography 1987*, p. 292.

10. Jim Naughton, *Taking to the Air: The Rise of Michael Jordan* (New York: Warner Books, 1992), p. 35.

11. *Current Biography 1987*, p. 293.

12. Michael Jordan, ed. by Mark Vancil, *Driven from Within* (New York: Atria Books, 2005), p. 33.

13. Halberstam, *Playing*, p. 151.

14. Krugel, *Michael Jordan*, p. 39.

15. Michael Jordan, ed. by Mark Vancil, *For the Love of the Game: My Story* (New York: Crown Publishers, 1998), p. 13, 20.

16. Krugel, *Michael Jordan*, p. 40–41.

17. Jordan, *Driven from Within*, p. 41.

18. Bob Greene, *Hang Time: Days and Dreams with Michael Jordan* (New York: Doubleday, 1992), p. 61.

19. Krugel, *Michael Jordan*, p. 55.

20. Jordan, *Driven from Within*, p. 41.

21. Krugel, *Michael Jordan*, p. 56.

22. Halberstam, *Playing*, p. 156.

23. Jordan, *Love of Game*, p. 23.

24. Halberstam, *Playing*, p. 157.

25. Ibid., p. 156.

26. Jim Naughton, *Taking to the Air*, p. 28.

27. Sam Smith, *The Jordan Rules: The Inside Story of a Turbulent Season with Michael Jordan and the Chicago Bulls* (New York: Simon and Schuster, 1992), p. 63.

28. Krugel. *Michael Jordan*, p. 75.

29. Ibid., p. 77.

30. Jordan, *Driven from Within*, p. 56.

31. Roland Lazenby, *Blood on the Horns: The Long Strange Ride of Michael Jordan's Chicago Bulls* (Lenexa, KS: Addax Publishing Group, 1998), p. 58.

32. Jordan, *Love of Game*, p. 27,

33. Lazenby, *Blood on Horns*, p. 59.

34. Jordan, *Love of Game*, p. 28.

35. Halberstam, *Playing*, p. 173.

36. *Chicago Sun Times*, April 21, 1986.

37. Jordan, *Love of Game*, p. 29.

38. Halberstam, *Playing*, p. 173.

39. Ibid., p. 186.

40. Mitchell Krugel, *One Last Shot: The Story of Michael Jordan's Comeback* (New York: St. Martin's Press, 2003), p. 28.

41. Halberstam, *Playing*, p. 187.

42. Krugel, *Michael Jordan*, pp. 127–128.

43. Ibid., p. 129.

44. Ibid., p. 133.

45. Ibid., p. 135.

46. *Newsday*, February 23, 1987, p. 72.

47. Krugel, *Michael Jordan*, p. 113.

48. Ibid., p. 121.

49. Ibid., p. 138.

50. *Current Biography 1987*, p. 292.

51. *Chicago Sun-Times*, May 26, 1988.

52. Jordan, *Love of Game*, pp. 50, 30.

53. Ibid., p. 38.

# Chapter 3

# THE ASCENDANT YEARS, 1988–1991

## THE BULLS CHARGE AHEAD (1988–1989)

Chicago possessed the nucleus of an outstanding team with Michael Jordan, Scottie Pippen, Charles Oakley, and Horace Grant but needed a physical center to overtake the Detroit Pistons. Bulls center Dave Corzine did not match well with Pistons center Bill Laimbeer. Chicago traded Oakley to New York in June for 7-foot 1-inch, 245-pound center Bill Cartwright and drafted Will Perdue of Vanderbilt University as his backup. Jordan lamented the departure of Oakley, who physically had protected him, and questioned whether Cartwright could fulfill that role.

Jordan began 1988–1989 scoring prolifically on the road, but the Bulls limped through November. He recorded 52 points and a season-high nine assists in a 110–104 victory over the host Boston Celtics on November 9 and 42 points against the victorious New Jersey Nets three nights later. In losses to the Philadelphia 76ers on November 16 and at the Denver Nuggets on November 26, Jordan scored 52 points. His determination surfaced in a setback at the Utah Jazz four nights later. After stealing a pass, he dunked the ball over guard Bobby Hansen to a thundering roar. Utah owner Larry Miller yelled at Jordan, "Why don't you pick on somebody your own size?" After pilfering the ball again, Jordan slammed it over 7-foot 4-inch defensive stalwart Mark Eaton and shouted back to Miller, "Was he big enough?"[1]

Chicago won 9 of 13 games in December. Jordan earned NBA Player of the Month honors, notching 42 points in a 116–103 romp over the Los Angeles Lakers at Chicago Stadium on December 20 and 43 points in a loss to the visiting Cleveland Cavaliers. *Time* called him "the hottest player in America's hottest sport" and proclaimed he moved in "a world without bounds. He gyrates, levitates, and often dominates. Certainly he fascinates. In arenas around the country, food and drink go unsold because fans refused to leave their seats for fear of missing a spectacular Jordan move to tell their grandchildren about."[2] His superlative performances spelled financial magic. The Bulls sold out more games in 18 months than they had during their entire history before Jordan's arrival.

Chicago's winning ways continued in the new year. Jordan scored 41 points in a 126–121 overtime home triumph over the Los Angeles Clippers on January 3, 48 points in a 104–101 win at the Atlanta Hawks a week later, and 42 points and eight assists in a 110–104 victory over visiting Boston on January 15. He scored a season-high 53 points against the triumphant Phoenix Suns six nights later at Chicago Stadium and reached a milestone on January 25 in a road setback to Philadelphia. His fourth-quarter bank shot with 5 minutes and 30 seconds left gave him 10,000 career points in just 303 games, fewer games than any other NBA player except Wilt Chamberlain. Chamberlain needed just 236 games to attain 10,000 career points. Jordan paced the East All-Stars with 28 points in the All-Star Game at Houston, Texas on February 12, but the West All-Stars still prevailed, 143–134.

The second half of the season brought Jordan continued success. On February 16, he tallied 50 points, including a season-high 17 free throws, to nip the Milwaukee Bucks, 117–116, at home. Jordan switched from shooting guard to point guard for the final 24 games, earning the NBA Player of the Month Award for March. Jordan recorded at least 10 points, assists, and rebounds in 11 games, and his teammates also contributed to the scoring. Because Jordan passed the ball more, defenders double-teamed him less. The Bulls won 11 of their first 14 games after his shift but dropped nearly all their remaining contests. His 48 points did not avert a loss to the Indiana Pacers on April 13.

Chicago placed a disappointing fifth in the Midwest Division at 47–35, 16 games behind Detroit. The Bulls won three fewer games than in 1987–1988, surrendering 105 points per contest. Jordan may have recorded the best all-around performance of his career, topping the NBA in scoring for the third consecutive year with a 32.5 point average. He boasted six of the NBA's top nine scoring performances, including the four best, but he became more than just a scorer, ranking third in the NBA in steals and tenth in assists. Jordan averaged a personal-best eight assists and a career-high eight rebounds and compiled 17 triple-doubles. Besides finishing second to Johnson in the NBA Most Valuable Player balloting, he repeated on the All-NBA first team and the NBA All-Defensive team and carried the Bulls to their fourth straight postseason appearance.

In the first round of the Eastern Conference playoffs, Chicago upset the Cleveland Cavaliers in five games. Cleveland had won 10 more games than the Bulls and swept all six regular season contests. Jordan averaged 39.8 points, 8.2 assists, and 5.8 rebounds in that series. Chicago surprised Cleveland, 95–88, in Game 1 on April 28 at Richfield Arena and 101–94 in Game 3 on May 3 at Chicago Stadium, with Jordan making 44 points. Although Jordan amassed an NBA playoff-high 50 points, the Bulls lost Game 4, 108–105, in overtime.

The dramatic May 7 finale at Cleveland marked Jordan's emergence among the NBA's great clutch performers. When Jordan boarded the plane for Cleveland, he predicted a Bulls victory. His confident attitude quickly spread to teammates. With Chicago trailing 100–99 and just three seconds left, Jordan took an inbounds pass, eluded two defenders, spun to the foul line, elevated, floated just long enough to regather his shooting posture, and drained an 18-foot series-winning jump shot over Craig Ehlo at the buzzer to stun 20,000 Cleveland fans. The moment became known in Chicago sport annals as "The Shot." Jordan tallied 44 points in the series finale.

In the Eastern Conference semifinals, Jordan performed spectacularly against the heavily favored New York Knicks. Chicago, fueled by the emergence of Pippen and Grant, upset New York, 120–109, in overtime in Game 1 on May 9 at Madison Square Garden and took a 3–1 series advantage with 111–88 and 106–93 victories in Games 3 and 4, respectively, on May 13 and 14 at Chicago Stadium. After recording six steals in Game 3, Jordan tallied 47 points and converted 23 of 28 free throws in Game 4. The host Bulls clinched the series with a 113–111 triumph in Game 6 on May 19, as Jordan made 40 points.

In the Eastern Conference Finals, however, Detroit eliminated the Bulls, 4–2. Chicago upset the Pistons, 94–88, in Game 1 at Detroit on May 21. Detroit, exhibiting punishing, physical play, double- and triple-teamed Jordan every time he touched the ball, preventing him from going to the baseline, hammering him when he drove to the basket, and forcing him to rely on inexperienced teammates. After the Pistons evened the series two nights later, Jordan's 46 points helped the Bulls eke out a 99–97 victory in Game 3 on May 27 at Chicago Stadium. Detroit regained the home advantage with an 86–80 triumph two nights later. Collins thought Jordan shot too much in the first four games and wanted teammates more involved offensively. Jordan, who interpreted his suggestion as criticism, shot just eight times in the Game 5 94–85 loss at

Detroit on May 31. The Pistons, demonstrating superior depth and balance, clinched the series with a 103–94 win in Game 6 at Chicago on June 2 and captured the first of two consecutive NBA titles.

Chicago drew some consolation from its defeat. Although not yet elevating his teammates to a championship level or winning an NBA title, Jordan nearly single handedly brought the Bulls to within two victories of reaching the NBA Finals. Chicago performed better against Detroit than the Western Conference champion Los Angeles Lakers, who were swept in the 1989 NBA Finals. Chicago boasted a more balanced squad, with Pippen emerging among the NBA's best all-around players.

## JORDAN MARRIAGE

By 1989, Jordan's personal life changed. He did not expect to marry or even develop an extensive dating relationship until his NBA career ended. Numerous women pursued the athlete who could not get dates in high school. Jordan dated actress Robin Givens before she married boxer Mike Tyson. Women even stood in front of his car and refused to move until he conversed with them. "It was hard for me to trust a woman's alleged affections because it was difficult to know whether she liked me for what I had or who I was," he explained. "I realized it was hard for many people meeting me to separate me the successful player from me that man."[3]

On September 2, 1989, Jordan married Juanita Vanoy, a former model, at the Little White Chapel in Las Vegas, Nevada. He was enamored by her refusal to fall for his star power when they first met at a Chicago restaurant in 1985. A mutual friend introduced them and invited them to a party. Vanoy recalled Jordan "asking how he could get in touch with me." Vanoy, who was employed by the same advertising firm that managed some of Jordan's endorsements, was four years older, more mature, and less adventurous. She usually wore elegant suits with gold jewelry, matching his. They developed a lasting relationship that transcended their age difference. "She always was very independent," Jordan observed. "She knew how to work and provide for herself." Vanoy admitted, "I was a little apprehensive about dating him at first because he was an athlete and he was younger. He proved his maturity to me, and he had this big heart. The more time we spent together, the more our personalities just clicked."[4]

Jordan valiantly sought to keep his lifestyle from intruding on their relationship. He proposed to Juanita on December 31, 1986 while eating seafood pasta, but they postponed marriage plans indefinitely. Juanita became pregnant and gave birth to Jeffrey Jordan in December 1988.

Several months later, she filed a paternity suit against Jordan and reportedly served him those papers right before a game.

Jordan took Juanita to Las Vegas, Nevada for a 3:30 A.M. September 2, 1989 wedding at which he wore jeans, loafers, and no socks and she wore blue jeans. They honeymooned in LaCosta, California, where he participated in a celebrity golf tournament and hosted a birthday party for his mother, Deloris. Jordan gave Juanita a five-carat diamond ring worth approximately $25,000.

The Jordans planned a 26,000-square-foot house on eight acres in a Chicago suburb where the family could find solitude. The mansion contained 22,000 square feet of living space, an indoor, full-court basketball court, indoor-outdoor pool, Jacuzzi, sauna, and ample driveway room for his dozen automobiles. Jordan wanted his children to see him play basketball whenever possible. He yearned to retreat from public view and hoped his marriage would give him some privacy. Juanita played the supportive wife, quiet in public but not afraid to express her opinions to Jordan when they were alone. She also tried to protect their relationship by limiting the incessant demands on his time. She would say no when his generosity and loyalty would not let him. "I have no problem saying no," Juanita told *Ebony*. "If someone doesn't step up and say no, there would be no time for his family. Everyone wants a piece of Michael."[5] The media concluded that Jordan really loved Juanita. After games, he especially enjoyed having candlelight dinners with her.

Jordan seemed devoted to Juanita at the time. "For us to get along and make it," he realized, "I had to come up to her level." Marriage gave him a new perspective on life. "We have a great relationship," Jordan observed. "She's like my mother and I mean that in the best possible sense. When I've got problems, even basketball problems, I can talk to her."[6] They frequented restaurants and movie theaters. Juanita managed the family finances.

Their son Jeffrey demonstrated Jordan's athleticism and Juanita's extroverted personality. "My sons are totally different," Jordan observed. "Jeffrey is very outgoing. He's a people person. He'll sit and talk to anybody." Jeffrey accompanied Jordan during his daily weight-training regimen at the family gymnasium. Jordan predicted that Jeffrey would play baseball or basketball because of his good eye-hand coordination and large hands. Juanita gave birth to another son, Marcus, on December 24, 1990, and a daughter, Jasmine, in December 1992. Marcus looked like Jordan and shared his independence. "Marcus is totally different because he's so independent," Jordan reflected. "If there's a woman around, he'll go right up and lie down next to her."[7] Jordan predicted that Marcus would play football because of his physical size. Jasmine looked like Juanita. She made Jordan more doting and sentimental. Juanita usually drove the children to the church in her parents' neighborhood on Chicago's South Side each Sunday.

Jordan focused on fatherhood as fervently as on winning an NBA title. He instilled in his children patience and understanding and wanted them to become more loving, sharing, and giving. He desired normal lives for them but could not take them to amusement parks, fast food restaurants, or movies because of his celebrity. Juanita transported them to school activities, medical visits, and Little League practice, helped them with their homework, and taught them ethical values.

Jordan gradually spent more time with his children. Besides taking them to school and practice, he often played with them. Jordan scheduled business commitments around family obligations. He wanted to share the responsibility of bringing up the three children with his wife. "I know she has had to give up things she's wanted to do," he realized. "Now, I want to be there."[8]

## THE THIRD TIME IS NOT THE CHARM
## (1989–1990)

In July 1989, Krause fired Collins and promoted 44-year-old Phil Jackson to head coach. Collins did not guide the Bulls to an Eastern Conference title, relied on Jordan too much offensively, and clashed with the younger players. Jackson practiced Zen Buddhism and espoused Lakota Sioux teachings, which said that teams, not individuals, win championships. Lakota warriors did not seek stardom, but rather helped others, regardless of the cost, so that the group could succeed.

Jackson wondered if Chicago could win an NBA title with Jordan. Only George Mikan's Minneapolis Lakers and Kareem Abdul-Jabbar's Milwaukee Bucks had captured NBA crowns with the league's leading scorer. A noncenter had never paced the NBA in scoring and led his team to an NBA title. Jackson claimed Jordan's playing style made defending against the Bulls easy for rival teams. He encouraged Jordan to shoot less often and to rely more on teammates to score.

Jackson installed a new system that fully involved all Bulls both offensively and defensively. He considered Chicago's offense too dependent on Jordan and planned to make him more of a team player. Jackson contended that Jordan would be a greater offensive threat as a player in the low post, taking advantage of a smaller defender with his pure strength and jumping ability. He believed that Tex Winter's triangle, motion offense best suited the Bulls, who lacked physical strength and size. Players continuously exchanged positions in the post as the defense rotated, relying on quick passes and few play calls. Jackson modified Winter's system by using pro-style screen rolls and post-up plays rather than triangles. He made the system flexible so that Jordan could still take advantage of scoring opportunities in clutch situations.

For the triangle system to work, however, Jackson needed to convince Jordan to support the program. He believed that the other players would follow Jordan's lead if he consented to follow it. Jackson found it challenging dealing with Jordan, whose drive to win an NBA title put considerable pressure on the organization. He sensed that the remaining Bulls felt uneasy about not fulfilling Jordan's expectations. According to Jackson, "his celebrity status isolated him from his teammates and made it harder for him to become the inspiring team leader the Bulls needed to succeed."[9] In early September, Jackson discussed his system with Jordan at his office. He encouraged Jordan to take fewer shots and pass the ball more to the open player. To win, the Bulls needed to score more consistently as a group. Jackson assured Jordan that his teammates could contribute substantially if given the opportunity. Paxson, Grant, and Cartwright were all 50-percent career shooters, and Pippen verged on greatness. Each player needed to move the ball around so that the Bulls could threaten anywhere on the court. "You've got to share the spotlight with your teammates because if you don't, they won't grow,"[10] he told Jordan. The Bulls needed to score consistently as a group to win.

Jackson even hinted that it might be a good idea if Jordan did not win the scoring title. He claimed that Chicago could not advance beyond the Eastern Conference without adopting the system. "Scoring champions rarely play for championship teams," he explained, because the best teams excel defensively in the playoffs and "can shut down a great shooter."[11] Detroit had limited Jordan's effectiveness by double- and triple-teaming him. Jackson argued that the system might make it easier for Jordan to score. Jordan, who liked Jackson and respected his basketball expertise, reacted skeptically. He still lacked confidence in his teammates except for Paxson and Pippen. He considered Paxson a dependable pure shooter and praised Pippen defensively but did not yet consider the latter a good pure shooter or clutch player. Jordan questioned whether Cartwright or Grant could fit within that system because "they can't pass and they can't make decisions with the ball." Besides contending that Grant "had trouble thinking on his feet," he did not consider Cartwright very dexterous and once jokingly accused him "of eating Butterfinger candy bars before practice."

Jackson understood Jordan's concerns, but assured him, "if you give the system a chance, they'll learn to be playmakers." He wanted Jordan's teammates to get involved at the offensive end "so they won't feel like spectators" and concluded "It's got to be a team effort."[12] Jordan insisted he was coachable and agreed to follow Jackson's advice, but he warned, "if we start losing, I'm shooting."[13]

Although trying to learn the triangle system, Jordan often abandoned it initially. Despite Jackson's admonitions, Jordan still led Chicago nearly every night in scoring. The Bulls experienced difficulty adjusting to the complicated triangle system. Jordan questioned the wisdom of using the triangle system in the NBA because of the lengthy time required to master it. He also argued that the talent, size, and speed of the newer NBA players made set plays passé.

Jackson's system altered Jordan's game and gave him less control over the offense, restricting his ability to play instinctively and conflicting with his pure, reactive style. Jordan believed that basketball benefited those who created their own shots. He loved playing creatively, making game-winning shots at the buzzer. Crowds energized him, and he knew the fans loved his big breakaway dunk, slashing baseline jam, and reverse hanging layup. No NBA player could match his quickness in reading a defense or scoring. Teammates recognized his talent, but they doubted Chicago could win an NBA title by relying on him so much.

Jackson forced the triangle system on the Bulls until they developed a cohesive rhythm. The system involved the entire team in implementing the offense. Defenders did not double- or triple-team Jordan nearly as often because he often rotated without the ball. Pippen, Cartwright, and Paxson became scoring options, and the offense gave Jordan more room to operate. Jordan conceded that the system occupied all the players and kept defenders honest. Jackson recalled that it took 18 months before the Bulls really felt at ease with it. Jordan estimated "it was another two-and-a-half years before everyone mastered its many nuances."[14]

Jordan inaugurated the new NBA season spectacularly with 54 points in a 124–109 overtime victory over Cleveland on November 3 at Chicago Stadium. Five nights later at Minnesota, his 45 points enabled the Bulls to defeat the Timberwolves, 96–84. After boasting a winning record in November, Chicago surged to an 11–3 mark in December. Jordan outmaneuvered defensive stalwart Rolando Blackman for 41 points in a 105–97 home triumph over the Dallas Mavericks on December 12 and tallied 38 points in a 124–113 victory over the visiting Orlando Magic two nights later. His 37 points helped overpower the Los Angeles Lakers, 93–83, on

December 19 at home. The next night, his 52-point masterpiece did not avert a heartbreaking loss at Orlando.

The Bulls continued their winning ways in January. Jordan tallied 43 points in a 127–116 win over visiting Orlando on January 5 and 45 points in a 107–95 road victory over the Charlotte Hornets one week later. He netted 44 points in a 132–107 home thrashing of the Golden State Warriors on January 18 and outscored Dominique Wilkins, 36–26, the next night to lead the Bulls to a 92–84 road triumph over Atlanta.

Chicago still trailed Detroit by six games at the All-Star break with a 28–19 slate. At the All-Star Game in Miami, Florida on February 11, Jordan lifted the Eastern Conference to a 130–113 victory over the Western Conference. Three nights later, Jordan netted 49 points in an overtime loss at Orlando.

After the All-Star break, Chicago adjusted better to Winter's triangle system, winning 24 of 27 games from February 18 through April 13. Jordan reflected, "we had all the pieces to the puzzle."[15] The Bulls inserted Craig Hodges at shooting guard and shifted Jordan to point guard. The streak started with a 111–98 romp at Milwaukee. All three Chicago losses ironically came at home to Utah, Detroit, and the Sacramento Kings. The Detroit setback hurt the Bulls' chances of overtaking the Pistons. Jordan scored 45 points in the Utah loss and 43 points in the Sacramento defeat. Chicago won all eight road games, recording their first-ever four-game Western Conference sweep.

The Bulls compromised between Winter's triangle system and Jordan's creative, instinctive play. Jackson realized the effectiveness of the triangle system depended on the extent to which Jordan innovated. The more Jordan involved his teammates, the more they elevated their play. Jordan performed brilliantly during that streak, recording seven straight triple-doubles with at least 10 points, rebounds, and assists. He played in the middle of the floor as a point guard, making it difficult for opponents to double-team him. Jordan notched 43 points in a 106–96 triumph over visiting Milwaukee on February 27 and 45 points in a 117–105 home win over Indiana on March 10.

Jordan torched Cleveland, equaling a career scoring high in a thrilling 117–113 overtime road triumph on March 28. His 69 points and 23 baskets marked NBA-season highs, and his 21 free throws ranked second. Cleveland surprisingly single-teamed him, but coach Lenny Wilkens could not find any defender who could stop Jordan's onslaught. Jordan shot so many times because Cavalier defenders left him open. His astronomical scoring did not guarantee victory because Chicago blew an 11-point fourth quarter lead. Jordan's prolific shooting disrupted team chemistry, permitting the Cavaliers to launch a comeback. "It's not that we don't want MJ to get points," Pippen remarked, "but it makes it tough for others to step up when they have to."[16] Two nights later, Jordan's 49 points let the host Bulls escape with a 107–106 nailbiter over New York.

Chicago owned a 47–23 record through March. Jordan made 47 points in a 111–103 triumph over the Miami Heat on April 1 at Chicago Stadium and 43 points to nip host Dallas, 109–108, six nights later. After recording a season-high eight steals at home against Milwaukee on April 13, he poured in 45 points in a setback at Boston a week later. Jordan, however, got too tired defending smaller, quicker point guards and wanted to return to shooting guard.

The Bulls finished the regular season with a franchise-best 55 wins and 27 losses, eight wins better than the year before, but four games behind Detroit. The Pistons won 25 of 26 games after inserting defensive ace Dennis Rodman at forward in January. For the fourth straight year, Jordan garnered the NBA scoring championship with a 33.6-point scoring average. He topped 40 points 22 times, averaged 6.9 rebounds and 6.3 assists, and paced the NBA in steals with 2.77 per game, finishing third in the NBA MVP balloting and making both the All-NBA first team and Defensive team. Pippen, who made his first All-Star team, and Horace Grant, who led the Bulls in rebounds, benefited most from Jordan's performance. Paxson capitalized on the constant double-teaming of Jordan, making more than 51 percent of his shots.

Chicago ousted Milwaukee, 3–1, in the first playoff round. Jordan's best scoring output of 48 points came in the Game 3 seven-point loss on May 1 at Milwaukee. The Bulls disposed of Philadelphia, 4–1, in the second round. Jordan exceeded his lofty standards, averaging 43 points, 7.4 assists, and 6.6 rebounds, and shooting nearly 55 percent. He scored 45 points in a 101–96 victory in Game 2 at Chicago Stadium on May 9 and in a Game 3 six-point setback at The Spectrum two nights later. The Bulls scored 45 points in one quarter in that defeat. Jordan established the NBA's playoff high with 49 points in a 111–101 triumph two days later, driving, dunking, posting up, burying jump shots, blocking shots, and defending well. He played some of the best basketball of his career, pacing Chicago in scoring in 13 of the first 16 quarters.

The Bulls met Detroit for the second consecutive year in the Eastern Conference Finals. Chicago had not reached the Eastern Conference Finals two straight seasons since 1974 and 1975. Jordan vowed to play more physically this time. "I wanted to start dishing out the punishment instead of taking it all the time,"[17] he asserted. The Pistons prevailed,

86–77, in Game 1 on May 20 and 102–93 in Game 2 two nights later at The Palace in Auburn Hills, Michigan. When the Bulls trailed Game 2 by 15 points at halftime, Jordan kicked over a garbage can and criticized his teammates for lacking mental toughness. He deplored the intimidation by Detroit stars Isaiah Thomas, Bill Laimbeer, and Rodman and implored his teammates to react physically and denounced his club's lackluster performance. The Pistons limited Jordan, who played with an injured hip and leg, to just 20 points, forcing him to attack the basket where their collapsing defensive schemes awaited him. Joe Dumars, who Jordan guarded, outscored him, 58–54, in those games.

The game signified a gradual change that had transpired in Jordan's leadership. In previous seasons, Jordan had led mainly through example rather than words. By 1990, he had been with Chicago longer than any of his teammates and had known the long, arduous road the Bulls had taken since 1984 to become a contender. He began criticizing teammates for not performing up to his expectations. "I had put in the time," he explained, "and I had earned the right to let my teammates know what I expected of them."[18]

Jordan ignored reporters after the second Detroit game and sat silently on the bus ride home. The frustrated star carried the weight of his team on his shoulders and claimed the Bulls had let him down when he was injured. He criticized teammates for either lacking focus or talent. Jackson interpreted Jordan's comments as a wakeup call for his teammates. He insisted that Chicago use its greater quickness to pass the ball and take open shots rather than penetrate the formidable Pistons' zone defense. The energized Bulls won Game 3, 107–102 on May 26 at home. Although Jordan scored 16 points in the first half, Chicago trailed 51–43 at halftime. He tallied 13 points in the third quarter, sparking a 17–6 run in the final 3 minutes and 30 seconds. Detroit attempted a fourth-quarter comeback, but Jordan countered with 18 points. His three-point field goal with the 24-second clock expiring shook Chicago Stadium in pandemonium. Jordan recorded 47 points and 10 rebounds; Pippen contributed 29 points and 11 rebounds. Jackson explained, "it wasn't the rules against Jordan, but that Jordan rules."[19] Two nights later, Chicago prevailed again, 108–101, handing the Pistons consecutive losses for the first time in two years, as Jordan scored 42 points.

The tougher, more aggressive Pistons exacted revenge in Game 5 on May 30, hammering visiting Chicago, 97–83, and limiting Jordan to 22 points. The Bulls played like champions in Game 6 two nights later, capitalizing on a 23-9 third-quarter run to prevail 109–91. Hodges and Jordan ignited the Chicago Stadium crowd with three-pointers.

Two days later at Auburn Hills, Jordan played his first Game 7 of an Eastern Conference Finals. The Pistons, led by Thomas, built a 48–33 half-time lead and overwhelmed the Bulls, 93–74, to clinch the NBA Finals berth. Jordan scored 31 points, 21 more than any teammate. Pippen, whose father had died during the Philadelphia series, suffered from a migraine headache and vision problems and made only one basket. Paxson limped on a badly sprained ankle and Hodges shot poorly.

Detroit used a suffocating defense, elevated its game to another level, exhibited superior mental toughness, and knew how to win. The defeat left Chicago, and especially Jordan, disconsolate. Jordan wondered if the Bulls would ever eliminate the Pistons and concluded that the management needed to make some changes. He wept at the back of the bus in perhaps the nadir of his career, questioning his teammates' mental toughness. The Pistons had exploited Jordan's impatience, stubbornness, and lack of faith in his teammates. Despite Jordan's brilliant performance, detractors stressed that his superstar mystique did not elevate the team to a world title.

Chicago held several glimmers of hope. The Bulls extended Detroit to seven games before the eventual NBA champions ousted them. Chicago reached the Eastern Conference Finals for the second straight year for the second time in franchise history. The Bulls won two more games against Detroit than the Western Conference champion Portland Trail Blazers won in the NBA Finals. Detroit had peaked, but the Bulls were improving. At age 28, Jordan was entering his prime years, combining awesome physical abilities with shrewder knowledge. His teammates, however, needed to believe in themselves, become tougher physically and mentally, not let the Pistons dictate the tempo, and learn how to win at Auburn Hills.

## JORDAN'S FIRST NBA TITLE (1990–1991)

The Bulls recognized three fundamental weaknesses. They needed a tougher, stronger front-court player, a reserve scorer to counter Detroit's bench strength, and a taller guard like Jordan. Chicago acquired forward Cliff Levingston from Atlanta to augment Pippen and guard Dennis Hopson from New Jersey to complement Jordan.

Jordan, tired of battling the physical punishment meted by the Pistons, vowed to strengthen himself. "Those guys are beating me to death," he protested, "I have to get stronger."[20] Tim Grover, a Chicago physical fitness trainer, put Jordan on a rigorous physical regimen to strengthen him for the late stages of games and reduce his injuries. He strengthened Jordan's upper body without reducing his lower body speed or elasticity. Jordan's weight gradually increased from 195 pounds to 215 pounds. Jordan initially worked out after practice, but switched to morning workouts at his home gym with Pippen. He missed only six games during the next seven years.

Winning an NBA championship obsessed Jordan, who always aspired to be the best. He was stronger, particularly in his shoulders and arms, enabling him to absorb and inflict punishment while driving to the basket. Pippen, who grew stronger and more committed, moved to point guard and handled the ball as much as Jordan, who returned to shooting guard. Cartwright, Paxson, and Grant joined Jordan and Pippen as starters for the 1990–1991 Bulls; reserves B. J. Armstrong and Stacey King logged considerable playing time. Other reserves included Perdue, Hodges, Hopson, Levingston, and Scott Williams. "This is the strongest team I've ever played on here,"[21] Jordan chirped.

The Bulls, however, began the season with losses to Philadelphia, Washington, and Boston. Charles Barkley of the 76ers outscored Jordan, 37–34, in the opening November 2 loss at Chicago Stadium. The next night, Jordan's last-second shot was blocked in the one-point Washington setback. He missed a 19-foot jumper with 20 seconds left in a two-point Boston triumph on November 6. Jackson recognized that the players relied far too much on Jordan in pressure situations. When Jordan became even more assertive offensively, the Bulls won the next four games. His 41-point masterpiece came in a 120–100 rout at Boston on November 9, and his long fallaway jump shot at the buzzer clinched an 84–82 nailbiter at Utah four nights later. Jordan's scoring outbursts did not trouble Jackson as long as they did not become habitual. "I knew he needed bursts of creativity to keep from getting bored," Jackson recalled. In addition, "his solo performances would strike terror in the hearts of our enemies" and "help win some key games."[22]

When Golden State defeated Chicago on November 15, Jordan blamed Jackson's triangle system for getting only two fourth-quarter shots. He questioned whether involving more players in the offense would bring the Bulls the success they aspired. Jackson played Jordan for only 28 minutes two nights later when the Bulls walloped the Seattle SuperSonics, 116–95. Jordan recorded 33 points and 7 steals in the first three quarters.

Losses to Portland and Phoenix followed. Jordan again criticized the triangle offense. He preferred to keep the ball, peruse the defense, and move when defenders neared him, splitting defenders for dunk shots. Jackson, though, still tried hard to persuade Jordan to take pressure off himself by relying more on his teammates, and he encouraged the other Bulls to shoot more when open.

During November, Jordan averaged more first-quarter points than any teammate averaged the entire game. On November 24, his 38 points sparked Chicago to a 151–145 triumph over Denver in one of the highest scoring games in franchise history. Jordan usually passed the ball in the first quarter because he never felt comfortable shooting at the outset, but he began taking more first-quarter shots. In the first quarter, Jordan tallied 15 points in a 24-point win over Washington on November 28 and 20 points in a 124–95 rout over Indiana two nights later.

Chicago feasted on a favorable December schedule mostly at Chicago Stadium, losing only 3 of 14 contests. Jordan netted 32 points in 30 minutes in a 120–85 thumping of host Cleveland on December 1. Three nights later, the Bulls vanquished visiting Phoenix, 155–127.

Jordan made one of his most spectacular athletic moves in a 108–98 victory over New York on December 7. After dribbling the ball through his legs three times and back near the foul line, he shifted the ball to his left hand and darted past Gerald Wilkins. Jordan pumped over 6-foot 10-inch Jerrod Mustaf and slammed the ball, dazzling the Chicago Stadium throng. He possessed an uncanny ability to exploit even the smallest of openings that the defense gave him.

After winning seven consecutive games, Chicago lost to Portland, the hottest NBA team, and Milwaukee. Jordan protested Jackson's decision to reduce his playing time to 36–37 minutes a game to preserve his stamina for the playoffs. He also complained that Winter's triangle offense forced Pippen and him to pass the ball too much. Some teammates countered that Jordan cared more about winning another scoring title than passing the ball to them.

The Bulls enjoyed their best effort in several years on December 14, trouncing the visiting Los Angeles Clippers, 128–88. Paxson uncharacteristically led Chicago with 26 points, and five others reached double figures. Pippen recorded a triple-double, and Jordan contributed 14 points. Chicago Stadium victories over Cleveland and Miami followed. "We're not winning because of talent," Jordan cautioned. "We're just beating bad teams."[23]

After Detroit trounced the Bulls at Auburn Palace on December 19, Chicago capped December with five consecutive victories. Jordan and Pippen barely missed triple-doubles, in a 114–103 win over the Los Angeles Lakers two nights later. Double-digit home victories ensued over Indiana and Detroit. The Bulls coasted to a 128–113 triumph over Golden State on December 27, as Jordan scored 42 points and Pippen added a career-high 34 points. The Bulls trounced Seattle, 116–91, on December 29, tallying 39 first-quarter points.

The new year began badly for the Bulls, with a humiliating setback to the Houston Rockets on January 3. Grant complained when Jordan and Pippen took 40 shots. Jordan, meanwhile, lamented Chicago's weak bench. When the Bulls built a 24-point lead at home against New Jersey five nights later, he left the game. The Nets, however, sliced the margin to 10 points, forcing Jackson to reinsert Jordan. Jordan finished with 41 points in the 111–102 triumph, but complained that the reserves were playing as individuals rather than trying to improve on their overall game. The reserves countered that they played too little to get into the offensive flow and charged that Jordan and Pippen did not try to run the triangle offense.

Chicago, nevertheless, captured seven consecutive contests in January, featuring Jordan's prolific offense, tenacious team defense, and athleticism. His 40 points lifted the Bulls over Philadelphia on January 9. He ironically scored career-point number 1,500 that night on a foul shot after making a picturesque shot from the field. Tim Hallam, Director of Media Services, did not find the moment very exciting because "it came on a free throw. Screws up my highlights film for next year."[24] Three nights later, Jordan tallied 12 of Chicago's last 14 points in a 106–95 triumph at Charlotte. On January 16, Jordan made 30 points as Chicago disposed of Atlanta, 114–105. The Bulls finished January 29–12, on pace to shatter the team record for victories.

During early January, Jordan informed teammates that he planned to play just five more seasons. Playing pro basketball was not enjoyable for him anymore because of the enormous public and media demands on his time. Jordan also criticized Chicago management for not trying to improve the team. He also wanted to spend more time with his family.

*Chicago Tribune* sportswriter Sam Smith claimed that Jordan increasingly seemed to operate under his own rules. Jordan expected special treatment as the Bulls' best player. He did not socialize very much with teammates, especially after Higgins and Oakley departed. Jordan slept comparatively little on road trips, often playing card games late at night with North Carolina friends Fred Whitfield and Fred Kearns. Unlike his teammates, he did not have to visit the trainer after reporting sick and missing practice. Jordan always reported to the team bus last because he did not like to wait. His friends rode the team bus and stayed in the team hotel on road trips, but other players did not enjoy that privilege. He employed his personal trainer Tim Grover, but teammates worked with team strength coaches Al Vermeil and Erik Helland.

Jackson, meanwhile, urged general manager Krause to acquire point guard Derek Harper from Dallas and trade reserves King, Armstrong, and

Hopson. Krause replied that he could not trade reserves very easily. The Bulls considered trading Levingston to Denver for Walt Davis, but Jackson questioned the latter's defensive skills. After New Jersey upset Chicago in late January, Jordan criticized Krause and wanted the Bulls to remove him as general manager. "We can't get anything done because of him." He concluded, "If I were general manager, we'd be a better team."[25]

Several Bulls' minority partners approached Jordan about getting Krause ousted. Jordan agreed to discuss the situation with owner Reinsdorf. Reinsdorf invited Jordan to his North Shore home just before the Bulls departed for San Antonio on January 31. He reminded Jordan that the Bulls occupied first place and that Krause had drafted Pippen and Grant and acquired Cartwright. Reinsdorf conceded that Krause often exhibited annoying behavior and did not always represent the Bulls well in public, but he liked his energy. Jordan countered that Krause did not evaluate talent well and lacked the personal skills to make major trades to help Chicago win an NBA title. He preferred having a former player as general manager. Other general managers had told him that they disliked dealing with Krause because he consistently tried to take advantage of them. Jordan denied that the team Krause had assembled could capture an NBA crown. Grant and Pippen had performed well, but neither excelled at playoff time. First-round selections Perdue, Armstrong, and King had contributed little. Jordan especially wanted Krause to acquire Davis from Denver to strengthen the bench scoring at playoff time. Reinsdorf replied that Krause was discussing several deals, but queried "how are we supposed to make a deal when you're knocking your players?"[26] Jordan was speechless. His conversation had little effect on Reinsdorf. He concluded that the Bulls would not make a trade.

Chicago's bench scoring problems continued on a lengthy road trip before the All-Star break. The Bulls led San Antonio, 82–75, after three quarters on January 31, but the Spurs launched a 13–2 run against their reserves in the next four minutes. Jordan scored three baskets to even the contest, but he fouled out with 36 points and the Spurs won 106–102. Although Chicago defeated Dallas the next night, Jordan was chagrined that the reserves blew another fourth-quarter lead. On February 3, the Los Angeles Lakers seized the lead against Chicago's reserves in the fourth quarter and won by 13 points.

Chicago won a pivotal game at Detroit on February 7. The Bulls led, 44–41, at halftime, but the Pistons seized a five-point advantage with four minutes remaining. Jordan scored 30 points, including Chicago's last 10 points, to eke out a 95–93 victory. "That's when we want to go to him," Jackson explained. "He's the best closer in the game."[27] Unlike previous games against Detroit, the younger players kept their focus and the Bulls got the close calls from the referees. Jordan triumphantly told the media "[a] monkey is off our back."[28]

Jordan traveled to Charlotte, North Carolina for the February 10 All-Star Game. NBA Vice President Rod Thorn urged him to compete in the slam-dunk contest because he symbolized the NBA's high-flying, acrobatic game. Jordan declined, however, because he was expected to perform more spectacularly each year. The East All-Stars, led by Jordan and Barkley, edged the West All-Stars, 116–114. Jordan scored a game-high 26 points as point guard, but committed 10 turnovers. Jackson marveled at his ability to score at will against the NBA's best, and Armstrong was amazed by how everything was so effortless for him.

Despite disagreements with management, Jordan still found solace on the playing court. The game relieved him from the media and other pressures. Jordan told *Chicago Tribune* columnist Bob Greene, "The basketball court for me, during a game, is the most peaceful place I can imagine. I truly feel less pressure there than anyplace I go." He added, "No one bothers me at all, even the other players on the court."[29]

Chicago performed superbly after the All-Star break, winning 18 of 19 games. The Bulls took five consecutive games between February 12 and February 19 over struggling Atlanta, New York, New Jersey, Cleveland, and Washington. Jordan questioned whether Pippen, Grant, and Cartwright could perform at that level against stronger teams in the playoffs. Chicago overwhelmed visiting Sacramento, 129–82, on February 22, as Jordan scored 34 points in 28 minutes and Pippen barely missed a triple-double. Pippen netted a career-high 43 points the next night in a 129–108 home romp over Charlotte, becoming Jordan's first teammate to tally at least 40 points in an NBA game. The host Bulls on February 26 routed Boston, 129–99, their biggest victory margin ever over the Celtics. Jordan and Pippen both compiled 33 points after three quarters, but the former notched six more fourth-quarter points. "The Bulls are the best team I've ever seen,"[30] Larry Bird declared. Chicago broke franchise records for most consecutive home wins with 16 and for victories in a month with 11, losing only to the Los Angeles Lakers in February.

The Bulls led Detroit by six games in the Central Division and shared the best Eastern Conference record with Boston. Although Jordan still dominated offensively, Chicago captured games with exceptional half-court defense, a quick transition game that allowed Pippen, Grant, and him to run, and excellent shooting. Jordan's 15 third-quarter points at home on March 1 vaulted the Bulls past Dallas, 109–86, for their eleventh consecutive victory, one short of the franchise record. The streak ended when an ankle injury sidelined Grant in a loss to Indiana.

Chicago embarked on another nine-game winning streak. At Chicago Stadium, the Bulls walloped Milwaukee, 104–86, on March 5 and overcame a 16-point deficit to best Utah, 99–89, three nights later. Jackson freed Jordan from the triangle system during the second half, letting him drive to the basket. Jordan, who enjoyed the freedom of the open court much more than taking jump shots in the restrictive triangle offense, blew by defenders, scoring 18 third-quarter points and 17 fourth-quarter points. He urged the Bulls to use an open court offense in the playoffs.

Lopsided victories came at Atlanta, 122–87, on March 10 and over visiting Minnesota, 131–99, two nights later. Jackson recorded his 100th career win against Minnesota, the quickest for any Bulls coach. Chicago had just won its thousandth game in franchise history and embarked on a three-game road trip. Jordan sank two free throws with five seconds left on March 13 to edge Milwaukee, 102–101. His 34 points elevated the Bulls past Charlotte, 105–92, two nights later. On March 16, Chicago overcame an 11-point deficit to best Cleveland, 102–98. The Bulls extended their winning streak to nine at home, vanquishing Denver, 121–108, on March 18 and Atlanta, 129–107, on March 20. Chicago reached 50 wins faster than any other team in franchise history, having suffered only 15 losses.

After Philadelphia snapped Chicago's winning streak on March 22, the Bulls responded angrily the next night because Reggie Miller of Indiana claimed they lacked talent beyond Jordan. Miller's remarks were posted above each player's locker. The Bulls whipped the Pacers, 133–119, for their 26th straight home win, second best in franchise history. Houston snapped the streak on March 25, overcoming Jordan's 34 points to whip the Bulls,100–90, and dropping Chicago to just 12–12 against the top 10 NBA teams.

The Bulls trounced New Jersey, 128–94, three nights later at the Meadowlands. Jordan tallied 28 first-half points, including 19 in the last five minutes, and added 14 third-quarter points before being taken out. His teammates, however, countered that he shot the ball too much and did not share the ball enough.

Two days later, Chicago lost a 135–132 double overtime heartbreaker at Boston. Jordan, Pippen, and Paxson launched a furious 14-point, fourth-quarter comeback to send the game into overtime. The Celtics seized a five-point lead in the first overtime, but Jordan made two foul shots and Paxson sank a three-pointer. After Boston surged to another five point advantage in the second overtime, the Bulls trimmed it to three with 15 seconds left. "The Boston Garden," the *Chicago Tribune* noted, "was a well of emotion now, a geyser, flooded with a fury of excitement."[31] Jordan, exhausted and double-teamed, missed two three-point shots in the waning seconds, but outscored Bird 37–34 in one of their final duels.

Jordan's scoring barrage continued at Chicago Stadium on April 2 with 44 points in a 106–102 victory over Orlando. *Chicago Tribune* columnist Bob Greene noted, "the Bulls as a unit had turned into something special. The rest of the team was no longer invisible."[32] The Bulls overcame an 18-point road deficit to defeat New York, 101–91, isolating Jordan on top of the floor. Chicago soon clinched its second Central Division title in 25 years. Jordan played a full round of golf on April 7 before scoring 41 points in an overtime loss to Philadelphia.

Jackson wanted to restrain Jordan's offense, getting teammates more involved before the playoffs. Although scoring under 30 points, Jordan still led the Bulls to consecutive victories over New York on April 9 at Chicago Stadium and at Indiana the next night. In the last road test on April 12, however, he netted 40 points in a setback at Detroit.

Chicago closed the regular season with four straight victories. The Bulls set a team record for triumphs with their 58th win, 103–94, over visiting Milwaukee on April 15. Jordan tallied a season-high 46 points, as Chicago's relentless defense prevailed. The Bulls clinched the best Eastern Conference record with a 111–101 victory at Miami two nights later, gaining home advantage throughout the Eastern Conference playoffs. Jordan tallied 41 points in a 115–99 romp at Charlotte. The Bulls also took the season finale, 108–100, on April 21 over Detroit at Chicago Stadium.

Chicago recorded 61 wins with just 21 losses, winning its first Central Division title since 1974–1975. The Bulls matched the team mark for most road triumphs and won 26 straight home games, sharing second on the NBA's all-time list. They were the highest scoring Bulls team in 20 years and their best shooting team ever at 51 percent. Chicago recorded the most blowout wins and the NBA's biggest victory margin per game, set team records for assists and three-point shooting, and played its best defense since the mid-1970s.

Jordan paced NBA scorers for the fifth straight season with a 31.5 point average and averaged 6.0 rebounds and 5.5 assists, notching his second NBA MVP Award, and repeating on the All-NBA first team and Defensive team. He dominated the Bulls offense, exceeding 40 points eight times. His scoring average dropped only because he attempted fewer foul shots. Only two other Bulls averaged in double figures. Pippen developed into an All-Star, averaging 17.8 points and leading the Bulls in rebounds and assists. Grant rebounded tenaciously, Paxson posed an outside scoring threat, and Cartwright improved inside.

Chicago swept New York in the first round. Aside from center Patrick Ewing, the Bulls held the advantage at every position. At Chicago Stadium, the Bulls trounced the Knicks, 126–85, in Game 1 and took Game 2, 89–79. Game 3 shifted to Madison Square Garden in New York, where the Bulls prevailed 103–94.

Chicago eliminated Philadelphia in the next round, although the 76ers' physical play presented a greater challenge. Despite Charles Barkley's 34 points, the Bulls took Game 1, 105–92. Jordan scored 29 points and involved his teammates more, building a 20-point, first-quarter lead. In one of its best shooting and rebounding playoff performances, Chicago won Game 2, 112–100. Jordan contributed 12 baskets and 9 assists.

After playing 36 holes of golf on his day off, Jordan experienced tendinitis in his left knee. The 76ers edged the Bulls, 99–97, in Game 3 at The Spectrum. Jordan converted 20 shots, including two brilliant, acrobatic drives in the last two minutes, but he missed three crucial free throws. Chicago played tenacious defense in Game 4, triumphing 101–85, on Mother's Day. Jordan made 25 points and 12 assists, and Grant and Pippen contributed 22 points and 20 points, respectively.

In the Game 5 finale at home, Pippen's 24 first-half points ignited a Bulls 100–95 victory. Although Barkley tallied 30 points, Jordan recorded Chicago's last 12 points and a playoff career-high 19 rebounds.

The Bulls held home court advantage against two-time defending champion Detroit in the Eastern Conference Finals this time. Jackson sent the NBA office a tape of the Pistons' past rough physical play against Chicago. The NBA office disliked Detroit's "bad boys" image, anyway.

Before a roaring Chicago Stadium crowd, the Bulls surged to a 20–8 lead in Game 1 on May 19. Mark Aguirre ignited a third-quarter Piston comeback, but Chicago won 94–83. Jordan fought even triple-teams to score 22 points, but Pippen contributed 18, Cartwright 16, and the bench an impressive 30. Reserves Perdue, Levengston, Armstrong, and Hodges paced a fourth-quarter onslaught, taking the load off Jordan. Jordan acted as a decoy, creating openings for Pippen, Grant, and the reserves. The Bulls realized they were more talented and better than Detroit and did not let the Pistons intimidate them.

Before Game 2 two nights later, Jordan received his NBA MVP Award at center court and seemed overcome emotionally amid the loud ovation. "The arena was packed and frenzied" and "almost claustrophobic."[33] Jackson wanted him to counter double-teams by letting other players score. Chicago outscored Detroit, 29–22, in the first quarter, with every starter netting at least four points. Pippen's 16 second-quarter points kept the Bulls ahead 49–41 at halftime. Chicago increased its lead behind Jordan's 12 third-quarter points and prevailed again, 105–97.

The Bulls' balanced scoring approach continued in Game 3 at The Palace. Chicago jumped to a 24–8 first-quarter advantage, but the Pistons rallied for a 38–36 second-quarter lead. Pippen and Cartwright helped the Bulls regain the lead, 51–43, at halftime. Chicago led by eight points after three quarters, but Detroit narrowed the gap to five points with 2 minutes and 31 seconds left. Vinnie Johnson stole the ball and planned a layup, but he realized that Jordan would block the ball, so he tried to pass the ball to Dumars. Jordan anticipated the move and forced Dumars to take a weak, off-balanced shot. "One of the great stops of all time,"[34] Jackson boasted. The Bulls won, 113–107, countering the Pistons' rough physical play with speed and quickness, and shooting 57 percent. Jordan led a balanced Chicago attack with 33 points, and Pippen contributed 26, Grant 17, and Cartwright 13.

Laimbeer and Rodman attempted to intimidate Paxson and Pippen in Game 4, but the tenacious Bulls withstood the pressure. "Jordan led the team at both ends of the court" by "driving relentlessly for the basket, sprinting down to lead the defense, making sure that Detroit's long domination of the Bulls would end by sundown."[35] Paxson scored 12 first-quarter points, putting Chicago ahead, 32–26. The Bulls built a 17-point, third-quarter lead and triumphed, 115–94, sweeping the series. Several Pistons left the court in the final seconds without shaking hands with the Bulls players. "It made the Pistons look to all the world like losers."[36] Jordan notched 29 points, and Pippen added 23 points and 10 rebounds.

Chicago had vanquished its long-time nemesis. The Bulls had retained their focus this time, playing through the intimidating tactics of the Pistons. During this series, they withstood the pressure without changing their original game plan. "That's when the Bulls started to get tough," Jordan claimed. "They won't attack me again because they know I'm not going to back down."[37] Jackson observed, "We completely disarmed them by not striking back. At that moment, our players became true champions."[38] Jackson, however, reminded the Bulls that their mission of winning an NBA title was not yet completed. On the plane ride home, Jordan sipped champagne and vowed to accomplish that mission.

Chicago faced the Los Angeles Lakers in the NBA Finals. Los Angeles, winners of 58 games, had captured five NBA titles in the 1980s, but injuries stymied James Worthy and Byron Scott this time. Laker starters had appeared in 123 NBA Finals games, but no Bull ever had. The finals matched superstars Johnson and Jordan, winners of the last five MVP awards. Jordan had always measured himself against Johnson. "Magic has the rings and the MVP awards,"[39] noted Jackson.

Los Angeles edged Chicago, 93–91, in Game 1 on June 2 at Chicago Stadium. The lead changed 22 times. The Bulls looked tentative, uptight, nervous, and slow in their defensive rotations. Jordan scored 15 first-quarter points to give Chicago a 30–29 lead. He frequently passed the ball to teammates, but they kept returning it to him. The Bulls retained the lead at halftime, 53–51. Los Angeles limited the Bulls to just 15 third-quarter points and surged ahead, 75–68, but Jordan ignited a 10–0 run to move Chicago in front, 78–75. The Bulls led until Sam Perkins sank a three-point shot with 14 seconds left. Ten seconds later, Jordan's 18-foot jump shot barely missed. Jordan scored 36 points and Pippen tallied 19 points, but their teammates relied on them too much for scoring.

Before Game 2 on June 5, Pippen signed an $18 million, five-year contract extension. The Bulls denied Johnson the ball and doubled teamed post-up players James Worthy and Vlade Divac. When Jordan accumulated two quick fouls guarding Johnson, Jackson assigned Pippen to defend against him. Pippen's long arms, quickness, and physical tactics bothered the Lakers star. Cartwright and Grant tallied 18 of the Bulls' 28 first-quarter points, and Chicago retained a 48–43 halftime lead. In the third quarter, the Bulls set an NBA Finals record by converting 17 of 20 baskets. Jordan and Paxson made all 10 of their shots, extending the third-quarter lead to 19 points.

The Bulls triumphed, 107–86, before the raucous Chicago Stadium crowd, as Jordan made 15 of 18 shots. He converted a spectacular shot, soaring to the basket to dunk the ball with his right hand. Sam Perkins blocked his path, so Jordan brought the ball back down, switched it to his left hand, glided to the left of the basket, stretched out his left hand, and banked the ball off the glass into the net before returning to the floor. Reporters "witnessed a basketball moment they would remember for the rest of their days" and "stared at the monitor, making sure it had been real."[40] *Chicago Tribune* reporter Sam Smith noted, "The crowd first gasped, for this was art, poetry without words, an instant for eternity. Then the crowd exploded."[41] Johnson admitted, "He can do the impossible, the unbelievable," and Jackson marveled that he had never seen Jordan do that before. The shot became an enduring video clip replayed thousands of times on various sports broadcasts, and it won an ESPY Award for Play of the Decade.

Chicago converted 61.7 percent of its shots, an NBA playoff game record. The Bulls' starters all scored in double figures, converting an amazing 73.4 percent in the second half. Jordan moved to point guard to direct the offense and spread the Lakers' packed-in defense. He led Chicago's onslaught with 33 points, but involved other teammates. Pippen totaled 20 points, 10 assists, and five rebounds, allowing Johnson only four baskets. Paxson made all eight of his shots for 16 points. "My job is to shoot the open jumpers," he said, "and when I'm in my rhythm, I feel like I'm going to make them all."[42] Jackson hoped that the Bulls would take two of three games at Los Angeles, but Jordan insisted that the Lakers could be swept there. Chicago enjoyed an advantage entering Game 3 on June 7. The Lakers inadvertently left 20 pages of their plays under their bench when they left the court after Game 2. The Bulls picked them up and studied them. Jackson instructed Jordan to pass the ball more to Paxson because Johnson had not defended him closely. Chicago led 48–47 at half-time, but the lead often changed hands in the second half. Vlade Divac's three-pointer put Los Angeles ahead, 92–90, with just 10.9 seconds left. "The Bulls were within seconds of a loss that could devastate their dreams." Jordan made a 14-foot jump shot with 3.4 seconds left to send the game into overtime, injuring his big right toe. *Chicago Tribune* columnist Bob Greene described the Forum as "suddenly going stony silent."[43] Despite the pain, Jordan still scored six overtime points. He drove the baseline for a basket with 1 minute and 54 seconds left to spark an 8–0 run, giving the Bulls a 104–96 victory and home-court advantage. "We feel really good to be in this position," he remarked. "When you play the Lakers, you are never really in control because they have been here before and know what it takes to win big ball games."[44]

In Game 4 two days later, Chicago used a suffocating defense. The Lakers led 28–27 after the first quarter, but Jordan's 11 second-quarter points gave the Bulls a 52–44 halftime lead. Chicago widened its lead in the third quarter, limiting Los Angeles to just 14 points. The Lakers lost resoundingly, 97–82, shooting a woeful 37 percent. Los Angeles tallied its fewest points in a playoff game in three years and its lowest finals score at home since the NBA introduced the 24-second clock in 1954. Despite his toe injury, Jordan scored 36 points and matched Johnson's 13 assists. The Bulls committed just five turnovers, another NBA Finals record.

Chicago concluded its march to the NBA crown in Game 5 on June 12, sweeping the Los Angeles Forum contests. The Bulls trailed 49–48 at halftime and tied the score, 80–80, after three periods. When Jordan took five of Chicago's first eight fourth-quarter shots, Jackson thought that he was trying to do it all himself. Jackson, who noticed that Johnson was leaving Paxson open to stop potential drives by Jordan and Pippen, asked Jordan twice, who was unguarded. Jordan really wanted the ball, but finally replied, "Paxson." Jackson instructed Jordan to pass him the ball. Paxson scored half of his 20 points, including eight points in a 10–3 run, in the last four minutes to give the Bulls a 108–101 victory. "Every time he got the ball," Perkins lamented, "he put it in. It killed us."[45] Pippen paced Chicago with 32 points, the first time in the playoffs Jordan had not led the Bulls in scoring; he had played all 48 minutes and scored 30 points.

Chicago achieved a milestone, faring 8–1 in the final two series and winning all five road games at Detroit and Los Angeles. Its defense held opponents to less than 100 points in 14 of 17 playoff games. After three agonizing playoff defeats, the Bulls finally conquered their archrival Pistons and kept the Lakers nearly 20 points below their normal NBA Finals average.

The excitement of winning his first NBA title nearly overwhelmed Jordan as he rushed to the locker room. Jordan remained in a state of disbelief. He collapsed into his seat before 10 million television viewers. His head fell into the lap of his wife, Juanita, as he cried unexpectedly on the championship trophy. Visibly teary-eyed, "Michael Jordan hugged the championship trophy as if it were a newborn baby."[46] He tried to remove the tears of ecstasy. "I never thought I'd be this emotional. I've never been this emotional publicly."[47]

The NBA crown ended Jordan's seven-year quest. "When I came here, we started from scratch," he recalled. "I vowed we'd make the playoffs every year, and each year we got closer. I always had faith I'd get this ring one day."[48] He averaged 31.2 points, being named unanimously NBA Finals MVP. During the postseason, Jordan averaged 31.1 points, 6.4 rebounds, and 8.4 assists. By winning his first NBA title, he silenced the skeptics who doubted he could ever lead his team to a championship. Critics complained that Jordan was too selfish, had not improved his teammates, and had directed his greatness toward his own glory. They had not pictured him as a great passer, teammate, or winner like Johnson. Jordan realized that Jackson's triangle system had worked.

Chicago was no longer called "Michael and the Jordanaires."[49] Capturing an NBA crown was the only way he could join the Magic Johnson-Larry Bird echelon. "That's why our first championship was a little sweeter," he claimed. "Beating Magic added credibility to that first title."[50] Jordan won recognition as more than just a great scorer and dunker, becoming the first scoring champion since 1971 to lead his team to the championship. He earned the seemingly elusive NBA title quicker than NBA greats Jerry West, Oscar Robertson, and Wilt Chamberlain. Other NBA stars, including Elgin Baylor, Dave Bing, and Nate Thurmond, never experienced an NBA title.

Jordan could not sleep that night because of his pure, unrestrained joy. After boarding the team bus for the ride to the Los Angeles airport the next morning, he remained in uniform clutching a champagne bottle and chewing on a large cigar. The Bulls gently passed the NBA Finals trophy from player to player. Jordan then slept with the trophy the remainder of the flight to Chicago. The next day, the city gave the team a noisy celebration at Grant Park.

The media showered Jordan with plaudits. Americans liked his "disciplined audacity," essayist Stanley Crouch observed, "because the improvisational hero is the great American hero."[51] According to *Time*, he alone surpassed the Mona Lisa and united "hard-court fundamentals with the improvisational creativity of the (inner-city) blacktop."[52] *Sports Illustrated*, which named Jordan 1991 Sportsman of the Year, wrote "The consummate player and the ultimate showman, Michael Jordan has captivated America and is about to conquer the world." A sports agent declared "he has a level of popularity and value as a commercial spokesman that is almost beyond comprehension. It is a singular phenomenon. It never happened before and may not ever happen again."[53]

By 1992, Jordan's $21.75 million in endorsements plus $3.25 million salary made him the world's richest athlete. He endorsed the Illinois State Lottery Commission and a profitable Chicago restaurant bearing his name. Six million Wilson basketballs with his signature had been sold. Nike's Air Jordans remained the world's most profitable sports shoe, and McDonald's named a hamburger the McJordan. In 1988, Jordan became the first basketball player pictured on a Wheaties box and acted as their spokesman. The NBA, Chevrolet, Coca-Cola, Gatorade, Hanes, Johnson Products, Ball Park Franks, Rayovac, MCI, and Bugs Bunny capitalized on his name, too. For many years, he has served as the real-life mascot for Nestlé Crunch, appearing on their products and in their advertising. His fame spread to numerous European, Asian, and Latin American nations through cable and satellites.

## NOTES

1. Mitchell Krugel, *One Last Shot: The Story of Michael Jordan's Comeback* (New York: St. Martin's Press, 2003), p. 50.

2. S. B. Donnelly, "Great Leapin' Lizards," *Time* 133 (January 8, 1989), pp. 50–52.

3. Mitchell Krugel, *Jordan: The Man, His Words, His Life* (New York: St. Martin's Press, 1994), p. 232.

4. Ibid., pp. 232–333.

5. Lynn Norment, "Michael and Juanita Jordan," *Ebony* 47 (November 1991), pp. 72–74.

6. Michael Jordan, ed. by Mark Vancil, *Rare Air: Jordan on Jordan* (San Francisco, CA: Collins Publishers, 1993), p. 67.

7. Ibid., p. 73.

8. Michael Jordan, ed. by Mark Vancil, *I'm Back! More Rare Air* (San Francisco, CA: Collins Publishers, 1995), p. 120.

9. Phil Jackson, *Sacred Hoops: Spiritual Lessons of a Hardwood Warrior* (New York: Hyperion, 1995), p. 172.

10. Ibid., p. 101.

11. Ibid., pp. 100–101.

12. Ibid., p. 101.

13. Sam Smith, *The Jordan Rules: The Inside Story of a Turbulent Season with Michael Jordan and the Chicago Bulls* (New York: Simon & Schuster, 1992) , p. 67.

14. Jackson, *Sacred Hoops*, p. 102.

15. Michael Jordan, ed. by Mark Vancil, *For the Love of the Game: My Story* (New York: Crown Publishers, 1998), p. 47.

16. Krugel, *One Last Shot*, p. 32.

17. Jordan, *Love of Game*, p. 47.

18. Michael Jordan, ed. by Mark Vancil, *Driven from Within* (New York: Atria Books, 2005), p. 93.

19. Smith, *Jordan Rules*, p. 22.

20. David Halberstam, *Playing for Keeps: Michael Jordan and the World He Made* (New York: Random House, 1999), p. 270.

21. Smith, *Jordan Rules*, p. 57.

22. Jackson, *Sacred Hoops*, p. 102.

23. Smith, *Jordan Rules*, p. 124.

24. Bob Greene, *Hang Time; Days and Dreams with Michael Jordan* (New York: Doubleday, 1992), p. 145.

25. Smith, *Jordan Rules*, p. 162.

26. Ibid., p. 168.

27. Ibid., p. 178–179.

28. Jackson, *Sacred Hoops*, p. 141.

29. Greene, *Hang Time*, p. 163.

30. *Chicago Tribune*, June 17, 1991, sec. 7, p. 3.

31. Smith, *Jordan Rules*, p. 226.

32. Greene, *Hang Time*, p. 191.

33. Ibid., p. 223.

34. Smith, *Jordan Rules*, p. 295.

35. Greene, *Hang Time*, p. 234.

36. Ibid., p. 237.

37. Jordan, *Driven from Within*, p. 100.

38. Jackson, *Sacred Hoops*, p. 144.

39. Smith, *Jordan Rules*, p. 302.

40. Greene, *Hang Time*, p. 243.

41. Smith, *Jordan Rules*, p. 312.

42. Craig Carter et al., eds., *The Sporting News Official NBA Guide 1991–92* (St. Louis, MO: The Sporting News, 1991), p. 11.

43. Greene, *Hang Time*, p. 250–251.

44. Carter, *NBA Guide 1991–92*, p. 12.

45. Ibid., p. 11.

46. Jackson, *Sacred Hoops*, p. 145.

47. Carter, *NBA Guide 1991–92*, p. 12.

48. Ibid., p. 10.

49. Jordan, *Driven from Within*, p. 36.

50. Jordan, *Love of Game*, p. 54.

51. Jim Naughton, *Taking to the Air: The Rise of Michael Jordan* (New York: Warner Books, 1992), pp. 10–11.

52. *Time* 137 (June 24, 1991), p. 46.

53. Jack McCallum, "The Everywhere Man," *Sports Illustrated* 75 (December 23, 1991), pp. 65–66.

As a player for the Chicago Bulls, Michael Jordan thrilled crowds with his innovative drives and dunks. Photofest.

Jordan led Chicago to six National Basketball Association titles in the 1990s and won five NBA Most Valuable Player awards. Photofest.

*Jordan remains one of the most popular, best known, and wealthiest athletes in the history of organized sports. Photofest.*

*Jordan accepts the Male Athlete of the Decade award with his son, Marcus, during the eighth annual ESPY Awards show at the MGM Grand Garden Arena in Las Vegas, February 14, 2000. Jordan was also named Athlete of the Century and Pro Basketball Performer of the Decade and became the first athlete to win two of the inaugural ESPY Decade Awards. © Reuters/ CORBIS.*

*As a Washington Wizards guard, Jordan (23) performs his legendary Air Jordan move for one of the last times, driving the lane past New York Knicks forward Clarence Weatherspoon (35) in the fourth quarter of Jordan's last NBA game at New York's Madison Square Garden, March 9, 2003. Jordan scored 39 points, including 19 of Washington's 22 points in a six-minute span of the second quarter, but the Knicks edged the Wizards, 97-96. © Reuters/CORBIS.*

# Chapter 4

# THE TRIUMPHANT AND TRANSITION YEARS, 1991–1995

## THE BULLS REPEAT (1991–1992)

In late 1991, *Chicago Tribune* reporter Sam Smith published an unflattering biography, *The Jordan Rules*, questioning Jordan's mystique. Smith, who had covered Chicago's games for three years, admired Jordan's greatness, but pictured him as a selfish, petulant, demanding perfectionist who criticized teammates when they did not meet his high performance standards and was very conscious of his corporate image.[1] Jordan deplored the book, which gave a distorted image of him, but realized that it showed the public a more human side to Jordan.

Jordan found it increasingly difficult dealing with the press and maintaining a role model image. "The media helps you become famous," he noted, but then "they break you down bit by bit." His major responsibility outside basketball and family was dealing "with the expectations and contradictions that come with being in the spotlight."[2] Jordan tried being a "positive image" and a "positive influence," but told *Sports Illustrated*, "I look forward to playing now, more than ever."[3] It was the only time he could avoid the endless scrutiny into his personal life. He found the basketball court his escape and haven.

Another incident, however, further damaged Jordan's image. In October 1991, Jordan, a lifelong Democrat, upset some teammates by skipping a White House ceremony hosted by President George H. W. Bush to honor Chicago for winning its first NBA title. The media portrayed Jordan as a registered Democrat who did not support the Republican president and reported that he played golf at his Hilton Island, South Carolina retreat. Jordan did not explain why he skipped the celebration.

In 1991, the Bulls enjoyed one of the best starts in NBA history. Chicago boasted virtually the same team except that backup shooting guard Dennis Hopson was replaced by Bobby Hansen. After losing two of its first three games, Chicago amassed 14 consecutive victories from November 6 through December 6. According to Jackson, "the Bulls were in such perfect harmony they rarely lost."[4] Jordan performed like a scoring machine, netting 46 points in a heartbreaking loss at the Milwaukee Bucks on November 2, 40 points in a setback to the visiting Golden State Warriors on November 5, and 46 points in a 132–113 road triumph over the Boston Celtics the next night. Bulls victories followed over the Dallas Mavericks, Orlando Magic, Detroit Pistons, Charlotte Hornets, Milwaukee Bucks, Golden State Warriors, Seattle SuperSonics, Denver Nuggets, and Los Angeles Clippers. His 40 points enabled Chicago to edge the host Portland Trail Blazers, 116–114, in double overtime on November 29.

The Bulls won 11 of 13 games in December to extend their season record to 24 wins and just 4 losses. The victory streak continued with triumphs over the Sacramento Kings, Cleveland Cavaliers, and Charlotte Hornets. The Philadelphia 76ers ended Chicago's run on December 7, edging the visiting Bulls' 103–100. The Los Angeles Lakers was the only other team to defeat Chicago that month, prevailing by 13 points on December 17.

The Bulls captured 13 consecutive victories from January 4 through January 25, elevating their season mark to 38–7. Losses at Milwaukee on January 3, the San Antonio Spurs on January 28, and the Houston Rockets on January 30 were the only blemishes that month. Jordan tallied 44 points in the Milwaukee defeat and 40 points in a 108–106 victory over the Miami Heat five nights later.

Chicago fared 9–4 in February. After defeating the Los Angeles Lakers on February 2, the Bulls endured consecutive road losses to the Utah Jazz in triple overtime on February 3 and Phoenix on February 5. Despite Jordan's 18 points, the West All-Stars trounced the East All-Stars, 153–113, on February 9 at Orlando, Florida. Jordan celebrated his 29th birthday on February 17 with an NBA-season-high 21 baskets and 46 points, but Cleveland nosed Chicago, 113–112.

The Bulls lost just twice in 14 March games to go 59–13 overall. Their lone setbacks came at home in heartbreakers to the Indiana Pacers on March 3 and Orlando, on March 21. Chicago won eight consecutive contests, including six away, from March 5 through March 19. Jordan tallied

40 points in a 90–71 triumph over the New Jersey Nets on March 17 and a season-high 51 points in a 106–100 win over the Washington Bullets. A week later, he netted 50 points in a 116–103 win over Denver at Chicago Stadium. A 44-point encore followed on March 28 in a 126–102 rout over visiting Cleveland. The Bulls won 8 of 10 games in April, falling only to host Boston on April 5 and Cleveland on April 14.

In 1991–1992, Chicago continued its dominance, setting another club record, winning 67 of 82 games. The Bulls registered 10 more victories than any other NBA team, never lost more than two consecutive games, and finished first in the Central Division, 10 games ahead of Cleveland. Assistant coach Johnny Bach proclaimed, "Only the Bulls can beat the Bulls."[5]

Jordan captured his third MVP Award; this was his second consecutive one. His leadership and all-around skills vaulted the Bulls to the fourth-best record in NBA history. Jackson relied on Jordan, along with Cartwright, as the liaisons with the team. Jordan garnered his sixth straight scoring title, but his average dropped to 30.1 points because his teammates enjoyed stellar seasons. Besides notching 50 points twice and four of the top seven NBA scoring performances, he also averaged 6.4 rebounds and 6.1 assists. His awards included making the All-NBA first team for the sixth straight season and the All-Defensive first team for the fifth consecutive time. *Sports Illustrated*'s Jack McCallum wrote that Jordan "stands alone on the mountaintop, unquestionably the most famous athlete on the planet and one of its most famous citizens of any kind."[6]

Scottie Pippen and Horace Grant performed admirably for the Bulls. Pippen, a first-time All-Star starter, averaged 21 points, seven assists, and nearly eight rebounds, even amassing more rebounds and assists than Jordan. Jackson lauded Pippen as an able floor leader and team motivator who kept teammates focused. Grant enjoyed his best season, averaging 14.2 points and nearly 10 rebounds. Bill Cartwright, B. J. Armstrong, and John Paxson also contributed. Armstrong helped younger players behind the scenes, and Paxson was a calming influence in the locker room.

Chicago swept Miami, 3–0, in the first round of the Eastern Conference playoffs. The Bulls thrashed the Heat, 113–94, on April 24 and 120–90 on April 26 at Chicago Stadium and 119–114 at Miami on April 29. Jordan soared for 46 points in Game 1 and a playoff high 56 points in the series finale.

The New York Knicks gave Chicago tougher competition in the Eastern Conference semifinals. The Knicks checked Jordan and Pippen with a big, very physical front line of Patrick Ewing, Charles Oakley, Xavier McDaniel, and Anthony Mason, upsetting the Bulls, 94–89, in Game 1 on May 5 at Chicago Stadium. The Bulls tied the series, 86–78, two nights later, 86–78, and whipped the Knicks, 94–86, in Game 3 on May 9 at Madison Square Garden. Knicks coach Pat Riley complained to reporters that the officials were showing favoritism to Jordan. The Knicks evened the series, 93–86, in Game 4 the next afternoon, not being whistled for shoving players with both hands or tackling dribblers. "Horace (Grant) compared the game to a Wrestling Federation match," and Jordan complained to Jackson "the officiating was so bad it would be impossible to win."[7]

Chicago prevailed, 96–88, in Game 5 on May 12 at Chicago Stadium, but host New York took Game 6, 100–86, two nights later. In the series finale on May 17 at Chicago, Jordan finally penetrated the Knicks' defense for 42 points to eliminate the Knicks in a 110–81 debacle. The Bulls, inspired by Jordan, intensified their defense and accelerated their tempo in the second half.

Pesky Cleveland battled the Bulls in the Eastern Conference Finals. Chicago took Game 1, 103–89, on May 19 at Chicago Stadium, but the Cavaliers overwhelmed the Bulls, 107–81, two nights later. Chicago prevailed, 105–96, in Game 3 on May 23 at Cleveland, but the Cavaliers evened the series, 99–85, two nights later. Chicago dominated Cleveland, 112–89, in Game 5 on May 27 at home and outlasted the Cavaliers, 99–94, on May 29 at Cleveland, to capture the series, four games to two.

The Bulls faced Portland, an open-court team with impressive play-off triumphs over Los Angeles, Phoenix, and Utah. The media considered Portland guard Clyde Drexler, who had finished second to Jordan in the MVP voting, a better rebounder, three-point shooter, and perhaps better passer. Jordan avoided saying anything to provoke Drexler, instead using the comparisons to motivate himself. He regarded Drexler a less complete player and recalled that Portland had not even drafted him in 1984. Jordan also ranked far better defensively and among the best NBA jump shooters. "Clyde," he noted, "had been seen as a version of me, not necessarily a better version."[8]

In Game 1 on June 3 at Chicago Stadium, Drexler allowed Jordan the outside shot. Jordan tied an NBA Finals mark, draining six consecutive three-pointers, tallying a record 35 first half points, and giving Chicago a commanding 66–51 lead. He finished with 39 points in the 122–89 romp, the 33-point victory margin falling just two shy of the NBA Finals standard. His three-point explosion surprised him because he had converted only 27 three-pointers the entire regular season. "Sometimes I fascinate myself," he disclosed. "I can't explain it. I just felt good and I kept shooting. I got into a zone."[9] Defensively, Jordan denied Drexler the ball.

Chicago appeared headed toward another home victory two nights later, leading, 92–82, with 4 minutes and 36 seconds left. The Trail Blazers forced the game into overtime and triumphed, 115–104, as reserve guard Danny Ainge scored an NBA Finals record-tying nine overtime points. Portland launched its comeback after Drexler, its leading scorer with 26 points, fouled out. Jordan paced the Bulls with 39 points, but no teammate exceeded 16 points.

The series moved to Portland's Memorial Coliseum for the next three games. Chicago's defense stifled the Trail Blazers in Game 3 on June 7. Jordan led the Bulls with 26 points in a 94–84 victory; Pippen contributed 18 points, eight rebounds, and seven assists. Portland evened the series in Game 4 three days later, scoring 19 of the final 27 points in a dramatic 93–88 comeback victory, as Chicago blew another substantial lead. Drexler and Jerome Kersey paced the Trail Blazers with 21 points apiece. Jordan topped the Bulls with 32 points, but uncharacteristically did not score in the final 10 minutes. Chicago regained home advantage with a 119–106 victory in Game 5 on June 12, enjoying first-half runs of 10–0, 7–0, and 12–4. Jordan exploded for 46 points and Pippen added 24 points, 11 rebounds, and 9 assists.

The Bulls won the NBA crown, 97–93, in Game 6 two nights later, launching the biggest fourth-quarter comeback in NBA Finals history. Chicago trailed 79–64 entering the final period, but held Portland to 14 points. The Bulls' starters were exhausted. Jordan rested at the start of the quarter, as Pippen and four reserves outscored the Trail Blazers, 14–2. The reserves, who had struggled earlier in the playoffs, erased a 17-point deficit. Jordan reentered with 8 minutes and 36 seconds left and collaborated with Pippen to score the Bulls' last 19 points. Twelve of his game-high 33 points, including Chicago's final six points, came that period. To Jackson's delight, the entire team contributed significantly to the triumph.

The Bulls became only the fourth NBA team to win two consecutive championships, joining the elite Minneapolis-Los Angeles Lakers, Boston, and Detroit. Those teams, however, depended less on a single player. Two inexplicable Chicago fourth-quarter collapses made the series appear much closer. The Trail Blazers committed too many turnovers and performed too inconsistently to dethrone the Bulls. Jordan conceded that Portland performed tough physically, but lacked the mental fiber to succeed. "Winning two or three titles in a row was always more mental than physical,"[10] he contended.

Jordan, who dominated the series, became the first player to win the NBA Finals MVP during consecutive seasons. He outplayed Drexler, averaging 35.8 points, second-highest for a six-game series. "Going into the series, I thought Michael had 2,000 moves," Drexler remarked. "I was wrong. He has 3,000." "To see him up close like this for a long series, you realize how great he is," Portland forward Buck Williams observed. "He is the best there ever was. No question about it. When they need him, he produces. You can't stop him. The pressure on him is unbelievable but he still comes through."[11] In 22 postseason games, Jordan averaged 34.6 points.

The team celebration lasted several hours. After locker room ceremonies, the players returned to the Chicago Stadium court with the trophy and displayed it to the crowd. Jordan, cigar in mouth, and his teammates elatedly jumped and danced on the scorer's table, convincing themselves that the first NBA crown was no accident. He dedicated this title to his teammates and coaches.

Jordan's commercial success also continued. During the 1992 Super Bowl, Nike ads teamed him with Bugs Bunny on a basketball court. Critics rated "Hare Jordan" the game's best advertisement. Nike CEO Phil Knight said, "We invested in six months worth of drawings and a million dollars in production costs to show Michael Jordan, probably the most visible representative of Nike, paired with a cartoon character."[12] Air Jordan still dominated the basketball shoe market.

Commercially, Jordan transcended all groups in racially and ethnically divided Chicago, showing concern for the needy, especially African Americans. He worked for the United Negro College Fund, Special Olympics, Ronald McDonald House Charities, and Starlight Foundation, which assists terminally ill children. In 1989, Deloris helped him establish the Michael Jordan Foundation to contribute to these and other philanthropies.

Jordan, meanwhile, protested that tabloids were invading his privacy by disclosing his cash wagers on the golf course. In 1991–1992, authorities seized $200,000, including a $57,000 check to Jordan, from cocaine dealer James Bouler, who associated with star athletes. Bouler claimed that Jordan loaned him the money to purchase a golf driving range, but police concluded the check covered his losses during high-stakes poker and golf matches at his Hilton Head, South Carolina retreat in October 1991.

Jordan's name also was linked to bail bondsman Eddie Dow. Dow, a nightclub businessman, often carried a stainless steel briefcase full of cash to work. In February 1992, four men murdered Dow and took $20,000 from his briefcase. They left three checks totaling $108,000 from Jordan for his Hilton Head losses. Jordan and Dow frequently had bet a thousand dollars per hole in their golf matches.

Sportswriters criticized Jordan for associating with these figures while betting considerable money. Jordan admitted making a "mistake" meeting with them, but defended his "right to associate with whoever I choose. There's nothing wrong with friendly wagers between friends."[13] He admitted, "The way I had been perceived up to that point really wasn't reality."[14] These incidents did not hinder his basketball performance or diminish his market value. Friends argued that betting gave him a release for his competitive, addictive instincts. The Bulls even switched to a private jet for away games after Jordan and his teammates upset other commercial passengers with their noise and card gambling.

After an investigation of Jordan's betting activities, the NBA in March 1992 concluded that he did not have a gambling problem and declared him innocent of any wrongdoing. The Beaufort, South Carolina Sheriff's Department believed that Jordan appeared to violate the law, but did not press charges because the incident had occurred a year earlier and no one had brought charges against him. Jordan apologized. "The letting down of people is something I don't want to encounter again," he disclosed.[15]

In October 1992, Jordan testified at Bouler's drug and money-laundering trial in Charlotte, North Carolina. He admitted that his $57,000 check to Bouler was payment for gambling debts from the October 1991 weekend. Jordan did not want the American public to learn about his activities. The U.S. Attorney did not want to grill Jordan on the witness stand because an intense examination might irritate the jury from his home state, where he remained very popular.

## OLYMPIC DREAM TEAM ODYSSEY (1992)

In 1992, the United States assembled its greatest basketball team ever at the Barcelona, Spain Olympic Games. The games spread Jordan's fame abroad because the worldwide media focused on the American Dream Team. For the first time, professional players from the United States were allowed to participate in the Olympics. Jordan did not relish playing because he had experienced two exhausting championship seasons. He needed time to rest and retreat from the public limelight. Jordan did not want to sacrifice time with his family or on the golf course during an off-season already shortened by the playoffs, but he realized that the games would showcase him, his teammates, the NBA, and basketball. He yielded to patriotic duty and the wishes of his corporate sponsors and the NBA front office, which used the Olympics to promote the NBA and Jordan's potent image to a broadening international market of basketball fans. He looked forward to being with Larry Bird, Magic Johnson, and the other stars. The NBA players relished participating on the greatest basketball contingent ever assembled.

Bird and Johnson captained the Dream Team. Jordan had become the most dominant NBA player by 1992, having led Chicago to two straight championships. Coach Chuck Daly wanted him to serve as tri-captain, but he deferred to Bird and Johnson because they had been the NBA leaders for more than a decade. The Dream Team also boasted NBA stars Charles Barkley, Scottie Pippen, Patrick Ewing, David Robinson, John Stockton, Karl Malone, and Chris Mullin. "This team has a mystique of quality built up over 15 years," Daly said. "You have Magic, Michael, and Larry. It won't be like this again." "This is the best team ever assembled," Barkley chimed. "I get amazed every day at the things I see. Whatever you want or need, we've got."[16]

Jordan enjoyed best the Dream Team practices. Pippen, Bird, Ewing, Mullin, and he played intense practice games against Johnson, Malone, Drexler, Barkley, and Robinson. After Johnson's team built a 14–0 lead over his squad, Jordan quickly took over the game, driving to the basket to score 12 consecutive points, rebounded tenaciously, stepped in the passing lanes for steals, and hounded Johnson defensively. Jordan's team assumed a 10-point lead and won, 36–30. The quality and intensity of play amazed Daly. Reporter Jan Hubbard queried Jordan as to why he was so obsessed with winning. Jordan smiled, "I try to make a habit out of it."[17]

The Dream Team breezed to a gold medal at the Barcelona Olympics, winning 14 games by 43.8 points per contest and always triumphing by at least 32 points. Team USA routed Croatia by 68 points and Lithuania by 51 points, and overwhelmed Croatia, 117–85, in the gold medal game. No foreign aggregate challenged the truly remarkable Dream Team.

A shoe controversy embroiled Jordan. The Dream Team was supposed to wear red, white, and blue U.S. warm-up suits with a Reebok logo on the medal podium. Jordan and Barkley, who endorsed Nike shoes, initially declined to wear the Reebok logo. "I don't believe in endorsing my competition," Jordan declared. "I feel very strongly about loyalty to my own company."[18] Several sportswriters criticized his decision. Shortly before the award ceremony, Jordan, Barkley, and Pippen went into the stands and collected American flags. When the Dream Team received their gold medals before an estimated 600 million television viewers from 193 countries, Jordan stood up for his convictions by draping himself in the U.S. flag to hide the Reebok emblem.

The Dream Team became the world's most renowned athletes in a rapidly internationalized sport. They resided in high-security seclusion rather than the Olympic Village. Throngs surrounded the American players wherever they went. The media and public particularly hounded Jordan. One Japanese writer asked him, "Mr. Jordan, how does it feel to be God?"[19] More than 200 people watched Jordan and Julius Erving golf at a Pyrenees Mountains course. Pippen attained superstar status at the Olympics, excelling both offensively and defensively.

## THE THIRD TIME'S THE CHARM (1992–1993)

Propelled by his talent, titles, commercials, and Olympic fame, Jordan became an icon of almost unrivaled national and international fame. He competed with himself as his fame grew. As his success magnified, the expectations Jordan created intensified. The greater his challenges, the harder he tried to excel. Jordan possessed the intelligence, inner fortitude, and concentration to handle these mounting pressures and realized that basketball generated his success, finding true peace in the game.

The Bulls looked mentally and physically fatigued at the October 1992 training camp. Jackson's cohesive unit was unraveling. Jordan and Pippen were exhausted after a two-year grind that included two NBA titles and an Olympic gold medal and practiced just once daily during the first week. Jordan, who also faced off-court distractions, already had told his father, James, that he needed a respite and contemplated retiring after the Bulls captured their second consecutive NBA title. The lure of a third straight title, something that neither Bird nor Johnson had ever accomplished, enticed him to play one more season.

The Bulls hoped to become the first team since the 1960s to capture three consecutive NBA titles, but that dream seemed unlikely. Several players missed part of training camp. Jordan and Pippen were fatigued, and Cartwright and Paxson underwent off-season surgeries for back and knee problems. Grant protested the special treatment accorded to Jordan and Pippen, and Armstrong wanted more playing time. Cliff Levingston and Craig Hodges had departed.

Chicago won its season debut at Cleveland, 101–96, on November 6, but lost its home opener to the Atlanta Hawks, 100–99, the next night. The Bulls captured six consecutive victories, including an overtime 98–96 home thriller over Detroit on November 11. Jordan confidently believed that he could always deliver regardless how insurmountable the situation. After taking an inbounds pass at halfcourt with four seconds left in overtime against Detroit, he dribbled twice, pulled up on Joe Dumars, and buried a running three-pointer to lift Chicago to victory.

The Los Angeles Lakers ended the Bulls winning streak on November 20, but Jordan tallied 54 points in the narrow overtime road loss. His torrid shooting pace continued in successive road victories, with 40 points against the Phoenix Suns on November 22 and 49 points against Golden State two nights later. After falling to the New York Knicks and Boston, Chicago returned home to defeat Portland and Boston. Dominique Wilkins outscored Jordan 43 points to 32 points for victorious Atlanta on December 8.

The Bulls took 11 of their next 13 games from December 9 through January 2, boosting their record to 22–7. Their only losses came to Houston and Philadelphia at home. At Chicago Stadium, Jordan notched 57 points in a 107–98 victory over Washington on December 23 and 42 points in an 89–77 win over New York on Christmas night before an NBC television audience. Thirty-nine-point performances followed against Miami on December 30 and Indiana four nights later.

January marked the only losing month for Chicago, which took only 7 of 15 contests. On January 16, Jordan greeted Shaquille O'Neal of Orlando in his first ever visit to Chicago Stadium with an NBA-season best 64 points. He made an NBA-season high 27 baskets, but his late-game turnover forced overtime and an eventual 128–124 setback. The Bulls trailed San Antonio decisively in the second half eight nights later when Jordan told his teammates to quicken the pace. He finished with 42 points, helping slice the deficit to four points.

Chicago compiled 10 victories in February, suffering only consecutive home losses to New York and Cleveland. On February 10, Jordan's 40 points sparked the Bulls to a 115–104 triumph at Indiana. At the All-Star break, Chicago owned a 35–17 record. Jordan paced the East All-Stars with 30 points in the All-Star Game at Salt Lake City, Utah on February 21; but the West prevailed, 135–132, in overtime.

The Bulls remained torrid in March, capturing 10 of 14 contests. Jordan tallied 52 points in a 123–108 rout of Charlotte on March 12 at Chicago Stadium and 47 points in a 126–101 conquest at Washington on March 20. Four nights later, he recorded 43 points in a 113–100 win at Philadelphia. Despite his 44 points, Phoenix squeaked by Chicago on March 30.

In April, Chicago reeled off nine victories in 13 games. Jordan netted 40 points and an NBA-season-high nine steals in a 118–105 win over New Jersey on April 2 and 47 points in a 119–105 victory over Milwaukee on April 16 at Chicago Stadium.

The Bulls finished 1992–1993 with 57 victories, eight fewer than the previous season. "We staggered through the season,"[20] Jackson explained. Despite 25 losses, however, Chicago repeated as Central Division titlists, three games ahead of Cleveland. Besides remaining tough and confident, the Bulls performed well in clutch games, fared very well on the road, and knew how to finish games.

Jordan captured his seventh consecutive NBA scoring crown, averaging 32.6 points. He became the best closer in NBA history, wanting his teammates to pass him the ball at crunch time. Jordan scored at least 40 points 14 times and at least 50 points 4 times. He repeated as steals leader, with 2.83 per contest, and averaged 6.7 rebounds and 5.5 assists. When one reporter asked him about his scoring prowess, Jordan reminded the media that he had led the NBA in steals again. Jordan again made the All-NBA first team and All-Defensive team. Pippen also proved invaluable, averaging 18.6 points and ranking 10th in steals.

Chicago began its quest for a third straight title, sweeping Atlanta in the first playoff round, 114–90 on April 30 and 117–102 on May 2 at Chicago Stadium and 98–88 on May 4 at Atlanta. In the next round, the Bulls eliminated Cleveland, 91–84 on May 11, 104–85 on May 13 at home, 96–90 on May 15, and 103–101 on May 17 at Cleveland.

New York held home advantage in the Eastern Conference Finals, having compiled three more victories than Chicago. The Knicks defeated the Bulls 98–90 on May 23 and 96–91 on May 25 at Madison Square Garden, endangering prospects for a third consecutive crown. Although Jordan scored 36 points in Game 2, New York played very physically and did not permit Chicago players to roam. When the series moved to Chicago Stadium, the Bulls prevailed 103–83 on May 29 and 105–95 on May 31. Jordan tallied 54 points, 51 percent of Chicago's total in Game 4. In Game 5 at New York two nights later, Chicago outlasted the Knicks, 97–94. The Bulls eliminated New York, 96–88, in Game 6 on June 4 at home, taking the grueling series, four games to two. Jackson claimed that losing the home advantage gave the players extra motivation.

Chicago entered the NBA Finals with an advantage against Phoenix, having faced intense physical pressure from the Knicks. The Suns held the home court advantage because they boasted five more victories than the Bulls. The series attracted among the largest television audiences in NBA history because of the heralded match-up between Jordan and Barkley, who had ended his streak of consecutive NBA MVP seasons. Jordan's perceived slighting in the MVP balloting fueled his competitive fire. Jackson believed Chicago needed to split the first two games at America West Arena, but Jordan predicted that the Bulls would win both games there. Jordan, who usually preferred to lead with action rather than words, fired up his teammates on the flight to Phoenix, imploring them to perform at a championship level. He believed that the Suns lacked the experience to win critical playoff games.

Jordan's message paid dividends. Phoenix became the first team in NBA Finals history to drop the opening two games at home. Chicago, benefiting from single coverage and freedom to roam, defeated the Suns 100–92 on June 9 and 111–108 on June 11. In Game 1, the Bulls cruised to a 34–20 first-quarter lead on Grant's 11 points and widened the margin to 19 points by halftime. The Suns sliced the lead to 88–85 with 4 minutes and 25 seconds left, but Jordan made 14 of his game-high 31 points in the final period. "It's all about history now," he proclaimed. "We're here to make history."[21]

In Game 2 on June 11, Jordan and Grant helped Chicago bolt to a 57–43 first-half lead. Phoenix inched ahead briefly in the fourth quarter, but the Bulls quickly regained control for a 111–108 triumph. Jordan tallied 42 points, 12 rebounds, and 9 assists, and Grant contributed a career playoff high 24 points. Pippen recorded a triple-double with 15 points, 12 rebounds, and 12 assists. Barkley countered with 42 points, but Phoenix could not handle Chicago's three-pronged assault.

The Suns shocked the Bulls by winning two of the three Chicago Stadium contests, including a 129–121 triple overtime marathon on June 13 in Game 3. Dan Majerle's six three-pointers and point guard Kevin Johnson's superb defense against Jordan proved crucial. After Jordan wearied several Suns defenders, Johnson shadowed him in the fourth quarter and overtimes. Jordan missed 15 of his last 24 shots, including 9 of 10 in the fourth quarter when Phoenix built a 99–88 lead. Grant's three-pointer tied the score at 103–103 and sent the game into overtime. Although netting 44 points, Jordan took 49 shots and missed a critical free throw in the first overtime. Johnson paced the Suns with 25 points.

Jordan dominated Game 4 on June 16, attaining a career NBA Finals-high 55 points. He scored 33 of Chicago's 61 first-half points, including 22 in the second quarter. Jordan drove past Johnson and around Barkley, moved the ball while in the air, and scored the decisive basket with 13 seconds left. His three-point play gave the Bulls a 111–106 victory and 3–1 series lead. Jordan outperformed Majerle nearly every time he handled the ball offensively. He did not want the Bulls to squander the golden opportunity to clinch another title. Although Jordan scored 41 points two nights later, Phoenix surprised listless Chicago, 108–98, in Game 5 at Chicago.

The Bulls seemed downcast boarding the plane for Phoenix. "It was a lot like a morgue," Chicago broadcaster Johnny Kerr recalled. Jordan hopped on the plane wearing dark glasses and smoking a huge cigar. "Hello, World Champs," he bellowed, "Let's go to Phoenix and kick some ass."[22] The player mood shifted instantly.

Jordan flew his family to Phoenix for Game 6. Chicago vaulted to an 11-point, second-quarter lead and was ahead, 87–79, after three quarters. The Bulls inexplicably missed their first nine fourth-quarter shots, going scoreless for nearly six minutes. The Suns moved ahead, 98–94, with 2 minutes and 23 seconds remaining. Chicago tallied only 12 fourth-quarter points, the least ever recorded for that period in the NBA Finals. Although his teammates were tense and unfocused, Jordan remained composed and scored the Bulls' first seven points of the quarter.

When Jackson called a timeout in the final minute, Jordan calmly agreed to seize the initiative. He ignited the surge with a driving layup to slice Phoenix's lead to 98–96. After Majerle unloaded an air ball, Grant passed the ball to a wide-open Paxson outside the three-point arc, carrying the triangle system to perfection. Jackson lauded him for making "a selfless play instead of trying to be a hero." Paxson converted the game-winning three-pointer with 3.9 seconds left to give Chicago a 99–98 lead, remarking, "this was the one that really counted." Jackson beamed, "In that split second all the pieces came together."[23] Grant blocked a last-second shot to preserve the victory, but Jordan had made possible the Bulls' third consecutive NBA title. He led the Bulls with 33 points, and Pippen contributed 21 points. Chicago set an NBA Finals record 10 three-pointers.

Jordan retrieved the basketball and raised it high above his head. No public teary displays followed. Jordan bolted to the chapel at America West Arena and prayed. He had wanted to make history by winning three consecutive NBA championships. NBA legends Johnson, Bird, and Isaiah Thomas never accomplished that feat. The Bulls became the first NBA team since the 1960s Boston Celtics to capture three straight NBA crowns. Jordan became the first player in NBA history to win three consecutive NBA Finals MVP awards, setting an NBA Finals record with a 41.0 point average.

Before celebrating with his teammates, Jordan taped a commercial for McDonald's on the court. A voice in the commercial said, "Michael, you've just won your third straight NBA championship. Are you hungry for a fourth?" He smiled, "I'm hungry for a Big Mac."[24] The advertisement was quickly fed by satellites to cable stations.

Jordan had attained a remarkable legacy. Johnson still held two more NBA titles, but won his with Kareem Abdul-Jabbar and James Worthy. Bird achieved his NBA championships with Robert Parish and Kevin McHale. Thomas might not have earned his two crowns without Joe Dumars. The third title did not come easily for fatigued Jordan. "Winning three in a row," he insisted, "was the hardest thing I've ever done in the game of basketball."[25]

By 1993, Jordan had reached the pinnacle of the basketball and business worlds. He had helped commissioner David Stern build the NBA into top-dollar entertainment. Jordan had become Chicago's most famous figure and the sport's most recognizable name, a marketable commodity so vast that Chicago cable television station WGN won a suit allowing it to televise more Bulls' games. Don Pierson of the *Chicago Tribune* wrote that Jordan was "The world's most visible athlete,"[26] and John Skorburg, Chicagoland Chamber of Commerce economist, pegged his value to the region at around $1 billion. The Bulls' value had risen from $18.7 million in 1985 to $200 million by 1993. Gatorade, Nike, and Hanes underwear signed Jordan to be their principal endorser until 2002.

During the 1993 Eastern Conference Finals, meanwhile, troubling newspaper stories resurfaced about Jordan's gambling activities. Jordan had enjoyed wagering since his North Carolina days, where he had bet in drills and horse games in basketball practice. After joining Chicago, he gambled with teammates on horse games in basketball practice and numerous card games on road trips. Gambling fulfilled his competitive instincts and relieved him from daily pressures. Jordan possessed a compulsive desire to win and always thought he could win. He considered himself a much better golfer than he actually was, often wagering $100 a hole and occasionally $1,000 a hole. If Jordan lost, he often continued playing and upped the stakes. "Michael doesn't have a gambling problem," his father James insisted, "he has a competitiveness problem."[27] None of his gambling involved basketball games. Jordan disliked constantly having to defend his personal actions and thought that some people expected too much of him.

Just before Game 2 of the 1993 Eastern Conference Finals, reporters learned that Jordan had spent the latter part of May 24 betting on blackjack at an Atlantic City, New Jersey casino. Jordan supposedly had lost $5,000 in a private pit the casino reserved for him and had gambled until 2:30 A. M., an allegation he vehemently refuted. Jordan insisted that he returned to his New York City hotel by 1 A. M. and slept sufficiently before Game 2. He needed to relax during the pressure-packed playoffs, but he could not remain in his New York hotel suite long because the telephone kept ringing. Jordan could not frequent Manhattan establishments because of his fame. He told former teammate Levingston that he would give a million dollars if he could walk down the street incognito.

Sportswriter Mike Lupica defended Jordan's right to privacy. "He's let no one down," Lupica wrote. Lupica prophesied that Jordan "will get tired of all this and walk away, and it will feel like he took the whole sport with him."[28] Jordan refused to talk with the media he believed mistreated him over the Atlantic City episode and let his father handle all press interviews for the remainder of the series. The NBA office fined Jordan and the Bulls $25,000 for boycotting the press, but he skipped media interviews until after Game 1 of the NBA Finals.

In late June, San Diego sports executive Richard Esquinas self-published, *Michael and Me: Our Gambling Addiction*. Esquinas claimed that he had won $1.25 million from Jordan during a 10-day golf and card-playing marathon. Jordan accumulated the large debt primarily because of betting double or nothing. According to Esquinas, Jordan negotiated the debt down to $300,000.[29] Although admitting knowing Esquinas, Jordan initially labeled the $300,000 figure "preposterous."[30] He eventually confirmed the figure.

The media raised troubling questions about Jordan. They wondered if he had violated NBA regulations by giving Bouler or Esquinas inside information on NBA basketball contests. Jordan adamantly denied that he had ever gambled on NBA games. The NBA examined the allegations and agreed that Jordan had not broken NBA rules. Reporters also criticized his selection of golf and poker associates. Jordan acknowledged needing to choose his golf companions more carefully.

## PERSONAL TRAGEDY (1993)

In July 1993, tragedy struck Jordan's family. His parents had moved in 1985 to Charlotte, North Carolina to be closer to a major airport. After attending the funeral of a friend in Wilmington, James drove the evening of July 22–23 toward Charlotte, where he planned to board a plane to Chicago to see Jordan. Somewhat tired, he pulled off Route 74 near Lumberton to rest. Daniel Green and Larry Demery, both 18-year-olds, robbed him and shot him once through the chest, killing him instantly. The murderers panicked when they discovered who their victim was, drove his auto 30 miles across the South Carolina line, and dropped his body in a swamp. They aimlessly drove for three days before abandoning the car in Fayetteville, North Carolina. A fisherman located James's largely decayed body on August 13. Officials connected his body with the abandoned car. The murderers were nabbed because they had used the car's cellular phone. Demery ironically wore a Jordan T-shirt when arrested. Green and Demery, who both had criminal records, were charged with the crime, convicted, and sentenced to life in prison.

The tragedy came at a trying time in Jordan's career. The murder devastated Jordan, who had built a close relationship with his father. After Jordan had become a Bulls' star, James had retired from his General

Electric post and often visited Michael in Chicago. His father's warm, friendly, amiable personality relieved Jordan of some pressure. "He was my best friend," Jordan eulogized. "He was a people person and he had a great sense of humor. He taught me a lot about life."[31] Jordan realized that he now had to make his own decisions without James. He kept his composure at the funeral until leaving the church and then he sobbed. He disliked the way the media reported the funeral and distrusted them thereafter.

Jordan, who had achieved his ultimate basketball goal in the 1993 NBA Finals, considered retirement for various reasons. He needed new challenges because the Bulls had overcome Detroit and accomplished the fabled third straight title. Jordan had silenced critics, who considered him a great individual rather than team player. "I knew it was time to move on," he realized. Jordan had lost his enthusiasm and motivation for playing basketball, having tired of the burden of being the sport's marquee figure and the grind of NBA life. Johnson and Bird had retired and Shaquille O'Neal had not become a superstar. The Dream Team run, nagging injuries, the onus of defending the NBA crown, and the quest for a third consecutive crown had drained him physically and mentally. Jordan's obsession to excel also exhausted him, as he had shot more often than any season since 1986–1987 and had scored prolifically in the post-season. He also seemed more aloof and less radiant in practices. He had lost his enthusiasm for practice and daily competition.

Disagreements with teammates contributed to his retirement decision. Grant had complained about Jordan's salary, which also strained the latter's relationship with Pippen. "There was a lot of jealousy on the Bulls by the end of that third championship season," Jordan lamented. "They'd talk about how I never was anything until they came around," he added. "I was just fed up with all of it."[32] Jordan's concern about the gambling disclosures and his father's murder may have affected his decision.

## JORDAN'S PURSUIT OF
## THE FIELD OF DREAMS (1993–1995)

At the same time, Jordan discussed his aspiration to try baseball. Playing professional baseball was his longtime dream. He considered baseball his favorite sport as a boy and often discussed it with his father, who had shared similar sentiments. James regarded baseball as Jordan's best sport and encouraged him to pursue it as a youngster. The sport had connected them when Jordan played Little League. Jordan had not played the sport since the 1980, during his senior year at Emsley A. Laney High School in Wilmington. He wanted to continue with baseball at North Carolina, but Smith nixed that idea. Jordan began receiving invitations to play for minor league teams in the early 1990s, but he did not have enough time during the off-season to accept. In January 1992, he told writer David Halberstam about wanting to play major league baseball. Jordan and James also discussed the idea that spring. He was ready to spend the summer of 1992 on baseball, but the Olympics and the quest for the third consecutive title that had eluded Bird and Johnson delayed his plans.

During the 1992–1993 season, Jordan reached his decision to retire. He informed Dean Smith in April 1993 that he was leaving basketball and waited for the right time to announce his decision. When the Bulls clinched the 1993 NBA Finals at Phoenix, Jordan told his family that he planned to quit basketball and play baseball instead. After the playoffs, he also let owner Jerry Reinsdorf know that he wanted to play baseball. Reinsdorf, who had known of Jordan's interest in baseball, persuaded him to take the summer before deciding what to do. "Neither one of us wanted to make a spectacle out of my desire to play,"[33] Jordan recalled.

Jordan started working out in August with former Chicago White Sox player Bill Melton and trainer Herm Schneider and the next month asked Jackson to give him a reason to continue playing basketball. Jackson replied that Jordan had a responsibility to use his God-given gift to benefit others. Jordan countered that he would retire sometime anyway: "God is telling me to move on. . . . People have to learn that nothing lasts forever."[34] Jackson did not give him a compelling reason for him to continue playing basketball. "And, I didn't have one, either,"[35] Jordan remembered.

When news leaked in October about his workouts, Jordan told teammates that he was quitting basketball. In a dramatic press conference at the Berto Center on October 6, he officially announced his departure from the Bulls. Jordan had lost his desire to play the game and declared, "I have nothing more to prove in basketball."[36] He denied that media pressure influenced his decision; he just wanted to pursue other endeavors and spend more time with his family and friends. Jordan relished recapturing his privacy and living in suburban Chicago away from media scrutiny. "Five years down the line, if the urge comes back, if the Bulls will have me, if David Stern lets me back in the league," he indicated, "I may come back."[37] When asked to name his special contribution to basketball, Jordan jokingly said his wagging tongue. At just 30 years old, he exited the game on his own terms at the pinnacle of his skills. His announcement sent shock waves throughout the NBA and appeared in front-page newspaper headlines worldwide. Not since fullback Jim Brown retired from the Cleveland Browns in 1965 had such a dominant athlete left a sport in his prime.

The media speculated that Jordan's gambling revelations and father's death had influenced his decision. An NBA investigation of his betting activities cleared him of any wrongdoing. Jordan switched to baseball while still grieving for his father, wanting to find solace by returning to another time.

Baseball proved more challenging than Jordan had anticipated. Jordan gave pitchers a sizable strike zone without having any compensating power and needed to retool his body and reflexes relatively late in his career. He was prepared to start in the minor leagues, but declared, "I always considered myself a great all-around athlete and I believed I could do anything if I set my mind to it. I was serious about making the White Sox team."[38]

Jordan signed a minor league contract for $1,200 a month with the Chicago White Sox, owned by Jerry Reinsdorf. In February 1994, he joined several Chicago players in walking through fielding drills at the Illinois Institute of Technology basketball court. When the White Sox began spring training in Florida later that month, 250 reporters saw Jordan take batting practice the first day. He was assigned to the Class AA Birmingham Barons of the Southern League, two levels below the major leagues.

Jordan found minor league life much more challenging than NBA life. In the NBA, he resided in suites at the Plaza and ordered room service lunches. With the Birmingham team, he lived in an ordinary room at the La Quinta Inn and ate peanut butter and jelly sandwiches in the clubhouse. The Barons dressed in small, humid locker rooms; received minimal meal money; and took lengthy bus rides. A decade older than some teammates, Jordan earned far more than their $850 monthly salary and $16 daily meal money. He also made an estimated $30 million in endorsements and $4 million in Bulls salary. Jordan initially traveled by private car, but bought the team a luxurious bus to travel to road games. He found the attitude of his teammates refreshing. Jordan had attained his dreams and financial security. "But these guys, they didn't have anything," he noted, "and they were the happiest guys in the world. . . . They were so pure, their dreams so real. They were fun to be around."[39]

Birmingham's home attendance soared, but Jordan struggled. Although his speed and base-running skills approached major league standards, his hitting and fielding barely reached Double-A standards. Jordan labored diligently to elevate his game at spring training, swinging a 34-ounce bat 300 or 400 times daily at 6 A. M. sessions and taking extra batting practice with hitting coach Walt Hriniak before and after the team practice. He batted around .300 the first month and enjoyed a 13-game hitting streak, but his average plunged when pitchers began throwing him more curves and sliders. Jordan swung awkwardly at breaking balls and possessed disappointing bat speed. *Sports Illustrated* advised, "Bag It, Michael! Jordan and the White Sox are Embarrassing Baseball."[40]

Jordan nearly quit midway through the season after striking out four times at Memphis, the last on three straight sliders with the bases loaded and two outs in the ninth inning. "I looked like a damn windmill," he recalled. "That was the lowest point."[41] Jordan asked manager Terry Francona if he had made the correct decision in opting to play baseball. He did not want to waste either his or the club's time. Francona assured him that every player experiences slumps and encouraged him to work through that stage. Jordan adopted a more natural swing and even enjoyed one memorable exhibition game for the White Sox in the annual Crosstown Classic against the Chicago Cubs at Wrigley Field, doubling and singling with two runs batted in. He gradually improved, hitting .259 the last month and exhibiting more power.

Jordan did not conquer the baseball world, batting only .202 with three home runs, 51 runs batted in, and 30 stolen bases, and striking out 114 times in 436 at bats in 1994. He did not have the reflexes to hit a 90-mile an hour breaking pitch and lacked strength in his thighs and legs, areas where baseball players usually get their power. An outfielder, he possessed a below-average arm and led the Southern League with 11 errors. On the other hand, only five other Southern Leaguers matched his 50 RBIs and 30 stolen bases. Jordan led Birmingham with 11 RBIs when the bases were loaded and 25 RBIs with runners in scoring position and two outs. His basketball frame did not adapt well to baseball, but he appeared more relaxed and relished freedom from the burdens of being a basketball legend. The baseball odyssey let him regain his innocence and examine his priorities.

In the 1994 Arizona Fall League, Jordan batted .252 and struck out once every four at bats for the Scottsdale Scorpions against rookie and minor league hurlers. His presence, however, enabled Scottsdale to attract 87 percent of the league's total attendance.

Jordan's basketball hiatus did not hinder his marketing skills. He remained articulate and retained his legendary status. In 1994, *Forbes* reported that Jordan led athletes in income for the third consecutive year. His marketing prowess remained undiminished because of his advertisements and the media frenzy surrounding him. Nike's annual sales rose to more than $4 billion while profits exploded. Those profits partly emanated from the $18 million Nike paid Jordan annually for his endorsement. McDonald's and Wheaties paid him $3 million annually, Sara Lee approximately $4 million, and Gatorade $2 million.

During 1994, Jordan did not completely forget basketball. He played occasional Sunday morning pickup basketball games with Birmingham teammates. B. J. Armstrong updated him about Chicago and the NBA. The Bulls moved across Madison Street from Chicago Stadium to the fancy $175 million United Center. The landmark Chicago Stadium had been an intimidating place for opponents and referees in crucial games with its loud crowd noise; the new United Center drew a far wealthier, less noisy audience.

In the last Chicago Stadium contest on September 9, Jordan participated in Scottie Pippen's annual charity basketball game to benefit Operation PUSH/Excel. After practicing intensively for a week at the Berto Center with Pippen and other former Bulls teammates, he dominated the game, making 24 of 46 shots for 52 points. Besides dunking the ball on a drive, Jordan converted a 15-foot fallaway jumper over Pippen. Pippen observed, "it didn't seem like he has lost anything."[42]

Chicago recognized Jordan's drawing power by placing a landmark one-ton bronze statue of him at the main entrance of the United Center. The statue displayed him in Nike shoes soaring through the air over a figure similar to Detroit Pistons center Bill Laimbeer, preparing to dunk the ball. The inscription read

**Michael Jordan Chicago Bulls 1984–1993**
The best there ever was
The best there ever will be[43]

The Bulls officially sponsored Jordan's retirement party on November 1, nearly 13 months after he quit basketball, at the United Center. This celebration honored Jordan and raised money to build the James Jordan Boys and Girls Club, a plush facility he was giving to Chicago's destitute West Side to honor his father. Celebrity Larry King uncovered the bronze statue. Jordan's three children helped him elevate his Number 23 jersey to the United Center rafters.

That winter, Jordan appeared more often at his Chicago restaurant and played gin rummy in suburban country clubs. After struggling in the Arizona Fall League and watching the Bulls that winter, he contemplated leaving baseball. The major league baseball strike, which began the previous August, remained unsettled by spring training, preventing him from working out to improve his skills. In early February 1995, Jordan visited Phil Jackson. Jackson reminded Jordan that the time left for him to play basketball was diminishing and wondered if he could return to the Bulls for the final 25 games of the NBA regular season. Jordan suggested 20 games instead. Jackson realized that Jordan was listening.

During spring training, major league baseball owners announced that they planned to use minor leaguers as replacement players to start the season. Jordan was forced to declare himself a strikebreaker or a minor leaguer and could not accept his status as just another player. He deplored the politics of the strike and disliked being trapped. "I didn't want to be used to draw fans into spring training games," he explained. "I decided to walk away instead of helping the owners."[44] Jordan abruptly quit baseball on March 3 and planned his return to basketball after a 16-month hiatus. He discerned that his baseball teammates were a decade younger and striving to attain a dream in a sport they adored. "I kind of lost that," Jordan admitted, "in what was happening to me two years ago with basketball. I was on a pedestal for so long that I forgot about the steps it took to get there."[45]

Jordan doubted he would have returned to basketball if not for the baseball strike. He enjoyed playing baseball, relished the opportunity to prove that he could play two sports well, and believed that his baseball skills were improving. But all he needed to get the urge to return to basketball was being around the court for awhile.

At approximately 6 A.M. on March 17, Jordan phoned Armstrong to meet him at the Berto Center. He told Armstrong that he had been practicing for several weeks and suggested they play one-on-one. Although in street clothes and shoes, Jordan still won, 10–7. "You still can't guard me," he chided Armstrong, " and I had shoes on."[46] The Bulls summoned reporters the next day to the Berto Center. Jordan did not attend the press conference; instead he had Chicago issue a terse release, "I'm back."[47]

Jordan rejoined the Bulls on March 19 against the Indiana Pacers at Market Square Arena in Indianapolis, wearing unfamiliar jersey Number 45. His familiar Number 23 already had been retired. Jordan, who considered his return as "a new beginning," indicated, "I didn't want to play with the last number my father had seen me wear."[48] He chose Number 45 because he had worn number nine or four plus five both in the Olympics and with Birmingham. Jordan missed 21 of 28 shots, scoring only 19 points in the double overtime 103–96 loss. He did not appear prepared physically and lacked consistency. The press claimed that "Air Jordan" had become "Fair Jordan."[49] The circus-like event was broadcast worldwide and attracted the largest television audience of any regular season NBA game in history.

Chicago, battling for a playoff spot with a 34–31 record, welcomed Jordan's return. Pippen had led the Bulls since 1993, and Armstrong and Steve Kerr started at guard. With the departures of center Bill Cartwright and power forward Horace Grant, Will Perdue, Luc Longley, and Bill Wennington split center duties and Croatian Toni Kukoc tried to adjust to the NBA at forward.

Jordan transformed Chicago into a playoff team with 13 victories in 17 games, including two season-best six-game winning streaks. On March 25, Jordan tallied 32 points and converted a 15-foot jump shot at the buzzer to nose the host Atlanta Hawks, 99–98. Three nights later, his 55 points sank the New York Knicks, 113–111, before 350 media representatives from 12 nations at Madison Square Garden. Jordan's talent shone abundantly that game. New York did not double-team him, assigning smaller guard John Starks to Jordan. "They let me get into that zone," Jordan recalled. "I always wanted to play well in New York because it's a basketball mecca."[50] The game, televised on Ted Turner's Atlanta station, attracted a record viewing audience for a basketball cable broadcast. Jordan made an NBA-season high 21 of 37 shots and added 10 free throws. Only Glen Rice of the Miami Heat netted more points in an NBA game that season. Jordan propelled Chicago into the playoffs with a 9–1 record in April.

The Bulls finished with a 47–35 record, third in the Central Division. Pippen, an All-NBA First Team selection, paced the Bulls in every offensive category, including scoring, rebounding, assists, steals, and blocked shots. Jordan appeared in 17 games, averaging 26.9 points and 5.3 assists. He complained, however, about his inconsistent scoring and lack of accuracy, lamenting "my shooting percentage was horrendous." Baseball had stretched his forearms, preventing him from controlling some of his basketball shots. "My rhythm was totally off,"[51] Jordan admitted. He needed to restore his shoulders, chest, and leg muscles to basketball condition.

Chicago eliminated the Charlotte Hornets, 3–1, in the first playoff round. Jordan tallied a playoff-high 48 points, including 10 overtime points, sparking a 108–100 victory in Game 1 on April 29 at Charlotte. "Well, maybe my step is not as slow as some people think,"[52] he reminded critics. Charlotte evened the series, 106–89, two nights later, but the Bulls prevailed, 103–80, in Game 3 on May 2 and 85–84 in Game 4 on May 4 at the United Center. Jordan's two game-winning free throws clinched that series.

Although Jordan averaged 31.5 points in the playoffs, the Eastern Conference champion Orlando Magic ousted Chicago in the next round. The Magic had won 57 regular season games and swept the Boston Celtics in the first playoff round. Center Shaquille O'Neal, forwards Grant and Penny Hardaway, and guard Nick Anderson proved too much.

In the Game 1 94–91 setback on May 7 at Orlando Arena, Jordan committed eight turnovers, missed a crucial free throw, lost the ball to Anderson with 17 seconds left, and threw the ball away on the Bulls' final possession. He admitted to not being in game condition and realized that his new teammates found it hard adjusting to him.

During Game 2 three nights later, Jordan tallied 38 points in his former uniform Number 23. The NBA fined the Bulls $100,000 for letting him switch numbers. Jordan made 11 of his first 13 second-half shots, enabling Chicago to even the series, 104–94. He scored 29 first-half points in Game 3 on May 12 at the United Center, but missed 9 of 13 fourth-quarter shots in the 110–101 loss. The Bulls salvaged a split at home, 106–95, two days later, The Magic regained the series lead with a 103–95 victory at Orlando on May 16. Chicago, facing elimination on May 18, led Game 6, 102–94, at home with 3 minutes and 24 seconds left. Orlando tallied the final 14 points and stopped Jordan at crunch time for a 108–102 triumph. "The end had come crashing down so suddenly,"[53] Jackson lamented.

An NBA title had eluded Chicago for a second consecutive year. Jordan hated losing to a six-year-old franchise and shouldered responsibility for the Bulls' fate. "He didn't look like the old number twenty-three,"[54] Anderson declared. Jordan naively believed he could return for 17 games and win a title, but he realized how much he needed to improve. Chicago needed a rebounding power forward and also a point guard to replace Armstrong, who was lost in the expansion draft. The Magic, meanwhile, defeated Indiana in the Eastern Conference Finals, but were swept by the Houston Rockets in the NBA Finals.

The sports media and some younger NBA players considered Jordan's championship days history and speculated that the time had come for him to surrender the NBA leadership torch. They kept saying that not only had Jordan lost a step and a fraction of mid-air hang time, but that he no longer could drive to the basket with such blazing speed. The critical comments gave Jordan extra incentive to return next season. He worked strenuously that summer to be in the best condition of his career, spending hours daily on his low-post game, jump shot, and three-point shot. Jordan developed a fall-back jump shot, faking a move to the basket and jumping up at the last second while falling back slightly, separating from the defender. Given his jumping and driving ability, his new shot proved nearly unguardable and helped him dominate younger players. He no longer relied on sheer physical ability, quickness, and explosiveness, adjusting with his knowledge of the sport and opponents. "Beating defenses this way is just as enjoyable as the other way,"[55] he learned.

Jordan retooled his game while starring in his first major motion picture, *Space Jam*. His connection with cartoons began in 1991, when he appeared in *Pro Stars*, an NBC Saturday morning cartoon. The show featured Jordan, Wayne Gretzky, and Bo Jackson fighting crime and helping children. Jordan also affiliated with Looney Tunes cartoon characters. A Nike commercial in the 1993 Super Bowl, where he and Bugs Bunny played basketball against some Martians, inspired the 1996 live action/animated movie *Space Jam,* which starred Jordan, Bill Murray, and Bugs Bunny in a mythical story set during his first retirement. "It was a good experience, but it's hard," Jordan discovered. "Start at eight, shoot till seven, six days a week."[56] *Space Jam* netted $230 million at the box office and more than $200 million in video sales. Jordan and Bugs Bunny later appeared in several MCI commercials.

Warner Brothers moved a wooden basketball floor from Long Beach State University to its Hollywood studio lot for Jordan to practice. Tim Grover assisted Jordan in a rigorous physical conditioning program. Besides lifting weights during lunch hour, Jordan played pickup games from 7:00 to 9:30 almost every night with Barkley, Reggie Miller, Chris Mills, Shawn Bradley, Muggsy Bogues, Nick Van Excel, Charles Oakley, and even Magic Johnson in a gymnasium he had made out of a sound stage. The games paralleled his summer workouts in North Carolina. "I could feel it coming back pretty quickly,"[57] he said.

## NOTES

1. Sam Smith, *The Jordan Rules: The Inside Story of a Turbulent Season with Michael Jordan and the Chicago Bulls* (New York: Simon & Schuster, 1992).

2. Phil Jackson and Hugh Delehanty, *Sacred Hoops: Spiritual Lessons of a Hardwood Warrior* (New York: Hyperion, 1995), p. 179.

3. Jack McCallum, "The Everywhere Man," *Sports Illustrated* 75 (December 23, 1991), p. 69.

4. Jackson, *Sacred Hoops,* p. 160.

5. Ibid., p. 164.

6. McCallum, "Everywhere Man," p. 64.

7. Jackson, *Sacred Hoops,* p. 165.

8. Michael Jordan, ed. by Mark Vancil, *For the Love of the Game: My Story* (New York: Crown Publishers, 1998), p. 60.

9. Craig Carter et al., eds., *The Sporting News Official NBA Guide 1992–93* (St. Louis, MO: The Sporting News, 1992), p. 24.

10. Jordan, *Love of Game,* p. 61.

11. Carter, *NBA Guide 1992–93,* pp. 24, 26.

12. Walter LaFeber, *Michael Jordan and the New Global Capitalism* (New York: W. W. Norton & Company, 1999), p. 84.

13. *Chicago Tribune,* March 21, 1992, sec. 3, p. 1.

14. Jordan, *Love of Game,* p. 59.

15. *Chicago Tribune,* April 1, 1992, sec. 4, p. 1.

16. Mike Meserole, ed., *The 1993 Information Please Sports Almanac* (Boston: Houghton, Mifflin, 1992), pp. 300–301.

17. David Halberstam, *Playing for Keeps: Michael Jordan and the World He Made* (New York: Random House, 1999), p. 302.

18. *New York Times,* August 2, 1992, sec. 8, p. 1.

19. LaFeber, *New Global Capitalism*, p. 85.

20. Jackson, *Sacred Hoops*, p. 167.

21. Craig Carter et al., eds., *The Sporting News Official NBA Guide 1993–94* (St. Louis, MO: The Sporting News, 1993), p. 24.

22. Halberstam, *Playing for Keeps*, p. 316.

23. Jackson, *Sacred Hoops*, p. 168.

24. *Chicago Tribune*, June 22, 1993, sec .3, p. 4.

25. Carter, *NBA Guide 1993–94*, p. 24.

26. *Chicago Tribune*, June 21, 1993, sec. 4, p. 7.

27. Halberstam, *Playing for Keeps*, p. 320.

28. *Chicago Tribune*, May 28, 1993, sec. 4, p. 7.

29. Richard Esquinas with Dave Distol, *Michael and Me: Our Gambling Addiction* (San Diego, CA: Athletic Guidance Center, 1993).

30. Mitchell Krugel, *Jordan: The Man, His Words, His Life* (New York: St. Martin's Press, 1994), p. 213.

31. Jordan, *Love of Game*, p. 80.

32. Michael Jordan, ed. by Mark Vancil, *Driven from Within* (New York: Atria Books, 2005), p. 129.

33. Jordan, *Love of Game*, p. 86.

34. Jackson, *Sacred Hoops*, p. 180.

35. Jordan, *Love of Game*, p. 82.

36. LaFeber, *New Global Capitalism*, p. 121.

37. http://www.sportingnews.com/experts/dave-kindred/20050613.html

38. Jordan, *Love of Game*, p. 86.

39. Michael Jordan, ed. by Mark Vancil, *I'm Back: More Rare Air* (San Francisco, CA: Collins Publishers, 1995), p. 103.

40. Bob Greene, *Rebound: The Odyssey of Michael Jordan* (New York: Doubleday, 1995), pp. 54–55.

41. Jordan, *I'm Back*, p. 104.

42. Mitchell Krugel, *One Last Shot: The Story of Michael Jordan's Comeback* (New York: St. Martin's Press, 2003) p. 42.

43. Mark Kram and Rebecca Parks, "Michael Jordan," in Shirelle Phelps, ed., *Contemporary Black Biography* 21 (Detroit, MI: Gale Research, Inc., 1999), p. 90.

44. Jordan, *Love of Game*, p. 90.

45. Krugel, *One Last Shot*, p. 44.

46. Halberstam, *Playing for Keeps*, p. 333.

47. Jordan, *I'm Back*, p. 110.

48. Jordan, *Love of Game*, p. 92.

49. LaFeber, *New Global Capitalism*, p. 127.

50. Jordan, *Love of Game*, p. 93.

51. Jordan, *Driven from Within*, p. 153.

52. Krugel, *One Last Shot*, p. 47.

53. Jackson, *Sacred Hoops*, p. 198.

54. Krugel, *One Last Shot*, p. 47.

55. "Michael Jordan," *Current Biography Yearbook* (New York: H. W. Wilson Company, 1997), p. 254.

56. Ibid., p. 254.`

57. Jordan, *Love of Game*, p. 95.

# Chapter 5

# THE PINNACLE YEARS,
# 1995–1998

## THE BULLS SOAR TO RECORD HEIGHTS
### (1995–1996)

Before the 1995–1996 season, Chicago acquired Dennis Rodman from the San Antonio Spurs. The eccentric, volatile Rodman, the NBA's best rebounder and skilled defender, gave the Bulls a power forward with strength, size, and agility. Rodman, known for tattoos, changeable multicolor hair, and various body piercings, signed a $2.5 million one-year contract. The Rodman acquisition gave Chicago a third outstanding defensive player and made it among the greatest teams in NBA history. His speed enabled the Bulls to run the floor quickly and wear down opponents with tenacious halfcourt defense. Free agent guard Randy Brown of the Sacramento Kings replaced Armstrong.

Jordan earned $3.9 million in 1995–1996, the last year of a six-year contract. He returned from Burbank in great shape and anxiously awaited the season, vowing to restore Chicago to championship status. "I felt like a kid coming out of college with something to prove."[1] Jordan's baseball experience made him more tolerant toward teammates. He realized his limitations in a sport important to him that he could not master, no matter how hard he tried. His unique natural basketball gifts and talents, including amazing eyesight and kinetic reactions, had not extended to baseball. According to teammate Steve Kerr, Jordan was a more contented player "pretty much at peace with his game now." Kerr especially was impressed with Jordan's refined fadeaway jump shot, where he turned and shot over smaller, quicker defenders. Jordan fell back as he released the ball and landed four or five feet behind where he started. "It's an unbelievably difficult shot to make, but you can't guard it, either." Kerr considered Jordan invaluable to the Bulls. "The combination of incredible talent, work ethic, basketball skills and competitiveness. It's just an unbelievable combination."[2]

Jordan's commanding presence and leadership through example inspired his teammates to play at a championship level. Kerr, Steve Colter, Scott Burrell, Toni Kukoc, and Luc Longley had joined the Bulls since Jordan left and had not won NBA titles nor, according to Jordan, "experienced the stages of being a champion. I'm just speeding up the process."[3] New teammates quickly observed that Jordan set very high standards for himself every time he performed. Jordan expected excellence whether in games or in practice.

Jordan played every preseason game as if it were a playoff contest. Kerr noticed, "he just took control of the entire team's emotional level and challenged every single player in practice to improve. Every practice, every shooting drill, everything was just a huge competition. He was so competitive that it just set up the tone for our season."[4] His teammates assumed valuable supportive roles. Scottie Pippen was relieved not to be the team leader and spokesman. Ron Harper shifted from primary shooting guard to defensive specialist, and center Luc Longley learned how to maximize his massive body. Kerr, an excellent pure shooting guard, took three-pointers when Jordan was doubled-teamed.

The Bulls dedicated the United Center grandly on November 3. Jordan enjoyed his best opening night since 1989, scoring 15 first-quarter points in a 105–91 romp over the Charlotte Hornets. Although trailing, 48–40, at halftime, Chicago capitalized on ferocious defense and outscored Charlotte, 40–18, in the third quarter. Jordan scored 19 third-quarter points, including 13 points in the final 4 minutes and 49 seconds. He finished with 42 points, including three-pointers, mid-range jump shots, and at least one dunk, adding seven assists and six rebounds. Jordan felt completely different than in the previous spring and played more instinctively. *The Chicago Tribune* the next morning declared that he had returned to form.

The Bulls' confidence soared with five consecutive victories. "There was no stopping us that season,"[5] Jordan declared. Chicago routed the Boston Celtics, 107–85, on November 4 and defeated the expansion Toronto Raptors, 117–108, three nights later at the United Center, boosted by Jordan's 38 points and 13 forced turnovers. The Orlando Magic ended the Bulls winning streak on November 14 at the Orlando Arena, as Penny Hardaway outscored Jordan. The next night, the Bulls trounced the Cleveland

Cavaliers, 113–94. TNT analyst Hubie Brown proclaimed the Bulls "the best defensive team in the history of the game."[6]

Chicago's dominance continued with six triumphs in seven games on the western road trip. Jordan helped the Bulls erase a nine-point fourth-quarter deficit on November 21, scoring 36 points in a 108–102 victory over the Dallas Mavericks. The next night, his 38 points and 9 rebounds vaulted Chicago past San Antonio, 103–94. Jordan recorded 34 points, including 15 of the Bulls' last 16 points in the final 3 minutes and 34 seconds, and added eight rebounds to overcome the Utah Jazz, 90–85, on November 24 before a packed Delta Center. Chicago, however, blew a 16-point lead against the Seattle SuperSonics two nights later, as Jordan experienced a rare off-night.

Jordan's 33 points enabled the Bulls to edge the Portland Trail Blazers, 107–104, the next night. Chicago looked lethargic in a 94–88 win over the expansion Vancouver Grizzlies on November 30, but Jordan rescued the Bulls with 19 points in the last six minutes for a game-high 29 points. His teammates sang "(I wanna) Be Like Mike," the happy Gatorade commercial, after the comeback. The western road trip ended December 2 with a 104–98 triumph over the Los Angeles Clippers. The Bulls led the NBA with a 13–2 record for their best start ever, 1.5 games ahead of Houston and Utah. "We had a swagger about ourselves because we were dominating," Jordan acknowledged, adding "we just picked opposing teams apart."[7]

After missing 13 games with a calf injury, Rodman returned with a 20-rebound masterpiece on December 6 against the New York Knicks at the United Center. Although trailing by 13 points at halftime, Chicago prevailed, 101–94. Two nights later, the Bulls whipped visiting San Antonio, 106–87. Rodman recorded 21 rebounds, the first time in eight years that a Bull attained 20 or more rebounds in consecutive games. Jordan described Chicago's success formula, "There are no jealousies on this team. No individual goals, only team goals. . . . We maintain our focus."[8] The winning streak extended on December 9, as Jordan's 45 points ignited a 118–106 triumph over the Milwaukee Bucks.

The host Bulls anticipated their December 13 rematch with Orlando, which had won six of eight games with Chicago since Jordan's return and 16 consecutive contests without injured star Shaquille O'Neal. Jordan outscored Hardaway, 36–26, in the Bulls' 112–103 victory. After defeating Utah, 100–86, on December 23, Chicago owned a 23–2 record. The host team, the Indiana Pacers, ended the Bulls' 13-game winning streak, 103–97, at home on December 26.

Chicago launched an amazing 18-game winning streak from December 29 through February 2, extending its record to 41–3. The Bulls on January 3 walloped the two-time defending NBA champion Houston Rockets, 100–86, at the United Center. Jordan contributed 27 points the next night in a 117–93 thrashing of host Charlotte. On January 13, Jordan netted 15 first-quarter points and outscored Philadelphia 76ers rookie sensation Jerry Stackhouse, 48–20. Although Jordan sat out the final nine minutes of the game, visiting Chicago still vanquished hosting team Philadelphia, 120–93. His 46 points lifted the Bulls over the Washington Bullets, 116–109, two nights later. Rodman recorded his first triple-double with 10 points, 21 rebounds, and 10 assists on January 16 in a 116–104 romp over Philadelphia at the United Center. Jordan tallied 15 of his 38 points in the fourth quarter, as Chicago rallied for a 92–89 win at Toronto two nights later. The Bulls fared 14–0 in January, just the ninth NBA team to finish an entire month undefeated. Chicago set an NBA record with a 41–3 mark as of February 2. The 1973 Los Angeles Lakers had won 39 of their first 43 contests.

The Bulls took four of six contests on another western road trip, defeating the Houston Rockets, the Sacramento Kings, the Los Angeles Lakers, and the Golden State Warriors and falling to the Denver Nuggets and the Phoenix Suns. After Chicago trounced the Lakers, 99–84, on February 2, Magic Johnson lauded the Bulls as the "best team I've ever seen. They're as good as our championship teams [were]. They're better than their three titles teams. They're scary, man."[9] The victory marked Chicago's 18th consecutive win, the longest winning streak of Jordan's career. Denver ended the streak with a six-point victory two nights later. The Bulls suffered their only two-game losing spell of the season, falling by 10 points at Phoenix on February 6. Jordan's 40 points elevated Chicago past Golden State, 99–95, the next night.

The Bulls stood 42–5 at the All-Star break. Jordan scored 20 points in just 22 minutes, leading the East to a 129–116 victory over the West in the All-Star Game at the Alamodome in San Antonio, Texas. In his first All-Star appearance since 1993, he made 8 of 11 shots to capture MVP accolades.

On February 15, Chicago blew a seven-point fourth-quarter lead against the Detroit Pistons and trailed 101–96 with 37 seconds left. After tying the game, the Bulls won 112–109 in overtime. Jordan scored eight of Chicago's 11 overtime points, including two quick jump shots and two foul shots, to clinch the victory and finish with 43 points.

Jordan and Pippen combined for 44 points and 40 points, respectively, in a 110–102 victory at Indiana, the first time in Bulls' history and sixth time in NBA history that teammates had attained at least 40 points in the same contest. They collaborated for 15 rebounds, 9 assists, 8 steals, and 2 blocked shots, making 30 of 55 shots and 7 of 11 from three-point range. John Jackson of the *Chicago Tribune* proclaimed, "Michael Jordan and Scottie Pippen are the best tandem in NBA history."[10] Rodman contributed 23 rebounds. Chicago extended his win-loss record to 47–5 two nights later, walloping visiting Cleveland, 102–76.

NBA aficionados, who marveled over Jordan's spectacular moves and Rodman's rebounding prowess, began debating whether the Bulls could win 70 games, how they compared other great all-time teams, and even if they were the best team ever. Chicago matched well with the 1973 Los Angeles Lakers except at the center position, where it could not match Wilt Chamberlain.

The Bulls' winning streak increased to seven, as the Atlanta Hawks fell, 96–91, on February 22. When Jordan recorded a game-high 34 points, Greg Boeck of *USA Today* penned, "In a remarkable comeback ... Jordan (has) dusted off his old skills to produce MVP numbers for himself and a run at history and another ring for the Bulls."[11] The Miami Heat upset Chicago, 113–104, the next night, but the Bulls thrashed Orlando, 111–91, on February 25 and Minnesota Timberwolves, 120–99, two nights later at the United Center. Chicago reached 50 victories quicker than any team in NBA history, bettering the 50–7 start by the 1982–1983 Philadelphia 76ers.

The Bulls lost just twice in March, raising their record to 62–8. Chicago demolished visiting Boston, 107–75, on March 2, as Jordan made 21 points, 8 rebounds, and 8 assists in just 32 minutes. Five nights later, the Bulls spanked Detroit, 102–81. After hitting 14 of his first 16 shots, Jordan finished with 21 baskets and 9 free throws for an NBA season-high 53 points. He recorded 11 rebounds, 6 steals, and 2 assists, shooting 75 percent. Pistons coach Doug Collins claimed that Jordan could not be defended against. Host New York humiliated Chicago, 104–72, on March 10, holding the Bulls to their lowest season point total.

Although a bad back sidelined Pippen, Chicago coasted over Washington, 103–86, on March 13 and Denver, 108–87, two nights later at the United Center. Rodman was ejected for a head butt against the New Jersey Nets, but the Bulls prevailed anyway, 97–93, on March 16. Jordan netted 37 points in 43 minutes, recording 16 rebounds, 4 assists, 3 blocked shots, and no turnovers. The NBA suspended Rodman for six games and fined him $20,000. Two nights later, Chicago overcame Philadelphia, 98–84. Jordan combined 38 points with 11 rebounds in 47 minutes, compensating for the Pippen and Rodman absences. Jackson ran numerous substitution patterns and called midrange timeouts to preserve Jordan's strength.

The Bulls defeated Miami twice and Charlotte and Orlando once each in early April, ascending to a 66–8 record. Chicago remained undefeated at the United Center and hoped to surpass the 40–1 mark set by the 1985–1986 Boston Celtics. Charlotte, however, upset host Chicago, 98–97, on April 8. After the Bulls blew a 15-point lead, Jordan tied the game, 96-all, with his 40th point. Harper converted a foul shot, but Dell Curry countered with free throws for the Hornets. Kukoc, Jordan, and Pippen missed shots in the waning seconds. Chicago celebrated Rodman's return, pulverizing visiting Philadelphia, 112–82, on April 12. Four nights later, the Bulls overcame an eight-point fourth-quarter deficit to record their 70th win, 86–80, against Milwaukee. A 110–79 home rout over injury-riddled Detroit followed on April 18. Purposefulness, concentration, and focus keyed the Bulls' success.

Chicago dropped its final home game to Indiana, 100–99, losing a share of the home season victory record with Boston. "That was important to us," Jordan stressed, "and I wanted it. It would have been something else for our team to be proud of."[12] Jackson rested the regulars frequently. Jordan sparked a furious 8–0 Bulls run to knot the contest at 99-all, but fouled Eddie Johnson in the last second. Johnson converted one free throw for the Pacers victory.

Chicago won the season finale against the Washington Bullets, 103–93, setting an NBA single-season record with 72 victories. The Bulls won three more games than the 1971–1972 Los Angeles Lakers and suffered just 10 losses. Chicago had become America's team. The Bulls, a collection of "mediagenic" stars, exhibited remarkable unity as a disciplined group, a whole greater than its charismatic parts. "Incredible,"[13] Jordan exclaimed.

In their first season together, Jordan, Pippen, and Rodman blended well, performing their specific roles and suppressing their egos. Jordan and Pippen both made the All-NBA first team and All-Defensive first team. Superbly conditioned Jordan led Chicago to its greatest single season ever while making perhaps the greatest personal comeback in sport history. He earned his fourth NBA MVP Award, surpassing Bird and Johnson and receiving a record 97 percent of the first-place votes. Jordan appeared in all 82 games, averaging 30.4 points and converting nearly 50 percent of his shots. In his first full season since returning to the NBA, he broke Wilt Chamberlain's record with his eighth NBA scoring title and paced the Bulls in steals (2.20 average) and minutes played (37.7 average). Jordan also snagged 6.6 rebounds and dished off 4.3 assists per outing while destroying his opponents psychologically. His return increased ratings 21 percent for Ted Turner's cable network, with the 15 Chicago telecasts attracting 50 percent more viewers.

Teammates played valuable supportive roles. Rodman equaled Moses Malone's NBA record with his fifth consecutive rebounding crown (14.9 average), making the NBA All-Defensive team. Chicago became the first aggregate since the 1970 New York Knicks to place three players on that squad. Kerr ranked second in three-point field goal percentage, and Kukoc won NBA Sixth Man honors as Rodman's substitute. Jordan, impressed with the dedication of his teammates, stressed, "most of them had something to prove. Not everyone had won a championship."[14] Jackson captured NBA Coach of the Year honors, passing Pat Riley as the NBA mentor with the highest winning percentage (.721). "Phil has [such] a calming influence on everybody," Jordan observed. "That's why he's the best."[15]

Chicago sailed through the NBA playoffs, losing only three games in four series. Harper's slogan "Seventy-two and ten don't mean a thing/without the ring"[16] motivated the Bulls for the postseason. Jordan reminded teammates that they needed 15 victories to recapture the NBA crown, but Jackson cautioned that the Bulls would lose some games. Chicago swept Miami, 3–0, in the first round. The Bulls dominated the Heat, 102–85, in foul-plagued Game 1. In Game 2, Chicago jumped to a 63–35 halftime lead and trounced Miami, 106–75. The little noisemakers given to the United Center throng made the sound deafening. The Bulls clinched the series blowing out Miami, 112–91, in Game 3.

Chicago took four of five games from New York in the second round. Despite a bad back, Jordan scored 44 points, including 23 in the first half of the Game 1 91–84 triumph. He hooked defenders with his elbows on offensive moves, pushed when officials did not notice, put his hip to unsuspecting guards, and slapped wrists so quickly that only slow-motion cameras could detect it. His 29 points sparked a 91–80 Bulls' Game 2 victory. He tallied 40 percent of Chicago's points in those contests, using his fadeaway jump shot. Jordan had perfected the shot so that it was virtually indefensible. The Knicks, however, blocked the cutting routes of the Bulls' triangle offense and stymied both Kukoc and Kerr.

Game 3 at boisterous, packed Madison Square Garden featured very physical play. Jordan scored Chicago's final 10 points to produce an 88–88 tie and tallied 46 points in 51 minutes, but the Knicks won in overtime, 102–99. In Game 4, the Bulls led 51–50 at halftime and prevailed 94–91. Jordan recorded 27 points, 8 rebounds, 8 assists, 2 steals, a blocked shot, and no turnovers; Rodman contributed 19 rebounds. Jordan poured in

35 points, as the Bulls clinched the Game 5 series finale, 94–81, at the United Center. Kerr sighed, "We feel like we're getting out of jail. The Knicks have had us locked up."[17]

Chicago swept Orlando in four games, avenging the 1995 setback. In Game 1 at the United Center on May 19, the Bulls jumped to a 10–0 lead and trounced the Magic, 121–83, for a franchise-record 38-point victory. Rodman recorded 21 rebounds and held Grant scoreless. In Game 2 two nights later, Jordan outscored the Magic, 17–16, in the third quarter and lifted the Bulls to a 93–88 triumph. The series shifted for Game 3 on May 25 to the Orlando Arena, where Chicago's stifling defense prevailed, 86–67. In the 106–101 series finale two nights later, Jordan made 16 of 23 shots and scored 45 points.

Chicago faced Seattle in the NBA Finals. The SuperSonics had won 64 regular season games, second best in the NBA, and possessed physical ability, but lacked a cohesive halfcourt game. In the postseason, Seattle eliminated Sacramento, defending champion Houston, and Utah. In Game 1 at the United Center on June 5, Seattle stayed close for three quarters. The Bulls applied pressure defense on a 15–2 fourth-quarter run, sparked by Kukoc's nine consecutive points, for the 107–90 victory. "The fourth quarter is about desire and putting on the defense,"[18] Jordan explained. His streak of nine consecutive NBA Finals games with at least 30 points ended, but he still tallied 28 points.

Two nights later, the SuperSonics experienced another second-half drought in Game 2. Chicago ended the third quarter with a 10–1 flurry, including two Kukoc three-pointers, for a 76–65 advantage and survived a subpar fourth quarter to escape with a 92–88 win. Jordan ended with 29 points, 6 rebounds, 8 assists, and 2 steals; Rodman added 20 rebounds and tied an NBA Finals record with 11 offensive boards.

The Bulls whipped Seattle, 108–86, on June 9 in Game 3 at Key Arena to seize a 3–0 series advantage, as Jordan unleashed 36 points. He scored 26 first-half points, six more than any SuperSonic made the entire game. In the final four minutes of that half, Jordan torched Seattle for 15 points and staked Chicago to a 62–38 lead. Longley, who posted a career playoff-high 19 points, observed, "When he gets like that, I find myself running up and down the court with a smile on my face. . . . You want to watch him like a fan."[19] *The Seattle Intelligencer* wrote the SuperSonics "were buried by Michael Jordan and the Bulls,"[20] and Jackson termed the performance spectacular. When Seattle coach George Karl observed, "I think that's the first time I ever saw Chicago with killer eyes," Jordan countered, "We have killer eyes every time we step on the floor."[21] Karl knew that no NBA team had ever overcome a 3–0 deficit to win a playoff series.

The Bulls' phenomenal toughness impressed Karl. Chicago knew when to intensify the defensive pressure and prey on an opponent's weaknesses. Besides possessing enormous skills, mental fiber, and emotion, Jackson's squad exhibited intelligence and focus.

In Game 4 on June 12, the host SuperSonics shellacked Chicago, 107–86. Shawn Kemp led Seattle with 25 points and 11 rebounds, and Jordan paced the Bulls with 23 points. Jordan admitted "we're entitled to one bad game. To dominate this team for four straight games was stretching it."[22]

Seattle also took Game 5, 89–78, two nights later, benefiting from an aggressive defense and the noisy Key Arena crowd. Gary Payton contributed 23 points, 9 rebounds, and 6 assists. Chicago shot poorly from three-point range, losing consecutive games by double figures for the only time that season. The SuperSonics double-teamed Jordan in the second half, limiting him to just 9 of his 26 points.

The United Center crowd of 24,544 was filled with tension for Game 6 on June 16. The more intense Bulls used a much more rigorous defense and more focused offense. Rodman excelled with 16 rebounds, 9 points, and 5 assists and drew Kemp into foul trouble. The Bulls never relinquished the lead after Pippen ignited the crowd to a deafening noise with a three-pointer to put the Bulls ahead, 12–10, seven minutes into the first quarter. Rodman tallied five points in a 12–2 third-quarter run, extending Chicago's lead to 64–47 with 6 minutes and 41 seconds left and capped the surge with a perfect backdoor pass to Jordan for a layup.

As the crowd roared and danced wildly in the aisles, the Bulls eliminated Seattle, 87–75. Although making only 22 points, Jordan contributed nine rebounds, a team-high seven assists, and two steals. At the final buzzer, he dove on the ball and hugged it to his chest with both arms. Jordan had come full cycle. Teammates jumped on him. His eyes were shut and his face reflected rapture and release. Jordan then ran through the boisterous crowd to the locker room alone. As his teammates celebrated at midcourt, Jordan sobbed on the carpeted training room floor. He considered it even more special that the final victory came on Father's Day, as memories of his late father, James, permeated his thoughts. He considered the NBA title a tribute to his late father.

Chicago celebrated its fourth NBA title exactly three years after winning its third crown. "It couldn't have played out any better," a determined Jordan reflected. The NBA Finals completed his return to the NBA's pinnacle. He regained his position as the sport's premier player, exhibiting his remarkable determination and skill in restoring the Bulls to championship status. "I felt like I had to win another championship before anyone would give credence to my return,"[23] he recalled. Jordan averaged 27.3

points, 5.3 rebounds, and 4.2 assists in the series and 30.7 points during the entire postseason. He surpassed Magic Johnson with his fourth NBA Finals MVP and became the first player since Willis Reed in 1970 to capture all three major NBA MVP awards during the same season.

Jordan was in superb physical condition and possessed phenomenal energy. Despite having only five to six hours of sleep nightly, he set an unbelievable standard for his teammates with his amazing consistency, boundless energy, and enormous drive. He had something to prove.

On his return to basketball, Jordan was more focused and mentally tougher. He still possessed amazing personal charm, wit, and intelligence to supplement his legendary athletic skills; retained relentless willpower; and maintained an unparalleled fierce competitive drive and compulsive passion both to excel and to dominate.

Jordan related better with his less talented teammates, crediting Jackson's spiritual values. Jackson encouraged him to learn patience and better understand his teammates, enabling them to improve. Jordan especially got along better with a more mature Pippen, relying on him much more because he needed to preserve his energy. He depended on Pippen to bring the ball up court and pass it to him when he wanted it, to control the game's pace, and to provide an alternative threat both offensively and defensively. At a Grant Park team celebration two days later, he declared, "The city loves me. And I love them."[24]

The 1995–1996 Bulls rank among the best all-time NBA teams with a combined regular and postseason record of 87 wins and just 13 losses. "This team established a new level of play," Jackson boasted, "and it's something all teams will have to chase." Jordan considered the 1996 Bulls title his favorite. "The historians will decide our place among the greatest teams. But we certainly accomplished everything we set out to do." He added "That's the first time I really came back and focused on my career without my father."[25]

## THE SECOND REPEAT (1996–1997)

Jordan's contract lapsed after the 1995–1996 season. Reinsdorf and David Falk, Jordan's representative, discussed new contract terms. Jordan advised Falk, "Don't go in and give a price." He instructed Falk to listen to Reinsdorf, but not negotiate. Jordan, who feared that lengthy negotiations would cheapen his accomplishments, was dismayed that Reinsdorf did not make an offer. He joined a conference phone call with Falk and Reinsdorf while competing in a golf tournament at Lake Tahoe. Jordan wanted a one-year contract exceeding $30 million and gave Reinsdorf one hour to consent. Reinsdorf countered with a two-year $55 million offer, $30 million for the first year and $25 million for the second year. Falk replied that Jordan would accept a one-year $30 million contract, but threatened to initiate discussions with the New York Knicks and warned that Jordan might play there. Although irked, Reinsdorf was forced to accepted Jordan's terms. "I thought they were pushing it,"[26] he complained. Reinsdorf upset Jordan by asserting he would later regret giving him the $30 million. Jordan knew how he had spearheaded Chicago to four NBA titles and was offended that the Bulls had underpaid him.

Jordan, meanwhile, enjoyed another spectacular season in 1996–1997, becoming the best-ever post-up, turnaround, fadeaway jump shooter in NBA history. He became the Bulls' best post player, holding off defenders with one hand, catching the ball with the other hand, and using his strong legs to turn and elevate for a clear shot. To make his shot impossible to stop, Jordan fell away from the basket just out of the defender's reach. This shot enabled him to score at least 40 points nine times and win his ninth straight scoring title.

Chicago started the season with 12 straight victories from November 1 through November 21. After conquering Boston on November 1, the Bulls returned home to defeat Philadelphia and the Vancouver Grizzlies. Their first major test came on November 6 at Miami, where Jordan shot 18 for 33 with 13 free throws for 50 points to spearhead a 106–100 victory.

Despite Jordan's 44 points, host Utah inflicted Chicago's first loss on November 23. Two nights later, Jordan scored 40 points in an 88–84 triumph against the Los Angeles Clippers. He tallied 35 points in a 97–88 road victory over San Antonio on November 30, reaching a milestone with his 25,000th NBA point. The Bulls' record soared to a 16–1 mark in a 107–104 nailbiter at Milwaukee on December 3, as Jordan scored 40 points. Chicago dropped consecutive games for the first time all season, barely falling to Miami for their first home loss on December 7 and losing the next night in Toronto. The Bulls set a franchise record at the United Center on December 17, when three players attained 30 points in the same game. Pippen netted 35 points, Kukoc 31 points, and Jordan 30 points in a 129–123 overtime thriller over the Los Angeles Lakers. On December 28, Jordan's 45 points, including a season-high 19 of 20 free throws, sparked a 102–97 triumph over visiting Cleveland to give the Bulls a 27–4 mark.

Chicago won 13 of 14 contests, including all seven home games, in January, extending its record to 40–5. Houston inflicted the only setback that month on January 19. Two nights later, Jordan scored a season-high

51 points to edge visiting New York, 88–87. The next test came February 2 in a road rematch with Seattle. SuperSonics Coach George Karl irritated Jordan by saying he looked older and was resorting to jump shots rather than playing physically underneath. Jordan lifted the Bulls to a 91–84 win, converting 19 of 28 shots for 45 points. "I may be older, but I'm also smarter,"[27] he retorted.

Jordan's brilliance shone on February 9 at Cleveland, where he became the first NBA player to record a triple-double in an All-Star Game, with 14 points, 11 rebounds, and 11 assists. The Eastern Conference downed the Western Conference, 132–120. At the United Center two nights later, Jordan tallied 43 points to squeak by Charlotte, 103–100. On February 18, Pippen, who likewise started in the All-Star Game, registered a career-high 47 points in a 134–123 triumph over visiting Denver. Six nights later, Jordan's 37 points spearheaded a 116–89 rout of Portland. The Bulls fared 10–2 in February, 12–2 in March, and 7–4 in April, but dropped their final two games.

Exhibiting similar talent and focus as they had previous year, Chicago dominated the NBA again with 69 victories and just 13 losses in 1996–1997. Although dropping three more contests, the Bulls captured the Central Division by 13 games and compiled five more victories than second-best Utah. Chicago boasted a 48–7 record with Rodman, who had missed 11 games for kicking a photographer and 16 contests with a sprained knee.

Jordan captured a record ninth NBA scoring title with 2,431 points and 29.6 point average, contributing 5.9 rebounds and 4.3 assists per game. He and Pippen were the highest-scoring NBA duo, with a combined 49.8 point average, making the list of 50 greatest players in NBA history, and Rodman captured his sixth consecutive rebounding crown. Although Jordan nabbed his usual postseason honors, Karl Malone of Utah nipped him in the NBA MVP balloting. Phoenix coach Danny Ainge, who praised Jordan's work ethic, intensity, and superior athleticism, declared, "Michael's the best player, without question, of all time."[28]

Jordan added to his "John Bunyan-esque" legend in the NBA playoffs, leading Chicago to a 15–4 mark. The Bulls swept Washington, 3–0 and eliminated both Atlanta and Miami, 4–1, returning to the NBA Finals. Jordan's 55 points inspired a 109–104 win over Washington at the United Center on April 27. Pippen injured his foot in the Miami finale, and Rodman continued his recovery from a sprained knee.

The Bulls hosted Utah at the United Center in the first two games of the NBA Finals. Chicago struggled in Game 1 on June 1, but the Jazz did not take advantage. The two teams were deadlocked at 82–82 with 35 seconds left. John Stockton misfired a three-pointer and Malone missed two foul shots. Pippen inbounded to Kukoc, who passed the ball to Jordan. After taking a crossover dribble, Jordan pulled up and sank a 20-foot jump shot over Byron Russell as the buzzer sounded to cap the 84–82 victory. He led the Bulls with 31 points, and Pippen added 27 points. Game 2 embellished Jordan's legend three nights later. Chicago seized a 16-point first-half lead and coasted to a 97–85 triumph. After a 20-point first half, Jordan finished with 38 points, 13 rebounds, and 9 assists. The Bulls' pesky defense disrupted Utah's methodical offense.

The next three contests were played at the Delta Center in Salt Lake City. In Game 3 on June 6, the Jazz rebounded with a 104–93 win. After Utah built a 24-point first-half lead, the Bulls narrowed the gap to just seven points in the fourth quarter. The Jazz persevered to snag their first-ever NBA Finals triumph. Chicago outperformed Utah during most of Game 4 two days later, when Jordan and several teammates suffered cramps and upset stomachs. A Bulls assistant accidentally gave them Gator Lode instead of Gator Ade, so that each player absorbed the equivalent of 20 baked potatoes during the contest. Chicago still led 71–66 with 2 minutes and 42 seconds left, when Stockton stole the ball from Jordan. Utah outscored the Bulls 13–2 to win 78–73, tying the series.

Three nights later, Game 5 featured one of the most incredible performances in Jordan's storied career. At 3:00 A. M. that day, Jordan experienced stomach flulike symptoms—nausea, vomiting, and dehydration—because of food poisoning from some bad pizza. He spent the entire day in bed and never got back to sleep. Jordan fought to stay awake when he arrived at the Delta Center. He looked listless and anemic. Jordan recalled, "I played that game on heart and determination and nothing else." He lacked nourishment, energy, and sleep. "I have never felt as awful physically as I did in that game,"[29] he admitted. Exhausted and eyes jaundiced, Jordan appeared unable to navigate the court on reentering in the second quarter. "I came in and was almost dehydrated. . . . I couldn't breathe."[30] He amazingly scored 17 points that half, slicing the deficit from 16 points to 4.

Jordan struggled through the second half. "I felt like I was going to pass out," he recalled. He kept thinking, "Get this game over so I can lie down." He was fouled with 46 seconds left and converted the first shot to knot the score at 85–85. After missing the second shot, Jordan rebounded the ball and passed it to Pippen. Pippen returned the ball to Jordan, who was wide open and sank a dramatic game-winning, three-point shot to clinch the 90–88 victory. "I didn't even know whether it went in or not," he confessed. "I could barely stand up."[31] When Utah called a timeout, Jordan started staggering toward the Bulls bench until Pippen picked him up and carried him off the floor. Jordan scored 38 points, including 15 last-quarter points, in 44 minutes to give Chicago a 3–2 series lead. When Jordan returned to the locker room, the doctors were concerned because he was cold, sweating, and needed intravenous fluids. Jordan struggled to a table, started drinking Gatorade, and lay down for approximately 45 minutes.

In the series finale on June 13 at the United Center, Jordan's offense propelled the Bulls to their fifth NBA title. He scored 39 points and grabbed 11 rebounds in Game 6, but many remember the shot that he did not take. The Jazz led 44–37 at halftime and 88–86 with 26 seconds left in the fourth quarter. Utah double-teamed Jordan, leaving Kerr open. As the crowd roared, Kerr took Jordan's pass and sunk a memorable 17-foot shot from just behind the foul line. Chicago triumphed, 90–86, for its fifth NBA crown in seven years, defeating the Jazz, 4–2. Michael again snagged NBA Finals MVP honors, averaging 32.3 points to 23.8 points for Malone in the NBA Finals and 31.1 points during the postseason. His legacy continued to grow with his astounding accomplishments.

At the victory celebration, Jordan pleaded with Bulls' management to keep the team intact for a possible third consecutive title in 1997–1998. The celebration, however, turned sour when a thief stole more than $100,000 worth of his jewelry, including his wedding ring, a watch, and a necklace.

Chicago signed Jordan for a record $33 million, keeping him the highest-paid athlete for a single season. David Falk wanted Jordan to receive a 20 percent raise, the maximum allowed, because he had accomplished everything that was expected of him. Since Reinsdorf opposed raising his $30 million salary, Jordan persuaded him to split the difference at $31.5 million.

In 1997, Jordan's earnings rose to $100 million. Nike, McDonald's, Oakley Sunglasses, Gatorade, Wilson Sporting Goods, Wheaties, Rayovac Batteries, and other companies carried his endorsements. He also profited from the film *Space Jam*, CBS-Fox Home Videos, WorldCom, and CBS Sports Line. Jordan introduced his exclusive clothing line, with $250 million projected gross revenues, and MJ, his new men's cologne. His fame spread internationally because satellites carried NBA games to at least 175 nations. When a Chinese firm asked 1,000 people to name the best-known Americans, Jordan trailed only Thomas Edison and finished ahead of Albert Einstein, Mark Twain, and Bill Gates.

## THE END OF A REMARKABLE ERA (1997–1998)

Jackson, Jordan, and Pippen engaged in an internal power struggle with Krause and Reinsdorf before the 1997–1998 campaign. Krause and Reinsdorf doubted that Chicago could capture another NBA title. The Bulls carried a player payroll exceeding $60 million, the highest in NBA history and more than twice the salary cap. Because the players were aging, Chicago needed to begin making personnel changes. Krause wanted to hire new players to prove the Bulls could win an NBA crown without Jackson and Jordan.

Krause wanted to fire Jackson, but Reinsdorf opted to retain him for another year. Jackson signed a one-year nearly $6 million contract in July 1997, but he disagreed with Krause over basketball philosophy. He did not want to stay longer if Krause planned to release the veterans and rebuild the team. Jackson also criticized Krause's abrupt management style and told him, "I'm just as much a reason for this team being successful as you are." Krause replied, "You're not coming back next season."[32]

Krause called a press conference at Chicago's training camp in October and announced plans to rebuild the Bulls after the 1997–1998 season. He stressed that Chicago had won two NBA titles with several new players after capturing three consecutive crowns with another aggregate. Krause insisted "coaches and players alone don't win championships, organizations do."[33] His comments irked both Jackson and Jordan.

The next day, Jordan told reporters that he would retire if Jackson left the Bulls. He assured the media, however, that Krause's comments would not affect the Bulls' court performance. The Bulls prided themselves on capturing consecutive NBA titles and five crowns in seven years. Jordan rejected Krause's contention that organizations win titles, stressing that the players accomplish those feats. He considered the Jackson-Krause feud an unfortunate way to finish the incredible Bulls' run and implied that Krause was causing his and Jackson's departure from the Bulls.

Krause's relations with Jordan and Pippen deteriorated, too. Jordan disapproved of Krause traveling on the Bulls bus to road games, fearing that the latter might gather information about their personal lives. He complained that Krause was "brusque" and "sets the players on edge with his presence. . . . We don't want to feel like we're under a microscope the whole time while we're working."[34] Jordan also disliked Krause's inclination to assume personal credit for drafting players or for player on-court accomplishments. Krause also feuded with Pippen, whose contract would expire after the 1997–1998 season. Pippen wanted an estimated $45 million over three seasons, an amount Krause considered excessive.

Jordan considered the 1997–1998 season "my biggest challenge ever" because "of the cards we've been dealt" and vowed to play all 48 minutes each game, if necessary, to capture the sixth crown. He prepared for a lengthy season spanning 82 regular season contests and possibly

15 playoff games. "I don't know what burnout is,"[35] Jordan explained. Doctors operated on Pippen's foot during training camp, sidelining him indefinitely.

Without Pippen, Chicago recorded just eight victories in its first 15 games. The Bulls performed better in crucial games but showed signs of age and too often lacked focus and mental toughness. Boston upset Chicago, 92–85, in the October 31 season opener at Boston Garden. The Bulls blew a significant first-quarter lead, as the youthful Celtics controlled the game's tempo by running and pressing. Three quick home wins followed over Philadelphia, San Antonio, and Orlando, but Chicago lost a heartbreaker at the Atlanta Hawks when Rodman's foul negated Jordan's basket.

After vanquishing New Jersey at the United Center on November 8, the Bulls suffered consecutive setbacks at Cleveland and to Washington at home. Jordan grumbled that Chicago resembled an expansion franchise and tried to carry too much of the burden in Pippen's absence, averaging 26 points but shooting only 38 percent.

The Bulls struggled on an extensive road trip, losing to Phoenix and needing double overtime to defeat the last-place Los Angeles Clippers, 111–102, on November 21. Jordan's "Jordanesque" rebound and basket off his missed free throw at the buzzer sent the latter game into overtime. He scored 13 consecutive points, including all nine of Chicago's second overtime points, and unleashed his season's biggest production with 49 points, the 150th time he had tallied at least 40 points in a game. The Bulls defeated Sacramento, 103–88, two nights later. Losses at Seattle and Indiana were followed by victories at Washington and Boston. During that road trip, Jordan eclipsed Elvin Hayes for fourth place on the NBA career scoring list with 27,313 points.

Despite Pippen's absence, Chicago fared 11–3 in December and remained the NBAs stingiest team defensively. On December 5, the Bulls celebrated their first game at the United Center in three weeks by limiting Milwaukee to 61 points, the fewest allowed an opponent in franchise history. Chicago's 100–82 victory over visiting New York four nights later marked another milestone for Jordan. He passed Moses Malone for third place on the NBA's career scoring list with 27,409 points, trailing only Kareem Abdul-Jabbar and Wilt Chamberlain. The December 15 contest with Phoenix marked Chicago's 500th consecutive sellout, the longest such NBA streak in NBA history.

The Bulls trounced the Los Angeles Lakers, 104–83, on December 17 at the United Center, making Jackson the quickest NBA coach to attain 500 career victories. Jackson accomplished the feat in 682 games, two fewer than Pat Riley. "He certainly still knows how to coach the game," Jordan reflected. Jordan likened Jackson to Dean Smith of North Carolina in their coaching philosophies, techniques, and caring attitudes toward players over management. "Players first, management, everything else is second," he observed.[36] "They both love basketball and maintain poise in pressure situations."

Jordan outscored sensational Lakers' guard Kobe Bryant, 36–33. Twelve Bryant points came after Jordan's fourth-quarter departure. The duo drained jump shots from the perimeter and drove for powerful dunks. Jordan relished competing against a much younger Bryant and matching baskets with him. He captured NBA Player of the Week honors later that month, with 47 points against Atlanta on December 27 and 41 points against Dallas two nights later.

The Bulls drew sellout crowds nearly everywhere in anticipation of Jordan's possible retirement. Jordan tallied 44 points in a 114–100 romp over visiting Milwaukee on January 2 and in a 90–89 squeaker at New York one week later.

Pippen rejoined Chicago at the United Center on January 10 after missing 35 games and gave the Bulls new offensive cohesion. Chicago finished 24–11 without him and had won 13 of 15 games. Although losing some leaping ability and explosive power, Pippen still scored 14 points in 31 minutes in an 87–82 victory over hapless Golden State. His return built team confidence and meant that opponents could no longer concentrate just on Jordan. At the United Center, Jordan netted 40 points in a 101–91 triumph over Seattle on January 13 and 45 points in a 106–100 win over Houston five nights later. Utah ended the Bulls' 17-game home winning streak on January 25.

During late January, Chicago opened a western trip with wins over Vancouver, Portland, and Golden State. Jordan's 31 points, however, did not avert a 112–87 thumping on February 1 by the young, quick Los Angeles Lakers, the Bulls' third worst loss since his comeback. The next night, Chicago walloped the Denver Nuggets.

Before the Utah game on February 4, Krause told the *Chicago Tribune* that coach Jackson would not return, but he hoped that Jordan would remain. "If Michael chooses to leave because there is another coach here," Krause said, "then it is his choice, not ours. We want him back."[37] Krause implied that he wanted to dismantle the Bulls, clear the salary cap, and begin rebuilding. Jordan disclosed that he would retire if Jackson departed. Despite Jordan's 40 points, Chicago blew a 24-point lead and lost 101–93. The Jazz swept the two-game season series and won home-court advantage for the playoffs.

The mid-season timing of Krause's comments surprised Jordan. Jordan wondered why the Bulls would not renew the contract of a coach who had won five NBA titles and commanded both the respect and understanding of his players. Although Bulls executives considered Jackson arrogant, Jordan told reporters, "What I see in Phil is an attitude to work with the players to achieve the best as a team. That means a lot to us."[38]

The Bulls stood 34–15 at the All-Star break. Although battling influenza, Jordan flew to New York for the All-Star Game. He led the All-Stars with 23 points, propelling the East to a 135–114 victory and earning his third All-Star Game MVP Award. He became the career All-Star steals leader, with 33, and ascended to third place on the all-time scoring list, with 234 points.

Chicago reeled off eight straight wins over Toronto, Charlotte, Atlanta, Detroit, Indiana, Toronto again, Washington, and Cleveland before Portland, on February 25, handed the Bulls just their third setback at the United Center. Chicago resumed its torrid pace, breezing through March with a 13–1 record. After Bulls' victories over Sacramento and Denver, Jordan's 42 points sparked a 102–89 triumph over New York at Madison Square Garden on March 8. Jordan, donning the same shoes he had worn in his 1984 New York debut, entertained a national NBC television audience with vintage drives to the basket, reverses, and dunks. Besides switching hands in trademark fashion for one layup, he turned in midair and flipped the shot over Terry Cummings's shoulder for another tally. Jordan did not really think about his moves and the animated crowd response. His acrobatic moves amazed teammates and spectators alike. The highly focused Bulls trounced Miami, 106–91, at home two nights later.

Jordan enjoyed a spectacular season, thrilling crowds with extraordinary performances. Fans crowded arenas to see him play his final games in various NBA cities. Although depending more on his fadeaway jump shot, Jordan still exhibited the leaping ability, body control, and confounding athleticism that amazed spectators. Jordan still possessed an uncanny ability to dominate virtually any game while scoring at least 40 points. "I don't know of another sports hero in our history who has been able to play at this level at his age," Jackson boasted. "Michael has just destroyed the concepts of what we think of as normal, of what a man his age should be able to do."[39]

Chicago enjoyed a season-high 13-game winning streak from March 14 to April 7. After blowing an 18-point lead with five minutes left in an overtime loss to Dallas on March 12, the Bulls played one of their best games against San Antonio. Chicago blitzed to a 10–2 lead and led 27–17 after the first period. The Spurs sliced the deficit to 40–39 by intermission, but Chicago triumphed, 96–86. Two nights later, the host Bulls outscored New Jersey, 30–10, in the third quarter to prevail 88–72. After winning a crucial game at Indiana, Chicago defeated Vancouver and withstood a furious comeback by Toronto. Jordan netted 30 points in a 104–87 romp at Milwaukee on March 29. Victories followed over Minnesota, Houston, and Washington. Jordan recorded 41 points against Minnesota on April 3 and 40 points against Houston on April 5, the second time he had attained 40 points in consecutive contests. Six days later at the United Center, the Bulls defeated Orlando to become the first NBA team to reach 60 victories. In the season home finale on April 18, Jordan converted an NBA season-high 22 free throws in 24 attempts to edge New York, 111–109.

Chicago finished the season 62–20, four games ahead of Indiana in the Central Division and tied with Utah for the best NBA record. Their regular and playoff game home sellout streak reached 542 games. The Jazz held home playoff advantage, having swept the Bulls in both regular season games. The Bulls also looked vulnerable because their starters showed advancing age.

Jordan captured his NBA record tenth scoring title and third consecutive crown with 2,357 points, averaging 28.7 points. He was named NBA MVP for the fifth time, All-NBA first team for the 10th time, and All-Defensive first team for the ninth time. At age 35, Jordan became the oldest NBA MVP recipient. The award convinced him that he could still perform at peak efficiency. Jordan broke Abdul-Jabbar's NBA record for most consecutive games scoring at least 10 points, with 840. He paced the Bulls in scoring 64 times and attained 40 or more points 12 times. Pippen regained his All-Star form, with a 19.1 point average, and Rodman captured his seventh straight NBA rebounding title.

Chicago swept New Jersey in the first playoff round. Although blowing a 14-point lead and being outrebounded in Game 1 on April 24, the Bulls squeaked out a 96–93 overtime victory at the United Center. Jordan made just 11 of 27 shots, but he converted 17 of 23 free throws for 39 points. He dunked the ball with 1minute and 30 seconds left and made a crucial foul shot to preserve the triumph. In Game 2 two days later, Chicago capitalized on Jordan's 32 points and Rodman's 16 rebounds to prevail, 96–91. The Bulls led by 20 points late in the third quarter but played sluggishly thereafter. Chicago performed much better offensively and defensively in Game 3 on April 29 at New Jersey. Jordan converted 15 of his first 18 shots and tallied 38 points in the 116–101 triumph. The Bulls had swept three straight first round series and fared 24–1 in first round games since 1991.

Chicago victimized Charlotte in the next round. The Bulls exhibited stellar defense in their 83–70 Game 1 win on May 3. Jordan sparked a 16–0 second-quarter run, and Chicago limited the Hornets to 32 second-half points. Charlotte was held to 49 points the first three quarters in Game 2 on May 6, but guards B. J. Armstrong and Dell Curry led a fourth-quarter surge to stun Chicago, 78–76. The Bulls' controlled the remainder of the series, stinging the Hornets, 103–89, in Game 3 on May 9 and 94–80 in Game 4 the next night at Charlotte. At the United Center in Game 5 on May 13, Chicago clinched the series, 93–84. Jordan finished with 33 points, including 11 in the fourth quarter, and Rodman nabbed 21 rebounds.

Chicago battled Indiana, coached by Larry Bird, in the Eastern Conference Finals. The Pacers were the sixth opponent and toughest foe the Bulls had faced in six Eastern Conference Finals. The Bulls took Game 1, 85–79, at the United Center on May 17 because their stellar defense forced Indiana to commit 26 turnovers and, with his size, strength, and quickness, Pippen disrupted the Pacers' offense. Chicago trailed, 40–37, at halftime, as Jordan shot poorly, but started the second half with a 10–0 run and never looked back.

Two nights later, the Bulls performed much better offensively in their Game 2, 104–98, win. Chicago led by seven points late in the fourth quarter, but Indiana quickly sliced the margin to three before Jordan's two key baskets thwarted the comeback. Jordan tallied 41 points, shooting 13 for 22 from the field and 15 for 19 from the foul line, with five assists, four steals, and four rebounds. Pippen contributed 21 points and disrupted the Pacers' defense, and the Bulls recorded 15 steals. Bird complained the officials gave Pippen free rein in defending point guard Mark Jackson.

Chicago lost two spectacular games at Market Square Arena over the Memorial Day weekend. The Bulls led both games in the fourth quarter, but Indiana seized control in the waning minutes. The Pacers took Game 3, 107–105, on May 23. Pippen committed two quick fouls, limiting his effectiveness. Chicago relied on jump shots rather than penetrating the basket and committed many fouls, and Indiana featured a stronger bench and younger players. Bird neutralized Jordan by rotating different defenders on him and playing him very physically and used fresh substitutes when the Bulls appeared fatigued. Chicago surprisingly weakened toward the end of the second and third quarters.

Two nights later, Indiana nipped the Bulls, 96–94, in Game 4. Chicago led 94–91 when Travis Best scored with just 33 seconds left. After Pippen missed two free throws, Reggie Miller converted a game-winning three-pointer from the top of the key with less than a second left. Jordan's desperation 26-footer at the buzzer barely missed.

The Bulls bolted to a 57–32 halftime lead and blew out the Pacers, 106–87, in Game 5 on May 27 at the United Center. Jordan tallied 29 points, surpassing 35,000 career regular season and playoff points, third behind Abdul-Jabbar and Chamberlain.

Indiana squeaked by Chicago, 92–89, in Game 6 two nights later at Market Square Arena, exploiting another late game rally and superior bench strength. The Pacer reserves outscored Chicago's bench, 25–8. Indiana pounded Jordan, exhausting him physically. Jordan tripped as he was driving toward the basket and lost the ball in the waning seconds, but the officials did not call what he considered a glaring foul. The Pacers extended the Bulls to a seventh game for just the second time in Jordan's title run.

Chicago held the crucial home advantage in Game 7 on May 31 and had fared 27–2 in playoff games at the United Center since 1996. The Chicago *Tribune* dubbed the contest "ONE FOR THE AGED" and queried "Bulls' vets too weary to survive?"[40] Jordan's first five points that Sunday vaulted him past Abdul-Jabbar as the top scorer in NBA playoff history with 5,763 points. Indiana surged to an early 20–8 advantage, forcing Jackson to abandon his six-man rotation. Jackson played Rodman longer to increase rebounding and inserted Kerr and Jud Buechler to inject more offense, helping Chicago move ahead 48–45 at halftime.

When Jordan admonished his teammates at halftime for lacking intensity, Kukoc responded with five third-quarter baskets. The Pacers punished Jordan every time he drove to the basket, hoping to exhaust him physically by the fourth quarter. During a timeout, Jordan ensured his teammates that they were going to prevail. He played the last seven minutes entirely on desire, penetrating heavy traffic in the lane, drawing several fouls, and converting five of seven free throws to capture an 88–83 win. Jordan made only 9 of 25 field goals and 10 of 15 free throws for 28 points, but he refused to lose a home contest that would prevent him from reaching another NBA Finals. "It's about heart," he declared. Besides holding Miller scoreless in the fourth quarter, Jordan added nine rebounds, eight assists, and two steals. The Bulls had won the Eastern Conference Finals for the third consecutive year and outlasted Indiana in a series in which the latter appeared headed toward victory.

Jordan relished returning to the NBA Finals against Utah. Although conceding that the Bulls were drained physically, he gave assurance that "our hearts are not tired."[41] The Jazz, paced by Malone and Stockton, swept the Los Angeles Lakers in the Western Conference Finals and waited 10 days for

Chicago to advance. Although not holding home advantage this time, the Bulls matched up better individually, concentrated better, and performed better away against playoff teams.

Utah seemed tight in Game 1 on June 3 at the Delta Center, and Chicago looked sluggish, partly because of the higher altitude. After battling through a 17-all first period, the Jazz jumped to a seven-point second-quarter lead and retained a four-point advantage with 55.4 seconds left. The Bulls tied the contest, 79–79, with just 14 seconds left and used their stifling defense to force overtime. Stockton's three-pointer, however, gave Utah an 88–85 victory, putting Chicago behind in the NBA Finals for the first time since 1991. The Jazz outplayed the Bulls both in the middle and among the reserves and committed fewer turnovers. Although scoring 33 points, Jordan tired in the second half and tallied only 13 points after intermission. He missed several late shots and even allowed the 24-second clock to expire once in overtime.

Two nights later, Chicago performed like champions in a 93–88 triumph over Utah. The Bulls extended their triangle offense in the first half, enabling numerous drives for easy buckets. Jordan converted 14 of 33 shots and 9 of 10 free throws for 37 points in that contest, making 17 points in the final quarter. The Jazz countered with several transition baskets and led 86–85 in the final two minutes. Jordan's layup with 47.9 seconds left put Chicago ahead. Utah tied the score 88–88, but Jordan's basket and free throw propelled the Bulls to victory and wrested home court advantage. At crunch time, Jordan hit four clutch baskets and five of six free throws. Chicago's guards restricted Stockton's movement and isolated Malone. "It was just a matter of executing down the stretch," Jordan affirmed. He added, "this time we executed and got to all the loose balls. We went to the free-throw line, and defensively we held tough. I think we have an inner peace and an inner confidence in ourselves on what we can accomplish."[42]

The Bulls overwhelmed the Jazz, 96–54, the largest victory margin in NBA playoff history, in Game 3 on June 7 at the United Center. Utah succumbed to nearly flawless defensive performances by Pippen, Jordan, and Harper, scoring the fewest points for an NBA team since the introduction of the shot clock. Despite suffering from back spasms, Pippen tallied 10 first-half points and stymied Stockton defensively. Chicago built a 49–31 halftime lead and widened the margin to 72–45 after three quarters, pilfering the ball, blocking passing lanes, and forcing the Jazz to take desperation shots. Shell-shocked Utah coach Jerry Sloan noted "It seemed like they scored 196,"[43] and Jackson lauded the Bulls' relentless defense.

Three nights later, the Bulls took Game 4, 86–82. Besides disrupting the Jazz's offense, Pippen netted 28 points, 9 rebounds, and 5 steals and sank 3 fourth-quarter three-pointers. Jordan made 34 points, including two clutch baskets in the final 2 minutes and 11 seconds to rebuff Utah's challenge. Chicago converted 17 of 24 free throws in the fourth stanza. Rodman's four free throws in the waning seconds accompanied his 14 rebounds and stellar defense on Malone. The Bulls held a 3–1 lead with Game 5 at the United Center.

Utah spoiled Chicago's celebration plans, prevailing, 83–81, on June 12. Malone enjoyed his best performance, converting 17 of 27 shots for 39 points and recording nine rebounds. Kukoc kept the Bulls close with 30 points, but Jordan hit only 9 of 26 shots and the ailing Pippen just 2 of 16 shots. Jordan's desperation 26-foot shot at the buzzer missed the rim. "I would have loved to have won it here at home," he confessed. "It would have been a great scenario."[44] Jackson, who blamed the loss on the pre-game hype and media buzz about clinching at home, told Jordan that the Bulls needed to seal the deal in Utah.

Jordan, exuding infectious confidence, carried the Bulls when they needed him most in Game 6 at the Delta Center two days later, trumping his courageous feats of the 1997 playoffs with perhaps the greatest clutch performance in NBA Finals history. Pippen's back spasms limited his to use as a decoy for 26 minutes. Before intermission, Jordan made 9 of 19 shots, including three of six three-pointers, for 23 points. The Jazz led 42–37 at halftime and 66–61 after the third quarter. Chicago tied the game, 77–77, with less than five minutes left, but Utah regained the lead, 83–79. Jordan, who often had conserved his energy for the last quarter, told himself, "We're going to win this game."[45]

During a timeout, Jackson instructed Jordan to start driving toward the basket. Jordan concurred that the lane was open because the Jazz did not have a center in the game at the time. He was fouled while driving and sank two foul shots with 2 minutes and 7 seconds left. The Jazz fouled him again with 59.2 seconds left, and he converted two more free throws to tie the score. During another respite, Jordan assured Jackson, "I've got my second wind now."[46] Jackson reminded him to follow through on any jump shot attempt. After Stockton sank a three-pointer with 41.9 seconds to put Utah ahead, 86–83, Jordan calmly drove down the right side, spun past Russell, and floated a soft layup over Antoine Carr to slice the margin to 86–85, with 37 seconds left.

The Jazz passed the ball to Malone in the low post with 20 seconds left before a raucous Delta Center crowd. "It was like I was watching everything unfold in slow motion on television,"[47] Jordan remembered.

The Delta Center crowd suddenly quieted as he came around Malone's blind side and made the most important steal of his career with 18.9 seconds left. Jordan did not call a timeout because he did not want to let Utah set up defensively. He slowly dribbled the ball down court to his right, being guarded by Byron Russell, and realized that Stockton could not leave Kerr to help defensively.

When the clock reached eight seconds, Jordan stutter-stepped, started dribbling right, and crossed over to his left. Russell lunged to his left and slipped while attempting to keep Jordan from driving past him. Jordan never contemplated passing the ball, stating "I stole the ball and it was my opportunity to win or lose the game."[48] He suddenly stopped, got a great look, used perfect elevation and form, and sank an easy jump shot with 5.2 seconds left to give the Bulls an 87–86 lead. He held his right hand to make sure to get the ball over the rim because his fadeaway jump shots had been short.

Jordan's shot was rebroadcast countless times. "Jordan stood poised," Roland Lazenby wrote, "his arm draped in a follow through, savoring the moment, inhabiting the moment, frozen in that moment. Photos of the shot would show in the soft focus a number of Utah fans suspended there in agony with him, their hands covering eyes and ears, the ball hanging there in air, ready to swish for an 87–86 Chicago win." Jordan held that pose for the NBA world to take one final picture. He visualized the court and anticipated how the defense would respond. "I saw the moment,"[49] he recounted. "I would have taken that shot with five people on me."[50] The whole sequence took just 13 seconds.

Stockton missed a desperation last second three-point shot to preserve the Bulls victory. Jordan and Jackson embraced at midcourt, whispering to each other. Jackson told him, "it was just a magnificent ending, and that I don't know how much more a person can do in this game."[51] He boasted "it was the best performance I've seen in a critical situation and critical game in a series."[52]

Chicago won its sixth NBA title in eight years and secured three consecutive titles for the second time, overcoming the Jazz, 4–2, in the NBA Finals. Jordan wrote the last great chapter of his magnificent Bulls career with a fairy-tale ending. He carried Chicago again with 45 points, outscoring Malone 16–6 in the last quarter. Jordan drove to the basket when necessary and made 10 foul shots. He earned NBA Finals MVP honors an unprecedented sixth time, averaging 35.5 points. No other NBA player had won the NBA Finals MVP more than three times. Commissioner David Stern lauded him.

When the Bulls returned to Chicago, a huge throng celebrated at Grant Park. Players and wives dined that night at Jordan's restaurant. Teammates stood and cheered Jordan, who had inspired them to soar to new heights. The moment symbolized the Bulls' extraordinary accomplishments and the end of a remarkable era.

After the season, Jackson rejected Reinsdorf's offer to let him remain as coach. Krause still resented Jackson because the latter did not accord him the same respect he wanted for enabling him to become among the top coaches in NBA history. Jackson, who knew it was time to leave, had unified the Bulls and given them focus. He had understood how each player fit into the group and had respected their individuality. Jackson had challenged Jordan rather than criticize him.

## THE LEGEND RETIRES (1991)

The NBA management and players engaged in a bitter labor dispute that delayed the 1998–1999 season by three months. Although Chicago needed both Jordan and Pippen back to remain a winning club, it traded Pippen to Houston in January 1999. Jordan, who vowed to stay only if Pippen returned, announced his retirement on January 13, one week after settlement of the owner- induced NBA player lockout. Reinsdorf re-raised Number 23 to the United Center rafters and gave Jordan his championship ring. Jordan insisted that his physical skills and passion for basketball remained strong and departed knowing that he could still perform. He rated the 1991–1993 Bulls better than the 1996–1998 aggregates and regarded his dramatic shots to defeat Cleveland in 1989 and Utah in 1998 as his favorite memories. Jordan considered parenting to be his new challenge, and he was 99.9 percent certain that he would not return to basketball. "I am not going to say never,"[53] he added. He did not give fans any reason, however, to believe the end had really come.

Jordan remained the world's most popular sports and commercial figure. In mid-1998, *Fortune* magazine estimated his impact on the American economy at more than $10 billion. Approximately $5.2 billion benefited Nike, which spun off the Jordan line into its own company, the "Jordan Brand." Jordan's line surged in sales by 57 percent in 1997–1998, although every other major Nike brand declined sharply. Numerous star athletes endorsed the Jordan Brand, which sponsors numerous sports programs. The sales of NBA-licensed clothing (especially Number 23 jerseys) increased by $3.1 billion. *Fortune* credited him with furnishing hundreds of millions of dollars in profit to television and cable companies. Jordan also made a commercial impact in France, Germany, South Africa, Japan, and other nations. He and agent David Falk had begun using a global communications company for selling numerous Jordan products. Jordan's fans watched his *Space Jam* film while sitting in their Hanes underwear and Nike shoes, eating Big Macs, drinking Gatorade, and buying his videos over their Jordan-endorsed cell phone.

Jordan capped off the decade by winning four ESPY awards in February 2000. ESPN named him Athlete of the Century, Male Athlete of the 1990s, and Pro Basketball Player of the 1990s. He also garnered Play of the Decade honors for his shot against the Los Angeles Lakers in the 1991 NBA Finals, when he switched the ball from his right to left hand while in mid-air before shooting.

# NOTES

1. Michael Jordan, ed. by Mark Vancil, *For the Love of the Game: My Story* (New York: Crown Publishers, 1998), p. 96.

2. Rick Telander, *The Year of the Bull: Zen, Air, and the Pursuit of Sacred & Profane Hoops* (New York: Simon & Schuster, 1996), p. 99; Roland Lazenby, *Blood on the Horns: The Long Strange Ride of Michael Jordan's Chicago Bulls* (Lenexa, KS: Addax Publishing Group, 1998), p. 31.

3. Ibid., p. 29.

4. Telander, *Year of Bull*, p. 56.

5. Jordan, *Love of Game*, p. 96.

6. Telander, *Year of Bull*, p. 63.

7. Jordan, *Love of Game*, p. 96.

8. Telander, *Year of Bull*, p. 77.

9. Ibid., p. 97.

10. *Chicago Tribune*, February 19, 1996.

11. *USA Today*, February 23, 1996, p. 106.

12. Telander, *Year of Bull*, p. 183.

13. Jordan, *Love of Game*, p. 97.

14. Ibid., p. 97.

15. Telander, *Year of Bull*, p. 185.

16. David Halberstam, *Playing for Keeps: Michael Jordan and the World He Made* (New York: Random House, 1999), p. 352.

17. Telander, *Year of Bull*, p. 221.

18. Mark Broussard et al., eds., *The Sporting News Official NBA Guide 1996–97* (St. Louis, MO: The Sporting News, 1996), p. 117.

19. Ibid., p. 118.

20. *The Seattle Intelligencer*, June 10, 1996.

21. Telander, *Year of Bull*, p. 242.

22. Broussard, *NBA Guide 1996–97*, p. 119.

23. Jordan, *Love of Game*, p. 101.

24. Telander, *Year of Bull*, p. 266.

25. Broussard, *NBA Guide 1996–97*, p. 119, 117.

26. Lazenby, *Blood on Horns*, pp. 69, 71.

27. Mitchell Krugel, *One Last Shot: The Story of Michael Jordan's Comeback* (New York: St. Martin's Press, 2003), p. 53.

28. *New York Times*, June 6, 1996, sec. 8, p. 1.

29. Jordan, *Love of Game*, p. 102.

30. Mark Broussard et al., eds., *The Sporting News Official NBA Guide 1997–98* (St. Louis, MO: The Sporting News, 1997), p. 119.

31. Jordan, *Love of Game*, p. 103.

32. *Ibid*, p. 66.

33. Lazenby, *Blood on Horns*, p. 101.

34. Ibid., pp. 40–41.

35. Ibid., p. 110.

36. Ibid., p. 165.

37. *Chicago Tribune*, February 5, 1998.

38. Lazenby, *Blood on Horns*, p. 188.

39. Ibid., p. 188.

40. *Chicago Tribune*, June 1, 1998.

41. Lazenby, *Blood on Horns*, pp. 258–259.

42. Mark Broussard et al., eds., *The Sporting News Official NBA Guide 1998–99* (St. Louis, MO: The Sporting News, 1998), p. 117.

43. Ibid., p. 117.

44. Ibid., p. 118.

45. Jordan, *Love of Game*, p. 77.

46. Halberstam, *Playing for Keeps*, p. 395.

47. Jordan, *Love of Game*, p. 108.

48. Ibid., p. 108.

49. Lazenby, *Blood on Horns*, p. 270.

50. Jordan, *Love of Game*, p. 108.

51. Walter LaFeber, *Michael Jordan and the New Global Capitalism* (New York: W. W. Norton Company, 1999), p. 133.

52. Broussard, *NBA Guide 1998–99*, p. 118.

53. Krugel, *One Last Shot*, p. 60.

# Chapter 6

# THE DISAPPOINTING YEARS, 1999–2006

## THE FULFILLMENT OF EXECUTIVE DREAMS (1999–2001)

Carpooling his three children to school and parental challenges did not keep Jordan fully occupied. In September 1999, Washington, D.C. sports tycoon Ted Leonsis met with Jordan for three hours at his downtown Chicago restaurant. Leonsis, builder of America Online, proposed making Jordan one of his partners. His firm, Lincoln Holdings, controlled the Washington Capitols hockey club and 44 percent of Washington Sports & Entertainment, which owned the Washington Wizards basketball club and other athletic teams. He asked Jordan to head the Wizards operations.

Leonsis introduced Jordan to Abe Pollin, who completed the deal. Jordan met Pollin in late December 1999 at the latter's Bethesda, Maryland home. According to one report, Jordan paid between $20 million and $30 million for 5 percent of the Wizards and 10 percent of Lincoln Holdings. Another report claimed that he received $30 million to $50 million worth of stock in Lincoln Holdings. Pollin held final authority on budgetary issues. Jordan kept his Chicago residence and plunged wholeheartedly into overhauling the struggling Wizards.

On January 19, 2000, Jordan officially joined the Wizards as president of basketball operations and pledged to assess the entire organization. Despite boasting the NBA's seventh highest payroll, the Wizards were the NBA's second-weakest team and had reached the playoffs just once in 12 seasons. In 1997, the Chicago Bulls swept Washington in the first round. His duties included mastering the collective bargaining agreement involving players' contracts and the salary cap; negotiating contracts with players' agents; organizing a preseason training camp; scouting international, college, and high school games and tournaments; hiring and dismissing coaches, scouts, and office staff; and meeting with the media.

Jordan fired head coach Gar Heard when the Wizards dropped to 14–30 and selected Darrell Walker from the Continental Basketball Association as interim coach. Walker finished the season with an even worse 5–33 record and was reassigned to the player personnel department. Jordan named Rod Higgins assistant general manager, Fred Whitfield player personnel director, and Leonard Hamilton of the University of Miami, a veteran collegiate coach, as head coach. John Paxson, his former Bulls teammate, Mike Jarvis, then St. John's University head coach, and Roy Williams, then University of Kansas coach, already had declined his invitation to become head coach.

Jordan met with the Wizard players during the off-season and practiced with them that fall at the University of North Carolina at Wilmington. He soon began making roster changes. Isaac Austin, Tracy Murray, and Dennis Scott were released at training camp. To Jordan's disappointment, Washington won only four of their first 16 games through November. On December 6, the Wizards blew a 19-point lead at home against the struggling Los Angeles Clippers, losing 93–88. After the game, Jordan denounced the players as "a disgrace to the fans" because of their "losers' mentality."[1] He hoped the Wizards would respond to his challenge, but they lost the next four games.

Washington fared 5–25 through December 29, worst in franchise history. Jordan tried to improve the Wizards, trading or releasing some highly paid, unpopular players. In November 2000, he acquired forward Tyrone Nesby from the Clippers for Cherokee Parks and Obinna Ekezie and reclaimed Ekezie three days later. Two months later, Jordan sent Juwan Howard, Calvin Booth, and Ekezie to the Dallas Mavericks for centers Christian Laettner and Etan Thomas, guards Courtney Alexander and Hubert Davis, and forward Loy Vaught. He believed that Nesby and Alexander were built in his mold, but the Wizards still lost 21 of their last 27 games. Disgruntled guard Rod Strickland was waived in mid-March. Hamilton resigned as coach after posting a 19–63 record, the worst in franchise history. Only center Jahidi White and guards Richard Hamilton and Chris Whitney lasted the entire season.

## THE ROAD TO WIZARDRY (2001–2002)

In mid-March, Rick Reilly of *Sports Illustrated* reported that Jordan was 90 percent committed to making a comeback with the Wizards.[2] He wanted to play for two years, instructing his teammates how to be mentally tough, win, and make the playoffs. Jordan, inspired by the comeback of Pittsburgh Penguins hockey star Mario Lemieux, began exercising six hours daily in suburban Chicago in February to return to playing condition. He needed to shed 25 pounds, work on backpedaling, and restore his jump shot and fadeaway shot. His knees swelled during the first practice games in March. Antoine Walker, Penny Hardaway, Ron Artest, Charles Barkley, Michael Finley, Jerry Stackhouse, Charles Oakley, and others participated in some pickup games with Jordan at Hoops the Gym, a Chicago gymnasium. Artest accidentally elbowed Jordan and broke some of his ribs, delaying his reconditioning program. In April, Wizards president Abe Pollin predicted that Jordan would return. Jordan exhibited spring in his legs, an efficient, laser-like shot, and improved peripheral vision, but his vertical jump had declined. After conducting his annual summer basketball camp, he resumed workouts with Walker, Marcus Fizer, and others at Hoops the Gym.

When the Wizards won the NBA draft lottery in May, Jordan selected Kwame Brown from Glynn Academy in Brunswick, Georgia. Brown had averaged 20 points, 13 rebounds, and 6 blocked shots his senior year. The Wizards brass viewed Brown as "the prize of the draft" with "the potential to be groomed over a few years into becoming the next NBA phenom."[3] Jordan liked Brown's competitiveness and ability to overcome adversity and hoped to train him to become the team leader and the foundation for a title contender, but that never happened.

Jordan also hired former Bulls and Detroit Pistons coach Doug Collins, who had been a television network basketball commentator, to replace Hamilton, a move many saw as foreshadowing his own return. Besides being competitive, Collins knew what role Jordan should play, how to motivate and improve the young Wizards, when to play a subservient role to Jordan, and how to discipline the younger players. Jordan selected "a known commodity he could command over a wild card who might exert an unwanted authority."[4]

Jordan spent late August in pickup games with 15 NBA players, including Mike Finley, Charles Oakley, Anafree Hardaway, and Tim Hardaway. Although Jordan uncharacteristically lost games, the experience prepared him for the Wizards training camp. He drove himself to the maximum and soon suffered tendinitis in his foot and knees. A late September press release announced his departure from executive responsibilities to return as a player.

Jordan headed for Washington's training camp in Wilmington, North Carolina in early October. His return as a player rejuvenated his spirits.

Jordan led the Wizards mostly by example and worked especially hard on Brown, trying to develop him in his own image. After practicing one week, he spent considerable time on the bench with ice wrapped around his knees. During eight exhibition games, Jordan scored 135 points in 158 minutes. He tallied 41 points, including 16 points in a six-minute span of the third quarter against New Jersey, but the Wizards still lost, 102–95. Washington needed to perform better without relying on him so much.

The Wizards dropped their October 30 season opener to the New York Knicks at Madison Square Garden. Two nights later, Jordan's 31 points and Richard Hamilton's 22 points vaulted Washington past the host Atlanta Hawks, 98–88. Washington won its November 3 home opener, 90–76, over the Philadelphia 76ers at the MCI Center. NBC televised the Wizards for the first time in five years, as Jordan contributed seven points and nine assists as a point guard.

Jordan struggled with his shooting and elevation during Washington's eight-game losing streak in November. Detroit fans booed him when the Pistons trounced the Wizards on November 4. "It's been quite a while since I took some heckling,"[5] he admitted. Jordan experienced frustration when attempting to stop the losing streak, making only 22 of 63 shots in the first three setbacks. Teammates did not get open for shots when he tried to pass to them. He tallied 32 points in a loss at the Boston Celtics on November 7, but Boston blocked three of his shots to stymie a fourth-quarter comeback. Jordan lamented that the inexperienced Wizards had not learned yet how to close games in the fourth quarter.

Washington dropped its next five games at home. Despite Jordan's 13 for 30 performance, the Golden State Warriors defeated the Wizards on November 9. Jordan complained that the Wizards were performing as individuals rather than as a team "Collective effort means team defense," he stressed. "Offense is not counting on one guy to score."[6] Although he ranked among the top 10 in scoring, Jordan led the NBA in shots taken and missed. He had converted a career-low 41 percent of his shots. Two nights later, Jordan missed his first eight shots and converted only 5 of 26 made shots in a setback to the Seattle SuperSonics. Seattle made Jordan work hard to get the ball and crowded him when he shot. His Chicago teams had not lost four consecutive games in 11 seasons. Teammates waited for him to regain his old form. Washington lost its fifth straight game on November 14 to the Milwaukee Bucks, but Jordan sank 50 percent of his shots for the first time. Milwaukee outscored the Wizards, 29–13, during one five-minute span when Jordan did not touch the ball. He complained that his teammates were not fulfilling their responsibilities.

"They take that paycheck twice a month, and along with that comes accountability."[7]

The Utah Jazz turned back Washington two nights later, although Jordan tied the NBA season-high with 44 points. The Jazz triple-teamed him with 4 minutes and 40 seconds left and blocked one of his shots with the score tied, triggering a 7–0 run. On November 20, the Charlotte Hornets bested the Wizards. Jordan tallied 30 points in a 13-for-23 performance; his teammates struggled mightily. He averaged 40 minutes of playing time per game during the losing streak, causing him to fatigue. The losing streak extended to nine games when Washington lost to the Indiana Pacers two nights later, as Jordan shot poorly. Jordan rationalized his subpar performances by saying that either "he had stopped himself" or "the *whole* defense is focusing on me."[8]

The bleeding stopped with an 88–84 double overtime victory on November 24 over visiting Boston. Jordan performed for 45 minutes but suffered pain in his swollen knee. Three nights later, the Cleveland Cavaliers trounced the Wizards. Although Jordan scored 18 points, he did not take a free throw for the first time in 162 games. He was not accustomed to losing and was dismayed that his young teammates seemed to accept it.

Jordan's physical conditioning seemingly abandoned him. At crunch time, he missed shots he usually made and committed uncharacteristic turnovers. In one contest, he seemed out of sync and converted just two three-pointers in 16 attempts. He expected his shooting accuracy to return when his legs strengthened and figured that shooting more would solve his problems.

Opponents used new Jordan Rules, denying him the ball so that he would tire more readily late in games. They guarded him with tall centers and forwards to exploit his dwindling vertical leap and prevent him from driving to the basket. Defenders also stayed on the floor until Jordan jumped.

The Wizards rebounded on November 28 with a 94–87 victory at Philadelphia. Although 76er Allen Iverson scored 27 first-half points, the triumph signified the return of Jordan's game. Jordan regained his old form, making 14 consecutive second-quarter points. When Philadelphia double-teamed him in the third quarter, Hamilton compensated with 16 points. Hamilton realized that playing with Jordan meant not being afraid to shoot. Other Wizards discovered that, if they hustled, Jordan would get them the ball, too. Jordan's 28 points, 7 assists, and fourth-quarter defense ensured the triumph.

Two nights later, Jordan converted his first five shots and hit four of seven fourth-quarter shots, including six points in a 12–2 run, to overcome a 13-point deficit and defeat the host Miami Heat, 84–75. A hyperextended right knee hindered him in a December 1 loss to the Orlando Magic. During the fourth quarter, Tracy McGrady blocked his jump shot. "MCI sounded like a tomb. Jordan lurched, buckled. His pain and limp became impossible to hide."[9] Collins removed him from the game perhaps too late. Jordan missed the next game at San Antonio, the first time an injury had sidelined him since the 1992–1993 season. He visited Dr. John Hefferon in Chicago, who put his knee through a magnetic resonance imaging exam and drained more fluid. Hefferon advised him to reduce his playing time and skip the second halves of consecutive games. Collins also wanted to reduce Jordan's playing time, but Jordan did not intend to miss second halves of consecutive games.

Despite Jordan's ailing knee, Washington tied a franchise mark with nine straight victories from December 6 through December 22. Collins rested Jordan eight minutes during both halves, four at the end of one quarter and at the start of the next. The strategy enabled him to preserve his energy for crunch time. The streak began with an 85–82 squeaker at the Houston Rockets. Hamilton recorded most of his 26 points in the first three quarters, and Jordan netted 10 fourth-quarter points. The Wizards defeated Dallas, 102–95, two nights later, building a lead without relying on Jordan. After Dallas tied the game, 80–80, early in the fourth quarter, Jordan made 15 points. On December 11, Washington triumphed, 91–81, over the host Memphis Grizzlies, 91–81. Hamilton notched 30 points, and Jordan contributed nine assists. Victories over Miami and New York extended the streak to five games.

Washington overcame a 19-point first-quarter deficit to conquer the Toronto Raptors, 93–88, on December 16. The Wizards played some of the best basketball in franchise history in the last quarter, outscoring Toronto, 20–3, during a 9-minute and 20-second interval. As they scored 14 of those points with Jordan on the bench, the Wizards finally showed signs of becoming the team he wanted. Hamilton tallied 27 points, outscoring Vince Carter, 16–4, over the final three periods. Kwame Brown made 10 rebounds and Chris Whitney sank several three-pointers in the final quarter. Jordan claimed that the Wizards had matured and had begun to heed his advice. "Winning is an attitude," he taught, "and if you step into every game with the attitude, you have a chance to win." Collins concurred, "I can deliver a soliloquy, but one word like that from Michael means everything."[10]

Washington achieved its largest victory margin in nearly two years, routing Atlanta, 103–76, three nights later at the MCI Center. In the second quarter, Jordan made nine consecutive baskets for 18 points. The

MCI crowd chanted "Joooorr-dan, Joooor-dan—less an exhortation than a feel-good mantra, more reverential than rabid."[11] Although the Wizards walloped Orlando, 93–75, on December 21 on the road, Hamilton suffered a groin injury that sidelined him for six weeks. The next night, Washington overcame a 16-point deficit at New York for its ninth straight victory. Jordan's clutch 18-foot jumper with just 3.2 seconds left edged the Knicks, 87–86, signifying the defining moment of his latest comeback and giving the Wizards a 14–12 record. Whitney noted, "This is what he came back for," and Hamilton observed, "he makes you believe anything is possible."[12]

The rebuilding process took only a month in Washington, as Jordan collaborated with Hamilton. He averaged only 21 shots in less than 35 minutes during the nine-game winning streak because his teammates shot more often. Brown contributed both points and rebounds, and center Brendan Haywood dominated the middle defensively. During that span, the Wizards limited opponents to 85 points per game.

The streak ended with a 99–93 setback at Charlotte on December 26. Washington blew a fourth-quarter lead, allowing Charlotte a 22–7 scoring run. The Wizards sliced the deficit from nine to four on Jordan's layup and three-pointer with 23.9 seconds left. Jordan tallied 12 of his 28 points in the fourth quarter but made a crucial turnover with 12.3 seconds left. The next night, Indiana pounded the visiting Wizards, 108–81, limiting Jordan to a career-low six points. For the first time in 866 NBA games since March 22, 1986, he did not score in double figures. Jordan sat out the final 17 minutes of the debacle.

Three nights later, Jordan established an MCI Center scoring record with a 51-point masterpiece in a 107–90 romp over Charlotte. He tallied Washington's first 13 points in less than six minutes and made 24 of its 29 first-quarter points. Jordan signaled teammates to pass him the ball. His 34 first-half points broke the franchise record of 33, set by Jeff Malone in 1988. Jordan added 11 third-quarter points, breaking his MCI scoring record of 44 points against Utah in November. His 21 of 38 shots shattered the Wizard mark for most baskets, and his 51 points marked the most by a 38-year-old, five better than Kareem Abdul-Jabbar's 1984 standard. "I certainly wanted to make a statement offensively,"[13] he explained. "Tonight, I'm pretty sure people are going to say I can still play the game."[14]

Jordan combined 50-plus and 40-plus point masterpieces for the first time since November 1992, recording 45 points in a 98–76 thrashing of visiting New Jersey on New Year's Eve. He made four straight shots and 10 consecutive points to turn a second-quarter deficit into a three-point halftime lead. In the third quarter, his four straight layups sparked a 22-point Wizard run. Jordan, who finished the third quarter with 42 points, noticed that most teams defended him one-on-one rather than double-teaming him. His knee felt the best it had felt all season. "Before, he used to just beat you with sheer will, skill, energy," Collins detected. "Now, he slices you just like a surgeon."[15] He added, "As Michael has gotten better, it's given the guys a little bit of a swagger."[16] The Wizards boasted a 17–14 record through December, an 11-game improvement.

On January 4, Chicago visited the MCI Center in Jordan's first confrontation with his former franchise. Jordan scored 19 second-quarter points, the same as the Bulls, putting ace defender Artest in foul trouble. The 20,674 spectators cheered him when he left shortly before halftime. Jordan hit his first third-quarter shot, extending the Wizards lead to 64–41, but the Bulls limited him to eight points thereafter and narrowed the gap to six points. Jordan finished with 29 points in 38 minutes, ensuring the 89–83 triumph and the Wizards' 12th win in 14 games. He passed an historic milestone when Artest fouled him at 5 minutes and 28 seconds of the third quarter. Jordan's two free throws gave him 30,000 career points. Only Kareem Abdul-Jabbar, Wilt Chamberlain, and Karl Malone had attained that monumental figure. Jordan especially enjoyed accomplishing the feat against his former team.

## MARRIAGE PROBLEMS (2002)

Three days later, Juanita filed a petition in Lake County Circuit Court in Waukegan, Illinois to divorce Jordan for "irreconcilable differences" and terminate their 12-year marriage. She requested "half of the marital property," which included a "25,000-square-foot mansion" and his "net worth of $400 million."[17] Her friends hinted that she had threatened him with divorce twice before. She may have concluded that he would never become a stay-at-home father, may have heard rumors of infidelity, or may have grown weary of playing second fiddle. Juanita had waited for Jordan's basketball career to finish and for family to take precedence. Jordan had vowed to spend more time with his family when he retired. Before they wed, Jordan had promised never to move her from Chicago or from her family. After returning as a player, he reportedly attempted to shower her with gifts, including a sapphire-and-diamond watch. Jordan admitted missing the time he had enjoyed with his family during retirement. He saw Juanita when Dr. Hefferon looked at his injured knee in early December and pledged to return often to Chicago to restore some semblance of family life.

The media circulated rumors of infidelity. A supermarket tabloid wrote about Jordan's secret relationship with a former lover, Karla Knafel, which Jordan admitted was true. According to the *New York Post*, Juanita hired a private detective to shadow him for four years and "spotted him in public with at least six women."[18] Rumors also spread about him soliciting dancers in gentleman's clubs. *The Chicago Sun-Times* headlined its front-page "So who gets the house?"[19]

Before a January 8 home game, Jordan admitted being physically drained and tried to concentrate on playing basketball. He still believed that Juanita would give the marriage one last try, if only for the children. Several weeks later, the couple agreed to attempt a reconciliation of their differences.

Washington's 96–88 triumph on January 8 over the Los Angeles Clippers marked an excellent team effort. During the first half, Whitney made propitious three-pointers, Popeye Jones rebounded well, and Jordan converted four consecutive jump shots. Hubert Davis tallied 14 of his 16 points in the third quarter. The Wizards squandered a fourth-quarter lead, but Jordan, Jones, and Whitney tallied 10 straight points at crunch time. Jordan almost recorded a triple-double with 18 points, 10 rebounds, and 8 assists, and teammates relied less on him. Jones, Haywood, and Jahidi White combined up front for 33 points and 22 rebounds.

Washington lost four consecutive games, including three to division leaders, in mid-January. The Wizards suffered from Hamilton's continued absence. After Milwaukee walloped the visiting Wizards on January 11, Washington returned home and fell to the Minnesota Timberwolves the next night. Jordan scored 35 points, including 26 in the first half, but Kevin Garnett and Chauncey Billups combined for 60 points. Jordan endured his second-worst shooting night against the San Antonio Spurs on January 15, missing 16 of 21 shots and six free throws in a home loss. The next night, New Jersey demolished the Wizards, 111–67. Jordan skipped the entire second half in Washington's worst game of the season.

A standing-room-only crowd greeted Jordan when he returned to Chicago's United Center to face the Bulls on January 19. His introduction drew a rousing 1-minute and 18-second standing ovation. He waved several times and bowed his head attempting to fight off tears. Both teams performed poorly in Washington's 77–69 win. Jordan did not resemble his past glory, hitting only 7 of 21 shots. "I'm not the same player," he admitted.[20] Although still thriving on competition, Jordan knew his physical limitations. He had played several minutes longer per game than Dr. Hefferon recommended, but he was missing a vast majority of his shots andcommitting numerous turnovers. "His performance had plummeted,"[21] noted *Washington Post* writer Michael Leahy.

Jordan, however, returned to old form before the All-Star break, averaging 30.7 points, 6.7 rebounds, and 6.1 assists in 10 games and usually performing well until tiring in the fourth quarter. On January 21 at Minnesota, he made six consecutive second-quarter baskets and scored 22 points before intermission. The Timberwolves triple-teamed him in the second half, forcing him to miss 13 of 15 shots in a loss. In the first quarter against Philadelphia the next night, Jordan recorded 19 of Washington's 23 points. He added 10 second-quarter points, giving him more points than anyone had scored in a half against the 76ers. Philadelphia limited Jordan to just one basket after intermission and defeated the Wizards.

Washington won its final six contests before the All-Star break, nearly all at the MCI Center. Jordan notched 40 points in a 94–85 victory over Cleveland on January 24. The contest featured Jordan's fourth 40-point performance, as he made 18 of 29 shots. Two nights later, Jordan tallied 41 points, hitting 17 of 30 shots in a 112–102 win over the Phoenix Suns and becoming the first NBA player to post consecutive 40-point games twice that season. "My legs, my moves, my first step are definitely coming back,"[22] he sensed. With Washington, Jordan had never enjoyed having such wide-open shots. Jordan led a furious rally on January 29 against Detroit, recording 14 of his 32 points in the fourth quarter. The Pistons barely survived, denying Jordan the ball in the waning seconds.

Two nights later, the Wizards trailed host Cleveland by one point with just 1.6 seconds left. Jordan was left open when the Cavaliers double-teamed Whitney and he made the clutch shot to nip Cleveland, 93–92. "*Everybody* in the gym knew I was gonna take the shot,"[23] he boasted. Washington bested Atlanta, 97–90, on February 1 and Indiana, 109–89, two nights later. In all, 17 of Jordan's 23 points came after intermission. On February 5, he held Vince Carter to four final-quarter points in a 99–94 triumph over Toronto. The Wizards truly played as a team in turning back the Sacramento Kings, 108–101, on February 7. Washington not only had won 23 of its last 34 games, but Jordan was one of just three NBA players averaging more than 25 points, 5 rebounds, and 5 assists that season.

Collins wanted Jordan to skip the All-Star Game on February 10 at Philadelphia to rest his swollen right knee. Jordan, who already ranked third in All-Star history scoring, made his 12th All-Star appearance, moving one ahead of Larry Bird and Magic Johnson and six behind Kareem Abdul-Jabbar. He hit three straight baskets and six of the Eastern Conference's first nine points in the first quarter, but he made only one more shot and missed an easy dunk shot. Jordan's eight points in 23 minutes marked his worst All-Star performance since 1985, as the Western Conference prevailed, 135–120.

The Los Angeles Lakers defeated Washington, 103–94, at the Staples Center on February 12, as Jordan made only 8 of 20 shots. After Sacramento routed the Wizards two nights later, Jordan made his third game-winner with a 17-footer in the waning seconds to edge Phoenix, 97–96, on February 15. His mother, Deloris, and sister, Roslyn, who had moved to Phoenix, witnessed that shot. Jordan struggled with just 11 points in a setback at Houston three nights later.

Jordan's tendinitis and arthritis in his swollen right knee forced him to miss the Detroit contest. New Jersey blanked him in the fourth quarter in a February 21 home loss, but he rebounded with 20 points before intermission and 37 points altogether in a heartbreaking loss to Miami two nights later. Before the next contest at Miami on February 24, doctors drained more fluid from his right knee joint in the locker room. Collins advised Jordan, who could hardly walk, to skip the game. Jordan suffered such excruciating pain that he went scoreless in the first quarter and left the court in the final quarter "dragging the right leg like it had a steel ball on it."[24] Collins had never seen him face such adversity.

Jordan realized that a few days of rest would not cure his condition. Wizards physician Dr. Stephen Haas performed 90-minute surgery on his right knee at Sibley Hospital in Washington, D.C. on February 27. He repaired torn and inflamed lateral meniscus cartilage and cleaned out some loose pieces. The cartilage had limited his ability to change directions or elevate for jump shots. Doctors predicted that Jordan would be sidelined three to six weeks. Washington lost 9 of 13 games without Jordan and faded from the playoff picture at 31–36.

Jordan rejoined to the Wizards on March 20 at Denver. Some doctors advised him to spend more time in rehabilitation, but he was anxious to return. He did not start for the first time in 883 NBA games, but Collins inserted him with three minutes left in the first quarter and played him for about eight minutes. Jordan missed seven of nine shots and scored just seven points, but his presence inspired Washington to rout the Nuggets, 107–75. The next night, he tallied 11 points in 22 minutes in a setback to the Utah Jazz. Jordan ignited a 13–0 third-quarter run at Toronto on March 24, but he missed a crucial shot in the waning seconds in a heart-breaking loss.

The Wizards returned to the MCI Center on March 26, vanquishing Denver, 103–87. The Milwaukee contest three nights later rejuvenated Jordan. He hit five consecutive first-quarter shots and tallied seven points in a two-minute span of the third quarter. The MCI Center crowd gave him a standing ovation after he recorded 34 points in just 26 minutes in the 107–98 win.

Losses to Dallas, the Los Angeles Lakers, Milwaukee, and Charlotte between March 31 and April 5 dropped the Wizards to 34–42, severely damaging their playoff hopes. Dallas blanked Jordan until he made two foul shots late in the third quarter. Jordan did not convert his first basket until the fourth quarter and netted three consecutive jumpers in the final four minutes, but he missed two shots in the waning moments. He wore a synthetic blue legging against Los Angeles to keep his knee warm and prevent stiffness. Los Angeles limited him to a career-low two points scored by a 21-foot second-quarter jumper during a career-low 12 minutes of playing time. Jordan sat out the entire second half of the shellacking so as not to risk further injury.

The swelling in Jordan's right knee forced him to leave the Wizards on April 3 in Milwaukee. Jordan could barely bend his knee and had never suffered such deep pain. The Wizards released a statement that Jordan would miss the remainder of the season because he needed two months to rest his knee. Jordan had never finished a season on the injured list before. His Wizards teammates learned the news when they boarded the team bus that afternoon for the Milwaukee game. Philadelphia eliminated Washington from playoff contention on April 12.

In his inaugural Washington season, Jordan led the Wizards in scoring (1,375 points), assists (5.2 average), and steals (1.42 average). His 22.9-point scoring average was the highest ever for an NBA player who was at least 39 years old and for any guard who was at least 35 years old. He led the Wizards to a 37–45 record, an 18-game improvement over 2000–2001. Although he missed 22 games, Jordan helped develop Hamilton and Alexander as scorers and Whitney as a passer and three-point shooter. He taught Washington how to win, sparking the Wizards to a 22–9 mark in December and January, but his club fared only 11–22 after his surgery and became his first team to miss playoffs.

Jordan made his biggest impact at the gate, where the Wizards paced the NBA in regular season attendance. MCI Center home attendance jumped 32 percent because of his comeback. The Wizards boasted a team-record 41 home sellouts and 38 road sellouts.

## JORDAN'S FINAL CURTAIN CALL (2002–2003)

Jordan kept a low profile for about three months. He saw his sons, Jeffrey and Marcus, play basketball for the Rising Stars AAU squad that practiced in Deerfield, Illinois, near his Highland Park estate. Jordan ate low-fat lunches, practiced with the Wizards draft picks, and exercised at Hoops the Gym. He spent part of the summer golfing and at casinos. Jordan told ESPN in late August that he could not endure another season in pain and notified the Wizards not to expect his return. He left open the possibility of changing his mind at the last minute. Jordan gradually strengthened his knee over the summer.

During the off-season, Washington made several roster changes. In September, the Wizards traded Hamilton to Detroit for veteran point guard Jerry Stackhouse. Hamilton challenged Jordan's learning-to-win rhetoric too much and did not want to be regarded as Jordan's sidekick any longer. Washington acquired small forward Byron Russell from Utah and point guard Larry Hughes from Golden State. Washington also drafted power forward Jared Jeffries from Indiana University, traded Alexander to the New Orleans Hornets, selected guard Juan Dixon of the University of Maryland, and obtained veteran forward Charles Oakley from Chicago.

The Wizards expected these moves to make them an Eastern Conference contender and planned to rely on Stackhouse, Brown, Hughes, and Oakley. Stackhouse demonstrated playoff scoring ability, and Hughes and Russell provided defensive skills. Washington added Patrick Ewing as assistant coach and planned to activate him if it needed a tall veteran for a playoff run.

In late September, Jordan announced his return to the Wizards. He was fitted with orthotic shoes to help his right knee and could decide when to play as the sixth man off the bench. Washington hoped Jordan could play himself into shape, return to the starting lineup by February, and lead the Wizards to the Eastern Conference playoffs. Jordan did not play until the fifth exhibition game and spent most of training camp tutoring younger players. He performed the less colorful role of the jump shooter, converting "like an aging Hollywood leading man" from "an action hero to a venerable character actor."[25]

Jordan performed inconsistently during the first few games. The Wizards lost the season-opener, 74–68, at Toronto on October 30, nearly plunging to an all-time franchise scoring low. Jordan tallied his eight points in the first half, missing six shots and two free throws in the fourth quarter. The Wizards routed Boston, 114–69, in the home opener the next night, as Jordan netted 21 points, including three consecutive jump shots, in 21 minutes.

After being blanked for the first three quarters and scoring just six points in a victory over Cleveland at the MCI Center on November 6, Jordan rebounded with 25 points to edge the Los Angeles Lakers, 100–99, two nights later and 27 points in a loss to Seattle on November 12. He recorded only six points four nights later, when the Wizards set a franchise record for fewest points allowed in a 95–65 rout over Miami.

Washington finished November with six consecutive losses, dropping to 6–10. When winless Memphis upset the visiting Wizards on November 23, Jordan complained about lack of playing time. On Thanksgiving Day, he revealed his intention to retire as a player at the end of the season. He notched 29 points in a loss at Indiana on November 29 in his last game as sixth man.

Jordan started 34 games between November 30 and the All-Star break, with Washington winning 18. He led the Wizards just nine times in scoring, making 50 percent of his shots only nine times. Washington snapped its six-game losing streak with a 103–78 rout over Milwaukee at home on December 3. Jordan amassed 25 points, including the first nine of the second quarter, to ignite the blowout. His 21 points the next night featured two crucial free throws to seal an 88–83 win at Detroit. In a season-high 40 minutes of playing time at Toronto on December 15, he missed eight of nine shots for just two points. Jordan still contributed to the 95–82 victory with nine assists and eight rebounds. He warned the media, however, not to question his scoring ability. Jordan responded with 30 points in a triumph at Atlanta on December 17 and 33 points in a win over visiting Memphis the next night.

Washington still performed inconsistently, owning a lackluster 24–25 mark at the All-Star break. The Wizards won five consecutive games, twice over Chicago, from December 31 through January 8. Jordan tallied 41 points, including 12 of Washington's first 13 fourth-quarter points, in a 107–104 double-overtime home win over Indiana at home on January 4. In his final game at Chicago on January 24, the United Center crowd gave teary-eyed Jordan a two-minute standing ovation when he delivered an emotional impromptu farewell speech in a 104–97 loss. Jordan even rang up 45 points in a 109–104 victory over New Orleans on February 1.

On February 9, Jordan appeared in his 13th All-Star Game at Phillips Arena in Atlanta, Georgia. The classic marked the highest rated NBA game the Turner Network Television had carried. Fans did not vote him as a starting guard for the first time, as he trailed Tracy McGrady by more than 230,000 votes and Allen Iverson by more than 70,000 votes. McGrady and Iverson both offered Jordan a starting spot, but he was resigned to substituting. Isiah Thomas plotted to get him to start. The public address announcer named Jordan as a last-minute starter, but he tried to wave off the call. The Eastern All-Stars refused to begin the game until Jordan agreed to start. He finished that quarter hitting just 2 of 10 shots.

Halftime featured a tribute to Jordan. Singer Mariah Carey serenaded him wearing dresses and miniskirts looking like jerseys chronicling Jordan's career with the Bulls, the Wizards, and Team U.S.A. After she sang her signature "Hero," the other All-Stars gathered around Carey's stage and joined the crowd in giving Jordan a two-minute standing ovation. Jordan delivered his farewell address: "I leave the game of basketball in good hands. So many great stars still in the game, so many great stars rising and playing the game. I passed on the things that Dr. J. and some of the great players—Magic Johnson, Larry Bird—passed on to me, I pass on to these All-Stars here as well as the rest of the players in the NBA. The game's going to be fun to watch and I'm going to sit back and enjoy watching it."[26]

The newer stars dominated after intermission. McGrady and Iverson mirrored Jordan with third-quarter scoring sprees. Jordan made two free throws, surpassing Abdul-Jabbar as the career All-Star scoring leader with 252 points. He showed flashes of past form converting six of seven second-half shots, giving him 18 points, but he missed a game-winning shot near the end with the score tied. After resting during most of the first overtime, Jordan made a jump shot with just 4.8 seconds left to put the East ahead, 138–136. Kobe Bryant, however, denied Jordan an opportunity to be the hero, sinking two foul shots to send the contest to second overtime. Jordan was too exhausted to play in the second overtime, in which the West prevailed, 155–145. Sam Smith of the *Chicago Tribune* wrote, "There are moments, but no more miracles."[27]

The Wizards struggled mightily after the All-Star Game, dropping 20 of 33 contests. A groin injury to Jerry Stackhouse forced Jordan to carry the offensive load for several games. On February 21, four nights after celebrating his 40th birthday, Jordan became the first 40-year-old to tally at least 40 points in an NBA game. He capped a 43-point performance with a left-handed layup, upsetting defending Eastern Conference champion New Jersey, 89–86, at the MCI Center. The game marked the 119th and final time he attained at least 40 points. Jordan took 30 of the Wizards' 56 shots, tallying nearly half of their points, and grabbed 10 rebounds. "He did virtually everything a player can do,"[28] Michael Leahy wrote. Jordan contributed 30 points in a home loss to league-leading Dallas on February 23 and 25 points in a 83–78 victory at Indiana two nights later. Despite a bruised left thigh, he notched 35 points, including the first 10 overtime points, in a 100–98 thriller over visiting Houston.

In late February, Jordan lamented, "I'm going down with no bullets left."[29] He defied injury through sheer determination and constant electrostimulation therapy. After hurting his back against Toronto on March 4, Jordan summoned trainers to his house that night to apply stimulation.

He barely got out of bed the next morning, but he kept the Wizards in playoff contention with a 99–80 win over the Los Angeles Clippers.

New York edged Washington, 97–96, in Jordan's Madison Square Garden finale on March 9, dropping the Wizards two games behind the final playoff spot. After making just two first-quarter shots, he scored 19 of the Wizards' 22 points in a six-minute span of the second quarter. He took only two third-quarter shots, but he sank consecutive baskets and two foul shots to slice the deficit to 96–94 with 9.6 seconds left. Shandon Anderson missed one of two free throws for the Knicks. Latrell Sprewell fouled Jordan, who converted both shots. Jordan did not repeat his second-quarter heroics, finishing with 39 points.

Jordan was frustrated as he continued to try to instill a winning attitude in the Wizards and criticized his teammates for lackluster performance. "It's very disappointing when a forty-year-old man has more desire than twenty-five, twenty-six, twenty-three-year-old people,"[30] he complained. Jordan wanted his teammates to keep up with him, but they did not desire to emulate him. In a crushing setback at Phoenix on March 21, he scored just 14 points and yet outplayed his teammates. "I'm not going to try to save this team,"[31] he told teammates at halftime. "My job is not to carry this team like I did in '84 for the Bulls."[32]

NBA franchises honored Jordan on his farewell visits. Denver gave him a motorcycle. On April 11, the largest crowd ever to attend an indoor sporting event in South Florida witnessed Miami president Pat Riley elevate Jordan's Number 23 uniform to the rafters of American Airlines Arena. The Heat had never retired a player uniform in their 15-year history. Washington recorded its last victory that night, defeating Miami, 91–87. Jordan nearly scored the winning basket against visiting Atlanta on April 12. His 13-foot jump shot with 18 seconds left put the Wizards ahead, 100–99, but the Hawks snatched the game at the buzzer.

Washington lost Jordan's home finale to New York, 93–79, on April 14. He led the Wizards with 21 points and 8 rebounds, departing with 2 minutes and 2 seconds left in the fourth quarter. The MCI Center erupted with applause that lasted beyond the final buzzer, lauding the player responsible for selling out the arena for 82 consecutive games. Jordan had rescued the franchise from a $20 million loss to a $30 million profit in two years. The Jumbotron broadcast kudos from Dean Smith, Pippen, and others. Wizards owner Abe Pollin gave Jordan a plaque and donated computer labs to 18 public high schools in Washington, D.C. Wizards teammates curiously did not give him a retirement present, nor did Jordan address the crowd.

The next night, Washington dropped its season finale at Philadelphia, 93–79. Jordan made one last jump shot, dunk, post-up shot, and fadeaway jumper before exiting with six minutes left. The usually hostile Wachovia Center crowd began chanting for him to return. Jordan reentered the contest with 2 minutes and 35 seconds remaining and was fouled 49 seconds later, converting his last two free throws for 15 points. When he left, the throng gave him a standing three-minute ovation before he bowed, waved, and thanked the crowd.

Jordan ended his legendary playing career at age 40, starting in 67 contests and being the only Wizard to appear in all 82 games. He paced Washington in points (1,640), baskets (679), steals (123), and minutes played (3,031), ranking 25th in NBA scoring with a 20.0-point average. Jordan averaged 6.1 rebounds, 3.8 assists, and 1.5 steals, shooting 45 percent from the field and 82 percent from the free-throw line. Besides scoring at least 30 points nine times and 40 points three times, he finished his storied career as the NBA's all-time leader in scoring average (30.12 points) and third on the NBA's all-time scoring list (32,292 points).[33]

Jordan, however, missed six potential game-winners and could not elevate his teammates to his standard. The Wizards remained in playoff contention until the last week, finishing fifth in the Atlantic Division with a 37–45 record. Washington won all four games,—in which Jordan, Stackhouse, and Larry Hughes each scored at least 20 points—but the team blew several fourth-quarter leads partly because Jordan could not close games. Washington led the NBA in attendance for the second straight season, averaging 20,173 fans at the MCI Center and 19,311 on the road. The Wizards sold out 78 of 82 games, including a franchise-record-tying 41 home contests.

What legacies did Michael Jordan leave with the Wizards? He had alleviated some financial pressures on the franchise and had assembled some young players, "a group that doesn't know how to apply their talents right now."[34] *Washington Post* columnist Michael Wilbon claimed that Jordan gave the franchise hope. The crowded MCI Center thought that a Wizard victory was possible in any of his games. Jordan improved the Wizard's financial situation enormously, netting gigantic profits through sold-out games and merchandise and removing the liabilities of long-term player contracts that gave the Wizards $5-$12 million of salary cap room entering the summer 2003. He also developed a sound scouting and personnel infrastructure, spending money wisely and hiring knowledgeable friends, including Rod Higgins as assistant general manager.

Jordan's player comeback, however, fell short of his superpower status. Unlike at Chicago, Jordan did not take the Wizards to an NBA title or even an NBA playoff. He enjoyed spectacular scoring performances against Charlotte and New Jersey, but he did not replicate the winning that had made him legendary. He had won six NBA championships, five MVP awards, and 10 scoring titles with the Bulls, but he ended his last season without sinking a game-winning shot.

Pollin and his aides conducted postseason exit interviews with Jordan's teammates. Some protested that Jordan influenced decisions on their playing time and even wanted Collins to bench players who would not pass the ball to him. Others complained that Jordan received credit when Washington won, and the rest of the team was blamed when the Wizards lost. Pollin, meanwhile, objected that Jordan remained in Chicago while serving as a Washington executive and devoted inordinate time to his business enterprises and other commitments.

Jordan assumed that he would resume his director of basketball operations position. He expected to become a major, if not majority, owner of the Wizards. According to Pollin, however, several MCI Center employees opposed his return to executive authority. The *New York Times* on May 4 quoted a Washington official who said that the Wizards were split between workers Jordan enlisted and those employees loyal to Pollin.[35] Jordan had strained relations with Wizards president Susan O'Malley, who conducted business operations and used him as a marketing tool. Jordan occasionally had resisted her requests for help in marketing and public relations activities. He had denied her request when he was headed toward the locker room to chat briefly with several season ticket holders.

Jordan dined with Leonsis and two of his partners for four hours on May 7 to discuss his future. Pollin had asked Jordan to develop a plan to end Washington's six-year playoff drought. Leonsis called Pollin the next morning to relate the details of the dinner. Jordan met with Pollin for 18 minutes that morning. Pollin told Jordan that he wanted to explore a different direction for franchise leadership, but Pollin did not explain what Jordan had done wrong or give him an opportunity to present his plan. Jordan had made some questionable administrative decisions, including drafting Brown and influencing Hamilton's trade to Detroit for Stackhouse. He reportedly told Pollin that he had anticipated becoming a Wizards owner, but Pollin supposedly replied that he did not want him as his partner. The firing stunned Jordan, who reportedly was not given any explanation.

Jordan, meanwhile, explored other basketball options. Robert Johnson, the first African American NBA owner, asked him to become an executive for the new Charlotte Bobcats franchise that would replace the departed

Hornets for the 2004–2005 season. Jordan declined the offer at that time because he was not given a share of ownership for free or final authority over basketball decisions. He attempted to acquire the Milwaukee Bucks from U.S. Senator Herb Kohl of Wisconsin in 2003, but Kohl ultimately did not sell that club. His attempts to acquire the Phoenix Suns and the Miami Heat did not materialize either.

Jordan watched a few Chicago Bulls games at the United Center and saw the 2004 All-Star Game in Los Angeles. He often was invited to other sporting events, including Chicago Cubs games; he kept in shape and played golf in celebrity charity tournaments. In January 2004, he hosted the Michael Jordan Celebrity Invitational Golf Tournament on Paradise Island in the Bahamas, near one of his favorite casinos. Jordan promoted his Jordan Brand clothing line and still associated with Nike, but his commercial impact had waned. Jordan lived in a world of fewer cheers and laurels and hoped to find the serenity that frequently eludes legends. The Jordan legacy still carries on. Jeffrey and Marcus, both left-handed, attend Loyola Academy, a Jesuit high school in Wilmette, Illinois, north of Chicago. Jeffrey, a 6-foot, 2-inch, 170 pound senior, resembles Jordan with his contagious smile, penetrating stare, and determined look and enjoys conversing with others. He has made All-Catholic League twice in basketball as a combination point and shooting guard and attended the 2005 Nike All-American camp at Indianapolis, Indiana, performing with the sons of other former NBA stars. He plans to play at the University of Illinois as a walk-on. Marcus, a 6-foot 3-inch sophomore who wears prescription sports goggles, is projected as a top conference, major college point guard with keen court awareness.

Jeffrey and Marcus share several personal qualities. Both demonstrate "an explosive first step, a fearless slashing style and the trademark Jordan competitiveness." They exhibit intelligence, maturity, and poise, play unselfishly, act politely, and blend well with teammates. Jeffrey reflected, "our parents did a good job of preparing us for what it was going to be like in high school and the media."[36]

Jeffrey and Marcus do not try to follow in their illustrious father's footsteps, however. Jordan attends most of their games and sometimes shouts encouragement, but does not interfere with Coach Bryan Tucker. He watches a lot of basketball video with them and often discusses their play following games, but insists, "I just want them to be themselves" and "to enjoy themselves."[37]

In October 2005, Atria Books published Jordan's inspiring memoir, *Driven from Within*. He discussed how authenticity, integrity, passion, commitment, and other qualities have influenced his life and described how challenging events have made him realize the importance of these qualities, pushing him to newer heights both on and off the court. Jordan also celebrated the people who have encouraged, supported, and tested him throughout his remarkable life.

In 2006, Jordan fulfilled his dream of sharing ownership of an NBA club in North Carolina. On June 15, he became second largest shareholder of the Charlotte Bobcats. Johnson, who had known Jordan for 17 years, named him part owner and manager of basketball operations, with final authority on player personnel decisions. NBA Commissioner David Stern beamed, "We're elated to have Michael back in the league, in both in an ownership and a management position, in an area of the country that's important to him and where his contributions have been so well recognized."[38]

Jordan's marriage, however, did not survive. He and Juanita had tried to resolve their differences after Juanita initially filed for divorce in 2002. Their reconciliation effort ultimately failed. The couple separated in February 2006, with Juanita remaining at their suburban Highland Park estate and Jordan living in Chicago. On December 29, 2006, they filed for divorce in Lake County Circuit Court, citing "irreconcilable differences." In a statement issued through their lawyers, Michael and Juanita announced that they "mutually and amicably decided to end their 17-year marriage." They retained joint custody of their three teenage children. Court papers did not disclose any monetary figures, merely indicating that Michael and Juanita had reached "a fair and equitable settlement" on the division of property, child support, parenting time, and other issues. The Jordans realized that "future attempts at reconciliation would be impracticable and not in the best interests of the family."[39]

## NOTES

1. Michael Leahy, *When Nothing Else Matters: Michael Jordan's Last Comeback* (New York: Simon & Schuster, 2004), p. 24.

2. Rick Reilly, "The Third Coming?," *Sports Illustrated* 94 (March 19, 2001), p. 124.

3. Leahy, *Nothing Else Matters*, p. 44.

4. Ibid., p. 43.

5. Mitchell Krugel, *One Last Shot: The Story of Michael Jordan's Comeback* (New York: St. Martin's Press, 2003), p. 109.

6. Ibid, p. 112.

7. Leahy, *Nothing Else Matters*, p. 135.

8. Ibid., p. 128.

9. Ibid., p. 154.

10. Krugel, *One Last Shot*, pp. 120–121.

11. Leahy, *Nothing Else Matters*, p. 178.

12. Krugel, *One Last Shot*, pp. 146–147.

13. Ibid., p. 153.

14. Ibid., p. 153.

15. Ibid., p. 156.

16. Leahy, *Nothing Else Matters*, p. 193.

17. *Chicago Tribune*, January 8, 2002.

18. *New York Post*, January 8, 2002.

19. *Chicago Sun-Times*, January 8, 2002.

20. Krugel, *One Last Shot*, p. 178.

21. Leahy, *Nothing Else Matters*, p. 215.

22. Krugel, *One Last Shot*, p. 187.

23. Leahy, *Nothing Else Matters*, p. 230.

24. Ibid., p. 261.

25. Ibid., p. 301.

26. NBA All-Star Game, Turner Network Television, Atlanta, Georgia, February 9, 2003.

27. *Chicago Tribune*, February 10, 2003.

28. Leahy, *Nothing Else Matters*, p. 365.

29. Krugel, *One Last Shot*, p. 275.

30. Leahy, *Nothing Else Matters*, p. 371.

31. Krugel, *One Last Shot*, p. 276.

32. Ibid., p. 276.

33. Zack Bodendieck et al., eds., *The Sporting News 2006–07 Official NBA Register* (St. Louis, MO: The Sporting News, 2006), pp. 379–381.

34. Krugel, *One Last Shot*, p. 279.

35. *New York Times*, May 4, 2003.

36. *USA Today*, February 1, 2007, p. C3.

37. Ibid., p. C3.

38. *USA Today*, June 16, 2006, p. C1.

39. *Chicago Tribune*, December 30, 2006; *Chicago Sun-Times*, December 30, 2006.

# Chapter 7

# THE LEGENDARY JORDAN

Michael Jordan's basketball talent manifested itself from the outset of his rookie NBA season. His ability to score at will, his breathtaking dunks, and his tenacious defense amazed both opponents and fans. What is his place in NBA history? How does he compare with the all-time great basketball players? In *100 Greatest Basketball Players* (1989), Wayne Patterson, Naismith Memorial Basketball Hall of Fame research specialist, and Lisa Fisher, Naismith Memorial Basketball Hall of Fame assistant public relations director, rated Jordan 13th all-time. Jordan had not yet led the Chicago Bulls to six NBA titles in eight years. Patterson and Fisher ranked the top 10 as (1) Wilt Chamberlain, (2) Kareem Abdul-Jabbar, (3) Bill Russell, (4) Larry Bird, (5) Oscar Robertson, (6) Magic Johnson, (7) Jerry West, (8) Julius Erving, (9) Bob Cousy, and (10) Rick Barry.[1]

Patterson and Fisher selected Chamberlain as the greatest player primarily because of his impact on the NBA record book. Chamberlain starred for 14 NBA seasons, holding or sharing 43 records on his retirement in 1973. He scored 100 points in one game, 19 better than anyone else, and averaged a record 50.4 points one season. Chamberlain remains the only NBA player to score more than 4,000 points in a season and was the first to reach 30,000 career points. Besides scoring at least 50 points in 118 games and 40 or more points in 271 games, he was the only player until Jordan to average more than 30 points a game for a career. His 55 rebounds against the Boston Celtics established an NBA record. Chamberlain was the fourth leading scorer in NBA history and its all-time leading rebounder with 23,924. He made the All-NBA first team seven times and appeared in 13 NBA All-Star games, leading his teams to five NBA Finals and two NBA titles. Chamberlain was named NBA Rookie of the Year in 1960, NBA Playoff Most Valuable Player in 1972, and NBA MVP four times, including three consecutive years. He led the NBA in scoring seven straight times, rebounding 11 times, and field goal percentage nine times, and never fouled out in 1,218 games.

How did Jordan fare after leading Chicago to six NBA titles in eight years? In 1999, ESPN named its Sportscentury top 50 athletes. Eight NBA players made the list including (1) Jordan, (13) Chamberlain, (17) Johnson, (18) Russell, (26) Abdul-Jabbar, (30) Bird, (36) Robertson, and (43) Erving. Jordan vaulted from thirteenth to first and Johnson from sixth to third, and Erving remained eighth. Chamberlain dropped from first to second, Russell from third to fourth, Abdul-Jabbar from second to fifth, Bird from fourth to sixth, and Robertson from fifth to seventh.[2] Peter Bjarkman, basketball historian from Lafayette, Indiana, and author of *The Biographical History of Basketball* (2000), considers Jordan the most celebrated NBA player of all time, but rates Oscar Robertson the greatest all-around player, Chamberlain the best offensive player, and Russell the best defensive performer.[3]

Does Jordan still maintain his top ranking? In March 2003, SLAM Magazine ranked him first among its top 75 NBA all-time players. Chamberlain remained second, and Robertson supplanted Russell and Johnson. They were followed by (4) Russell, (5) Johnson, (6) Bird, (7) Abdul-Jabbar, (8) West, (9) Shaquille O'Neal, and (10) Erving.[4] In *The Mad Dog Hall of Fame* (2006), Christopher Russo, sports radio talk show co-host on WFAN in New York City, and Allen St. John, sports columnist for the *Wall Street Journal*, rated the top-10 NBA players of all time. Jordan retained first, and Russell moved ahead of Chamberlain and Johnson. They were followed by (3) Chamberlain, (4) Abdul-Jabbar, (5) Johnson, (6) Bird, (7) Cousy, (8) Robertson, (9) West, and (10) O'Neal.[5]

Russell surpassed Jordan in certain phases of the game, leading Boston to more championships and proving a more dominant force defensively. He led the Celtics to 11 NBA championships, including eight straight; made the championship round in 12 of 13 NBA seasons; and never missed the playoffs. Jordan made the championship round just six times and missed playoffs twice in 15 NBA seasons. Russell revolutionized the game with his defensive wizardry and outstanding team play. He paced the NBA in rebounding for four years and in career playoff rebounding with 4,104, averaged more than 20 rebounds in 10 seasons, and ranked second on the all-time rebounding list with 21,620. Jordan never approached these figures, averaging 6.2 career rebounds and never exceeding 8.0

rebounds during any season.[6] Russell's renowned shot blocking skills and dominating defense presence disrupted opposing offenses.

Chamberlain outperformed Jordan in some categories, too. He proved a more intimidating athlete and the greatest offensive machine basketball has ever witnessed. Jordan never came close to scoring 100 points or making 55 rebounds in a game, never averaged 50 points or 27.2 rebounds nightly for an entire NBA season, never scored 50 points in a playoff game as a rookie, nor scored more than 40 points more than 270 times. Chamberlain enjoyed four seasons with higher point averages than Jordan's best of 37.1 points. He outrebounded Jordan 22.9 to 6.2 per game and enjoyed 118 50 point games to 31 for Jordan. Chamberlain led the NBA nine times in field-goal percentage, something Jordan never accomplished, and concentrated primarily on rebounding and defense after winning seven scoring titles. Jordan made the All-NBA Defensive team nine times, but he focused more on offense.

Robertson, Abdul-Jabbar, Johnson, and Bird made major contributions, too. Robertson led the NBA six times in assists, ranks third in career free throws made, fourth in career assists, and ninth in career scoring average and compiled the most career rebounds for an NBA guard, including Jordan. Abdul-Jabbar won six NBA titles and MVP awards, made 10 championship series appearances, ranks third on the NBA career rebounding list, and leads the NBA in career scoring. Johnson won five NBA titles, scored more than 17,000 career points, ranks third in career assists, played all positions well, and helped revive the NBA in the 1980s. Bird finished his NBA career with three NBA titles, two NBA Finals MVP awards, and three consecutive regular-season NBA MVP awards and also helped revive the NBA in the 1980s.

Nevertheless, Jordan transcended Chamberlain, Russell, Robertson, and the others as the greatest NBA player of all time, performing on a level unsurpassed in NBA history. He edged out Chamberlain for the highest scoring average (30.1) in NBA history; Robertson averaged 25.7 points and Russell 15.1 points. Jordan, like Russell, left a winning legacy, essentially leading Chicago to six straight NBA titles. He played crucial roles in the Bulls' winning three consecutive championships two times. Chicago might have defeated the Houston Rockets during the two years in between if Jordan had not left the Bulls. Although a prolific scorer and rebounder, Chamberlain played on only two NBA title teams. Robertson performed on only one NBA championship squad. Jordan holds the NBA record with 10 scoring titles, tying Chamberlain with seven consecutive scoring crowns. His scoring titles came in his first 10 full seasons. Russell and Robertson never led the NBA in scoring. Jordan converted more theatrical winning shots at crunch time, too. A hush often came over arenas when he touched the ball in the final seconds. Jordan promoted the sport more effectively than the more reserved Abdul-Jabbar and won more NBA titles and awards than Johnson and Bird.

Jordan scored the most career points (32,292) and the most single-season points (3,041, 1987) for an NBA guard, besting Robertson. Aside from Chamberlain, no other player tallied more than 3,000 single-season points. Robertson recorded a season-best 2,480 points, and Russell never attained 1,500 points in a season. Although a better rebounder than Jordan, Robertson never ranked among NBA leaders defensively. Jordan excelled defensively and, in 1987–1988, became the only scoring leader named NBA Defensive Player of the Year the same year. He enjoyed perhaps the greatest all-around season in NBA history, winning NBA MVP, All-Star Game MVP, and scoring championships. During that same season, Jordan scored 40 points in the All-Star Game, tallied 59 points in one game, and recorded 10 steals in another. Chamberlain enjoyed a better offensive year in 1961–1962, but paid little attention to defense. Jordan recorded thirty-one 50-point games, trailing only Chamberlain. He was feared around the NBA as its greatest clutch performer and was the Bulls' primary threat in the final seconds of a close game.

Jordan was the best performer in NBA playoff history, the lone NBA player to win six NBA Finals MVP awards. Chamberlain achieved that award just once. Jordan compiled the highest career NBA playoff scoring average (33.4 points, 179 games), scored the most points in an NBA play-off game with 63 against Boston in 1986, and holds the highest single-series playoff average (41.0 points, 1993). He leads the NBA All-Star players in career scoring average, averaging 20.2 points in 13 games, and in 1997 recorded the classic's first triple-double. During the playoffs, he always demanded the ball at crunch time. Jordan made the NBA All-Defensive first team nine consecutive full years that he played. He won the NBA MVP Award five times, a feat shared by Russell and surpassed only by Abdul-Jabbar who had six.

Jordan came closest to the ideal basketball player, combining body and mind. Basketball players wanted to be like him. He possessed more physical skills than any other player, exhibiting a virtually flawless game. He could drive inside, convert the 20-foot jumper, penetrate, pass, rebound, and play tenacious defense. Few players could defeat him one-on-one. He resembled Russell with an impenetrable will to win and also possessed exceptional concentration and focus.

Problems occasionally confronted Jordan; he often intimidated players not performing at his level or not hustling. He did not always serve as the best role model off the court, visiting an Atlantic City casino between playoff games and losing considerable money gambling on the golf course. His final comeback with the Wizards did not meet his expectations. But these flaws do not diminish his truly exemplary accomplishments.

Some NBA aficionados question the historical greatness of the Bulls teams. Aside from Jordan, Pippen, and Rodman, Chicago did not have exceptional players. The Bulls did not have to play any all-time great teams like Boston of the 1960s to win their NBA titles. Still Chicago conquered the teams it needed to for six NBA titles and two "three-peats". During that span, the Bulls won 25 of 26 playoff series.

Jordan's legend extends beyond his NBA records. He changed the game by becoming the most effectively marketed athlete of his generation. He spread the appeal of the NBA to corporate America and overseas as his era's biggest, most recognizable athlete. Nike and other companies rode the coattails of Air Jordan's legend. Jordan helped Nike sell a million sneakers at $100 each. His 1998 $32 million NBA single-season contract represented only a portion of his annual earnings and a small fraction of the revenue he generated for the NBA and the corporate giants who employed him. Jordan's flamboyant playing style enhanced his following, as he mastered the show-time moves captured in the 10-second video highlight films. The NBA promoted Jordan, basing its popularity on his image as the greatest sports-world showman in history. He generated instant crowd thrills with his drives, dunks, and other moves and sold countless books, newspapers, videotapes, NBA game tickets, and hours of television time.[7]

How does Michael Jordan assess his legacy? He ranks himself among the great NBA players, but rejects the theory that "there is only one greatest player."[8] Jordan, who considers greatness an evolutionary process, acknowledges, "a player will come along who will be able to build on what I have accomplished, just as I built on the example of great players before me."[9] Different players have shown different aspects of greatness. Some players have exhibited many of those same aspects. "I proved a great offensive player can play great defense," he admits. "But somebody will come along who plays even better offense and defense than me."[10] That remains to be seen.

## NOTES

1. Wayne Patterson and Lisa Fisher, *100 Greatest Basketball Players* (New York: Crown Publishers, 1989).

2. ESPN Sportscentury Top 50 Athletes, December 26, 1999.

3. Peter C. Bjarkman, *The Biographical History of Basketball* (Chicago, IL: Masters Press, 2000).

4. "SLAM Magazine's Top 75 NBA Players," March 2003.

5. Christopher Russo and Allen St. John, *The Mad Dog Hall of Fame* (New York: Doubleday, 2006).

6. For the regular season, playoff, and career statistics of Jordan and the other NBA players, see, Zack Bodendieck et al., eds., *The Sporting News 2006–07 Official NBA Register* (St. Louis, MO: The Sporting News, 2006) and Ken Shouler et al., *Total Basketball: The Ultimate Basketball Encyclopedia* (Wilmington, DE: Sport Media Publishing Company, 2003).

7. For Jordan's economic impact, see Walter LaFeber, *Michael Jordan and the New Global Capitalism* (New York: W. W. Norton & Company, 1999).

8. Michael Jordan, ed. by Mark Vancil, *For the Love of the Game: My Story* (New York: Crown Publishers, 1998), p. 111.

9. Michael Jordan, ed. by Mark Vancil, *Driven from Within* (New York: Atria Books, 2005), p. 12.

10. Jordan, *Love of Game*, p. 111.

# Appendix

# MICHAEL JORDAN STATISTICS

## Collegiate Career

| Year | Team | G | FGM | FTM | TRB | AST | PTS | PPG |
|------|------|---|-----|-----|-----|-----|-----|-----|
| 1981-82 | North Carolina | 34 | 191 | 78 | 149 | 61 | 460 | 13.5 |
| 1982-83 | North Carolina | 36 | *282 | 123 | 197 | 56 | 721 | 20.0 |
| 1983-84 | North Carolina | 31 | *247 | 113 | 163 | 64 | 607 | 19.8 |
| TOTALS | | 101 | 720 | 314 | 509 | 181 | 1788 | 17.7 |

*Includes three point field goals
Source: Basketball-Reference.com

## NBA Career Regular Season

| Year | Team | G | FGM | FTM | TRB | AST | STL | PTS | PPG |
|------|------|---|-----|-----|-----|-----|-----|-----|-----|
| 1984-85 | Chicago | 82 | *837 | 630 | 534 | 481 | 196 | **2313** | 28.2 |
| 1985-86 | Chicago | 18 | *150 | 105 | 64 | 53 | 37 | 408 | 22.7 |
| 1986-87 | Chicago | 82 | *1098 | 833 | 430 | 377 | 236 | **3041** | **37.1** |
| 1987-88 | Chicago | 82 | *1069 | 723 | 449 | 485 | **259** | **2868** | **35.0** |
| 1988-89 | Chicago | 81 | *966 | 674 | 652 | 650 | 234 | **2633** | **32.5** |
| 1989-90 | Chicago | 82 | *1034 | 593 | 565 | 519 | **227** | **2753** | **33.6** |
| 1990-91 | Chicago | 82 | *990 | 571 | 492 | 453 | 223 | **2580** | **31.5** |
| 1991-92 | Chicago | 80 | *943 | 491 | 511 | 489 | 182 | **2404** | **30.1** |
| 1992-93 | Chicago | 78 | *992 | 476 | 522 | 428 | **221** | **2541** | **32.6** |
| 1994-95 | Chicago | 17 | *166 | 109 | 117 | 90 | 30 | 457 | 26.9 |
| 1995-96 | Chicago | 82 | *916 | 548 | 543 | 352 | 180 | **2491** | **30.4** |
| 1996-97 | Chicago | 82 | *920 | 480 | 482 | 352 | 140 | **2431** | **29.6** |
| 1997-98 | Chicago | 82 | *881 | 565 | 475 | 283 | 141 | **2357** | **28.7** |
| 2001-02 | Washington | 60 | *551 | 263 | 339 | 310 | 85 | 1375 | 22.9 |
| 2002-03 | Washington | 82 | *679 | 266 | 497 | 311 | 123 | 1640 | 20.0 |
| TOTALS | | 1072 | 12192 | 7327 | 6672 | 5633 | 2514 | 32292 | 30.1 |

* Includes three-point field goals
Boldface indicates statistical categories in which Jordan led the NBA
*Source*: Basketball-Reference.com

## Playoffs

| Year | Team | G | FGM | FTM | TRB | AST | STL | PTS | PPG |
|------|------|---|-----|-----|-----|-----|-----|-----|-----|
| 1984-85 | Chicago | 4 | *34 | 48 | 23 | 34 | 11 | 117 | 29.3 |
| 1985-86 | Chicago | 3 | *48 | 34 | 19 | 17 | 7 | 131 | 43.7 |
| 1986-87 | Chicago | 3 | *35 | 35 | 21 | 18 | 6 | 107 | 35.7 |
| 1987-88 | Chicago | 10 | *138 | 86 | 71 | 47 | 24 | 363 | 36.3 |
| 1988-89 | Chicago | 17 | *199 | 183 | 119 | 130 | 42 | 591 | 34.8 |
| 1989-90 | Chicago | 16 | *219 | 133 | 115 | 109 | 45 | 587 | 36.7 |
| 1990-91 | Chicago | 17 | *197 | 125 | 108 | 142 | 40 | 529 | 31.1 |
| 1991-92 | Chicago | 22 | *290 | 162 | 137 | 127 | 44 | 759 | 34.5 |
| 1992-93 | Chicago | 19 | *251 | 136 | 128 | 114 | 39 | 666 | 35.1 |
| 1994-95 | Chicago | 10 | *120 | 64 | 65 | 45 | 23 | 315 | 31.5 |
| 1995-96 | Chicago | 18 | *187 | 153 | 89 | 74 | 33 | 552 | 30.7 |
| 1996-97 | Chicago | 19 | *227 | 123 | 150 | 91 | 30 | 590 | 31.1 |
| 1997-98 | Chicago | 21 | *243 | 181 | 107 | 74 | 32 | 680 | 32.4 |
| TOTALS | | 179 | 2188 | 1463 | 1152 | 1022 | 376 | 5987 | 33.4 |

G = Games; FGM = Field Goals Made; TRB = Total Rebounds; AST = Assists; STL = Steals; PTS = Points; PPG = Points Per Game

*Source:* Basketball-Reference.com

## Awards

Member, NCAA Division I title team, 1982
Member, All-NCAA Tournament team, 1982
*The Sporting News* National College Player of the Year, 1983
NCAA Consensus First Team All-American, 1983-1984
Consensus National College Player of the Year, 1984
Naismith Award, 1984
Wooden Award, 1984
Member, Olympic Gold Medal U. S. Olympic team, 1984, 1992
NBA Rookie of the Year, 1985
All-NBA Second Team, 1985
NBA Slam Dunk champion, 1987-1988
All-NBA First Team, 1987-1993, 1996-1998
NBA Most Valuable Player, 1988, 1991-1992, 1996, 1998
NBA All-Star Game Most Valuable Player, 1988, 1996, 1998
NBA Defensive Player of the Year, 1988
NBA All-Defensive First Team, 1988-1993, 1996-1998
Member. NBA title team, 1991-1993, 1996-1998
NBA Finals Most Valuable Player, 1991-1993, 1996-1998
Member, NBA 50th Anniversary All-Time team, 1996
ESPN Athlete of the Century, 2000
ESPN Male Athlete of the 1990s, 2000
ESPN Pro Basketball Player of the 1990s, 2000
ESPN Play of the Decade of the 1900s, 2000

# ANNOTATED BIBLIOGRAPHY

This biography draws from many sources. Jordan's four autobiographies provide numerous anecdotes and photographs from his life both on and off the court. *Rare Air: Michael on Michael* (1993) describes his daily life with the Bulls and answers frequently asked questions. *I'm Back!: More Rare Air* (1995) examines why Jordan left basketball to pursue a professional baseball career and why he returned to the Bulls. In *For the Love of the Game: My Story* (1998), he reviews the highlights of his career with the Bulls. In *Driven from Within* (2005) he reveals how his phenomenal success came from within and those who guided him. His skill, work ethic, philosophy, personal style, competitiveness, and presence have carried over from the basketball court into his entire life.

David Halberstam, in *Playing for Keeps: Michael Jordan and the World He Made* (1999), gives the best biographical account of Jordan's epic life. Halberstam studies the impact of Jordan's career, detailing the forces that shaped him into history's greatest basketball player and the larger forces that made him internationally known. His narrative of astonishing power and human drama brims with revealing anecdotes and penetrating insights. Jim Naughton, *Taking to the Air: The Rise of Michael Jordan* (1992) provides an excellent detailed account of Jordan's early life, North Carolina years, and rise to success with the Chicago Bulls and astutely assesses his impact on American society.

In three different works, Mitchell Krugel chronicles Michael's most notable games. *Michael Jordan* (1988) reviews his family life, North Carolina years, and Chicago career through 1987. *Jordan, The Man, His Words, His Life* (1994) features interviews and conversations with Jordan about his

Bulls career through 1993, highlighting his first three title years. *One Last Shot: The Story of Michael's Comeback* (2003) probes how and why Jordan risked his unparalleled status as the NBA's greatest player to come back for two seasons with the Washington Wizards and pictures him as a man forever playing for one last shot.

Three books illuminate Jordan's North Carolina basketball career. In *A Coach's Life* (1999) Dean Smith, with John Kilgo and Sally Jenkins, describes how the legendary coach taught Jordan discipline and other values and assesses his impact on the Tar Heel basketball program. In *March to the Top* (1982) Art Chansky, with Eddie Fogler, details how Jordan helped Smith win his first national championship, and his *The Dean's List: A Celebration of Tar Heel Basketball and Dean Smith* (1997) puts Jordan's North Carolina years in the broader context of the Smith era.

Several books highlight specific phases of Jordan's career with Chicago. Bob Greene, *Hang Time: The Days and Dreams of Michael Jordan* (1992) adeptly captures Jordan's daily life and innermost thoughts during the Bulls' first championship season in 1990–1991. His sequel, *Rebound: The Odyssey of Michael Jordan* (1995) features Jordan's basketball retirement and baseball interlude. Sam Smith's *The Jordan Rules: The Inside Story of a Turbulent Season with Michael Jordan and the Chicago Bulls* (1992) provides a critical analysis of Jordan's 1990–1991 season. According to Smith, Jordan disliked the Bulls' triangle offense, often played by his own rules, and clashed with management. His provocative sequel, *Second Coming: The Strange Odyssey of Michael Jordan—From Courtside to Home Plate and Back Again* (1995) probes why Jordan left the Bulls in 1993 to try baseball and returned to basketball 18 months later. Rick Telander, in *The Year of the Bull: Zen, Air, and the Pursuit of Sacred and Profane Hoops* (1996), recaptures Chicago's record-breaking 1995–1996 season. He describes how Jordan restored his position as the sport's greatest player and relates the legend's inner thoughts about his teammates and rivals. In *Blood on the Horns: The Long Strange Ride of Michael Jordan's Chicago Bulls* (1998), Roland Lazenby examines how the Bulls battled through the 1997–1998 season to win their sixth NBA championship in eight years and probes Jordan's growing rift with management.

The *Chicago Tribune* details Jordan's regular season and playoff games with the Chicago Bulls from 1984 through 1993 and 1995 through 1998, and the *Washington Post* examines his two seasons with the Washington Wizards from 2001 through 2003. The *New York Times* adds perspective on Jordan's basketball career. The annual editions of *The Sporting News*

*Official NBA Guide* and *The Sporting News Official NBA Register*, along with Ken Shouler et al., *Total Basketball: The Ultimate Basketball Encyclopedia* (2003), furnish his regular-season statistics between 1984 and 2003 and his playoff record between 1985 and 1998.

Jack McCallum, Curry Kirkpatrick, and other *Sports Illustrated* writers provide numerous insightful articles on Jordan's professional basketball career. *Ebony*, *Esquire*, *Gentleman's Quarterly*, *Newsweek*, the *New Yorker*, *People*, and *Time* also contributed important articles.

Walter LaFeber, in *Michael Jordan and the New Global Capitalism* (1999), adroitly assesses how Jordan's numerous commercial endorsements changed the global marketplace.

## BOOKS

Bjarkman, Peter C. *The Biographical History of Basketball*. Chicago, IL: Masters Press, 2000.

———. *The Encyclopedia of Pro Basketball Team Histories*. New York: Carroll and Graf Publishers, 1994.

Chansky, Art. *The Dean's List: A Celebration of Tar Heel Basketball and Dean Smith* New York: Warner Books, 1996.

———. with Eddie Fogler. *March to the Top*. Chapel Hill, NC: Four Corners Press, 1982.

Daly, Chuck with Alex Sachare. *America's Dream Team: The Quest for Olympic Gold*. Atlanta, GA: Turner Publishing, 1992.

Esquinas, Richard with Dave Distol. *Michael and Me: Our Gambling Addiction*. San Diego, CA: Athletic Guidance Center, 1993.

Greene, Bob. *Hang Time: Days and Dreams with Michael Jordan*. New York: Doubleday, 1992.

———. *Rebound: The Odyssey of Michael Jordan*. New York: Doubleday, 1995.

Halberstam, David. *Playing for Keeps: Michael Jordan and the World He Made*. New York: Random House, 1999.

Isaacson, Melissa. *Transition Game: An Inside Look at Life with the Chicago Bulls*. Champaign, IL: Sagamore Publishing, 1994.

Jackson, Phil with Hugh Delehanty. *Sacred Hoops: Spiritual Lessons of a Hardwood Warrior*. New York: Hyperion, 1995.

Jordan, Michael. *Driven from Within*, ed. by Mark Vancil. New York: Atria Books, 2005.

———. *For the Love of the Game: My Story*, ed. by Mark Vancil. New York: Crown Publishers, 1998.

———. *I'm Back: More Rare Air*, ed. by Mark Vancil. San Francisco, CA: Collins Publishers, 1995.

———. *Rare Air: Michael on Michael*, ed. by Mark Vancil. San Francisco, CA: Collins Publishers, 1993.

Krugel, Mitchell. *Jordan: The Man, His Words, His Life.* New York: St. Martin's Press, 1994.

———. *Michael Jordan.* New York: St. Martin's Press, 1988.

———. *One Last Shot: The Story of Michael Jordan's Comeback.* New York: St. Martin's Press, 2002.

Lazenby, Roland. *Blood on the Horns: The Long Strange Ride of Michael Jordan's Chicago Bulls.* Lenexa, KS: Addax Publishing Group, 1998.

LaFeber, Walter. *Michael Jordan and the New Global Capitalism.* New York: W. W. Norton & Company, 1999.

Leahy, Michael. *When Nothing Else Matters; Michael Jordan's Last Comeback.* New York: Simon & Schuster, 2004.

Naughton, Jim. *Taking to the Air: The Rise of Michael Jordan.* New York: Warner Books, 1992.

Patterson, Wayne and Lisa Fisher. *100 Greatest Basketball Players.* New York: Crown Publishers, 1989.

Rappoport, Ken. *Tales from the Tar Heels Locker Room.* Champaign, IL: Sports Publishing LLC, 2002.

Russo, Christopher and Allen St. John. *The Mad Dog Hall of Fame: The Ultimate Top-Ten Rankings of the Best in Sports.* New York: Doubleday, 2006.

Shouler, Ken et al. *Total Basketball: The Ultimate Basketball Encyclopedia.* Wilmington, DE: Sport Media Publishing Company, 2003.

Smith, Dean with John Kilgo and Sally Jenkins. *A Coach's Life.* New York: Random House, 1999.

Smith, Sam. *The Jordan Rules: The Inside Story of a Turbulent Season with Michael Jordan and the Chicago Bulls.* New York: Simon & Schuster, 1992.

———. *Second Coming: The Strange Odyssey of Michael Jordan—From Courtside to Home Plate and Back Again.* New York: Harper Collins Publishers, 1995.

Telander, Rick. *The Year of the Bull: Zen, Air, and the Pursuit of Sacred & Profane Hoops.* New York: Simon & Schuster, 1996.

## ARTICLES

Breskin, David. "Michael Jordan," *Gentleman's Quarterly* (March 1989), pp. 319–397.

Callahan, T. "The Greatest of Them All," *Newsweek* 114 (December 4, 1989), pp. 80—81.

Coplon, Jeff. "Legends, Champions?," *New York Times Magazine*, April 21, 1996, pp. 32–35ff.

Deford, Frank. "One of a Kind," *Sports Illustrated* 76 (June 22, 1992), pp. 48–50.

Donnelly, J. B. "Great Leapin' Lizards," *Time* 133 (January 9, 1989), pp. 50–52.

Halberstam, David. "A Hero for the Wired World," *Sports Illustrated* 75 (December 23, 1991), pp. 76–81.

———. David. "Jordan's Moment," *New Yorker* 124 (December 21, 1998), pp. 48–55.

Kirkpatrick, Curry. "A Towering Twosome," *Sports Illustrated* 59 (November 28, 1983).

———. "In an Orbit All His Own," *Sports Illustrated* 67 (November 9, 1987), p. 116.

———. "Nothing Could Be Finer," *Sports Illustrated* 56 (April 5, 1982).

———. "The Unlikeliest Homeboy," *Sports Illustrated* 75 (December 23, 1991), pp. 70–75.

———. "Up, Up, and Away," *Newsweek* 122 (October 18, 1993), pp. 64–67.

Kornbluth, Jesse. "Michael Jordan," *People* 39 (May 17, 1993), pp. 81–87.

Leehrson, C. "An Air of Superstardom," *Newsweek* 113 (May 29, 1989), pp. 58–60.

Lupica, Mike. "Let's Fly Again," *Esquire* 123 (May 1995), pp. 52–54ff.

McCallum, Jack. "Air Jordan, Air Bulls," *Sports Illustrated* 68 (May 16, 1988), pp. 32–36.

———. "The Desire Isn't There," *Sports Illustrated* 79 (October 18, 1993), pp. 28–32.

———. "The Everywhere Man," *Sports Illustrated* 75 (December 23, 1991), pp. 64–69.

———. "Going Out in Style," *Sports Illustrated* 98 (February 17, 2003), pp. 32–38.

———. "Helping Hands," *Sports Illustrated* 73 (December 17, 1990), pp. 40–43.

———. "Indelible Impression," *Sports Illustrated* 90 (January 25, 1999), pp. 82–93.

———. "Lift Off," *Sports Illustrated* 95 (November 12, 2001), pp. 52–55.

———. "Michael Jordan," *Sports Illustrated* 81 (September 19, 1994), pp. 52–57.

———. "Mission Impossible," *Sports Illustrated* 71 (November 6, 1989), pp. 44–51.

———. "Reaching for Greatness," *Sports Illustrated* 76 (June 22, 1992), pp. 12–21.

———. "Shining Moment," *Sports Illustrated* 74 (June 24, 1991), pp. 38–43.

———. "They're History," *Sports Illustrated* 78 (June 28, 1993), pp. 17–21.

———. "Un-fath-om-able," *Sports Illustrated* 70 (May 15,1989), pp. 26–33.

"Michael Jordan Leaps the Great Divide," *Esquire* 114 (November 1990), pp. 138–216.

"The Michael Jordan Nobody Knows," *Ebony* 49 (December 1993), pp. 128–138.

Reilly, Rick. "The Third Coming?" *Sports Illustrated* 94 (March 19, 2001), p. 124.

"SLAM Magazine's Top 75 NBA Players," March 2003. Press release.

Starr, Mark. "I Have Nothing Left to Prove," *Newsweek* 122 (October 18, 1993), pp. 68–70.

Stengel, Richard. "I'll Fly Away," *Time* 142 (October 18, 1993), pp. 114–116.

Taylor, Phil. "Resurrection," *Sports Illustrated* 82 (March 27, 1995), pp. 18–23.

———. "Six Shooter," *Sports Illustrated* 88 (June 22, 1998), pp. 38–47.

———. "To the Top," *Sports Illustrated* 86 (June 23, 1997), pp. 30–41.

———. "Vintage," *Sports Illustrated* 84 (June 24, 1996), pp. 28–33.

Telander, Rick. "Ready … Set … Levitate!" *Sports Illustrated* 65 (November 17, 1986), pp. 18–24.

———. "Senseless," *Sports Illustrated* 72 (May 14, 1990), pp. 37–38.

Verducci, Tom. "Keeping His Guard Up," *Sports Illustrated* 81 (December 12, 1994), pp. 94–97.

Wertheim, L. Jon. "Three's a Charm," *Sports Illustrated* 96 (January 14, 2002), pp. 48–51.

Wolff, Alexander. "55," *Sports Illustrated* 83 (November 13, 1995), pp. 108–121.

———. "In the Driver's Seat," *Sports Illustrated* 61 (December 10, 1984), pp. 36–42.

Wulf, Steve. "Err Jordan," *Sports Illustrated* 80 (March 19, 1994), pp. 20–23.

## TELEVISION

ABC-TV Oprah, October 29, 1993.

CBS-TV Eye to Eye with Connie Cheung, July 15, 1993.

CBS-TV 60 Minutes, October 23, 2005.

ESPN Best of the Decade ESPY Awards, February 14, 2000.

ESPN Sportscentury Top 50 Athletes, December 26, 1999.

## NBA VIDEOS

"Above and Beyond"(1996).

"Come Fly with Me," (1990).

"His Airness" (1999).

"On and Off the Court" (1993).

## WEB SITES

Answers Corporation. www.answers.com

Charlotte Bobcats. www.bobcatsbasketball.com

Chicago Tribune. www.chicagotribune.com

CNN/Sports Illustrated. www.sportsillustrated.cnn.com

Electric Foundry, LLC. www.worldathletes.com

The Entertainment and Sports Programming Network. www.espn.com

NBA Media Ventures, LLC. www.nba.com

Nike.com. www.jumpman23.com

Sporting News. www.sportingnews.com

Sports-Reference.com. www.basketball-reference.com

United States Olympic Committee. www.usoc.org

USA Today. www.usatoday.com

# INDEX

## About the Author

DAVID L. PORTER is the Louis Tuttle Shangle Professor of History at William Penn University, where he has taught since 1976. He has a BA in history from Franklin College of Indiana, an MA in history from Ohio University, and a PhD in history from the Pennsylvania State University. Porter has authored or edited 15 books on sports history and the U.S. Congress and specializes in sports biography and baseball history. His most recent works are *Basketball: A Biographical Dictionary* (2005), *Latino and African American Athletes Today: A Biographical Dictionary* (2004), *The San Diego Padres Encyclopedia* (2002), *Biographical Dictionary of American Sports: Baseball, Revised and Expanded Edition* (2000, three volumes) and *African American Sports Greats* (1995). Porter also writes a weekly sports column for the *Oskaloosa Herald*. He and his wife, Marilyn, live in Oskaloosa and have two grown children and three grandchildren.